ISSUES IN BIOMEDICAL ETHICS

The Future of Human Reproduction

ISSUES IN BIOMEDICAL ETHICS

General Editors
John Harris and Søren Holm

Consulting Editors
Ranaan Gillon and Bonnie Steinbock

The late twentieth century has witnessed dramatic technological developments in biomedical science and in the delivery of health care, and these developments have brought with them important social changes. All too often ethical analysis has lagged behind these changes. The purpose of this series is to provide lively, up-to-date, and authoritative studies for the increasingly large and diverse readership concerned with issues in biomedical ethics—not just healthcare trainees and professionals, but also philosophers, social scientists, lawyers, social workers, and legislators. The series will feature both single-author and multi-author books, short and accessible enough to be widely read, each of them focused on an issue of outstanding current importance and interest. Philosophers, doctors, and lawyers from a number of countries feature among the authors lined up for the series.

The Future of Human Reproduction

Ethics, Choice, and Regulation

Edited by
JOHN HARRIS
and
SØREN HOLM

CLARENDON PRESS · OXFORD

OXFORD
UNIVERSITY PRESS

Great Clarendon Street, Oxford OX2 6DP

Oxford University Press is a department of the University of Oxford.
It furthers the University's objective of excellence in research, scholarship,
and education by publishing worldwide in

Oxford New York

Athens Auckland Bangkok Bogotá Buenos Aires Calcutta
Cape Town Chennai Dar es Salaam Delhi Florence Hong Kong Istanbul
Karachi Kuala Lumpur Madrid Melbourne Mexico City Mumbai
Nairobi Paris São Paulo Singapore Taipei Tokyo Toronto Warsaw

with associated companies in Berlin Ibadan

Oxford is a registered trade mark of Oxford University Press
in the UK and in certain other countries

Published in the United States
by Oxford University Press Inc., New York

British Library Cataloguing in Publication Data
Data available

Library of Congress Cataloging in Publication Data
The future of human reproduction : ethics, choice, and regulation /
edited by John Harris and Søren Holm.
(Issues in biomedical ethics)
Includes bibliographical references and index.
1. Human reproductive technology–Moral and ethical aspects.
2. Human reproductive technology–Government policy. 3. Human
reproductive technology–Social aspects. I. Harris, John, 1945– .
II. Søren, Holm. III. Series.
RG133.5.F93 1998 176—dc21 98–16389
ISBN 0–19–823761–8
ISBN 0–19–825076–2 (Pbk.)

Printed in Great Britain
on acid-free paper by
Biddles Ltd
Guildford and King's Lynn

Acknowledgement

This book was made possible by the award of a project grant from the Commission of the European Communities Biomedicine and Health Research Programme (BIOMED I) Directorate General XII. The editors and contributors gratefully acknowledge the generous support of the European Commission and in particular of Dr Christiane Bardoux.

Contents

Notes on Contributors

INEZ DE BEAUFORT is Professor of Medical Ethics at the Erasmus University, Rotterdam.

MARGARET BRAZIER, OBE, LL B, of the Middle Temple, barrister, is Professor of Law at the University of Manchester, and Legal Studies Director of the Centre for Social Ethics and Policy. She has written extensively on both medico-legal problems and the law on torts.

JUSTINE C. BURLEY is a Research Fellow at the Institute of Medicine, Law and Bioethics, University of Manchester, and Lecturer in Politics at Exeter College, University of Oxford.

CHARLES A. ERIN is Senior Lecturer in Applied Philosophy and Head of the Centre for Social Ethics and Policy, University of Manchester.

FLEUR FISHER is a medical doctor and was Head of the British Medical Association's Ethics, Science and Information Division.

MARIE FOX is Senior Lecturer in Law at the University of Manchester. Her research interests are primarily in the field of feminist legal theory.

JONATHAN GLOVER is Professor of Medical Ethics at King's College, London. He is the author of some of the most influential books in moral philosophy and biomedical ethics including *Causing Death and Saving Lives* (London: Penguin Books, 1977).

JOHN HARRIS is Sir David Alliance Professor of Bioethics at the University of Manchester and Research Director of the Centre for Social Ethics and Policy, University of Manchester. He has published widely on bioethical issues.

SØREN HOLM holds degrees in medicine and health care ethics. He is Senior Research Fellow at the Department of Medical Philosophy and Clinical Theory, University of Copenhagen.

MAURIZIO MORI lectures in philosophy at the State University of Milan, and is editor of *Bioetica: Rivista interdisciplinare.*

SIMONE BATEMAN NOVAES is Professor of Sociology and full-time researcher at the Centre de Recherche Sens, Éthique, Société of the Centre National de la Recherche Scientifique, Paris, and is a member of the French National Ethics Committee. Professor Bateman specializes in ethical questions raised in medicine, particularly in the area of reproduction and sexuality.

TANIA SALEM has a Ph.D. in social anthropology from the Universidade Federal do Rio de Janeiro, and is a tenured professor of the Department of Health Policies and Institutions/Institute of Social Medicine/Universidade Estadual do Rio de Janeiro.

GAMAL I. SEROUR, FRCOG, FRCS, is Professor of Obstetrics and Gynaecology and Director of the International Islamic Center for Population and Research, Al-Azhar University. Professor Serour's research interests include human reproduction, medically assisted conception, high-risk pregnancy, and bioethics in human reproduction.

ANN SOMMERVILLE heads the BMA's Medical Ethics Department.

BONNIE STEINBOCK is Professor of Philosophy at the University of Albany/SUNY, New York, and is a Fellow of the Hastings Center and its current Vice-President.

GUIDO M. W. R. DE WERT is an ethicist and is Senior Investigator in Bioethics at the Institute for Bioethics, Maastricht.

Introduction

JOHN HARRIS AND SØREN HOLM

During recent years doctors and scientists have presented us with a growing range of treatments and technologies which enable us to control our
reproduction. The development of effective contraception in the 1960s
made it possible to control the timing and number of our children, but
the new reproductive technologies promise us far greater control. A very
incomplete list of the possibilities would note that infertile couples can
now have children, sometimes even their genetic children, the normal
reproductive span of women can be extended, fertilized eggs can be tested
for genetic disease before they are placed in a woman's womb, stored
gametes and embryos can be used after the death of the donor, and eggs
can be retrieved from aborted fetuses or ovaries transplanted like any
other organ transplant. These developments have prompted widespread
public debate and legislation in many countries. One constant feature of
these debates has been the conflict between private choice and public
regulation. Each of the new reproductive techniques is of benefit to some
people, but at the same time it offends the moral sensibilities of others.
How should society strike a balance between these different considerations? This is not a question which can be solved once and for all, and
indeed we have perhaps glimpsed only the earliest and most imperfect
manifestations of the new reproductive technologies, but it is a question
which we cannot avoid.

This book brings together the work of an international group of
scholars and researchers from a number of different fields and perspectives, all looking at different aspects of the interface between reproductive choice and public regulation. The authors approach the issue of
reproductive choice from a number of different angles. Some use philosophical analysis, some prefer a more sociological approach, and some
draw on history or religion. The writing styles are also diverse, ranging
from what might be termed 'standard academic' through the classical

essay form to the overtly literary. This diversity in approach and style in itself illuminates the central theme of choice.

Although none of the articles presents direct legal analysis it is characteristic that very few escape making repeated references to legal regulations. The field of reproductive choice is entangled in legal controversy, and, as a number of the authors point out, the legislative process in this area has not always been characterized by wisdom and rationality.

The first chapter by John Harris considers a range of the new reproductive technologies, and argues forcefully that most of the ethical arguments raised against these technologies are weak or flawed. We should therefore 'be cautious about needlessly denying ourselves the benefit of such advance and such technology, particularly when it offers much needed and much desired treatment or offers a legitimate extension of human choice'. Harris discusses a number of recent *causes célèbres* and defends a radical conception of reproductive autonomy.

The chapter by Maurizio Mori continues this line of philosophical argument by looking more closely at the way in which we classify stages of early human life, and especially at the claim that the individual human life begins at conception. He argues that this claim rests on a conceptual confusion. Once this confusion is cleared away, he suggests, we will be able to see the issues surrounding reproductive choice in a new and clearer light.

Jonathan Glover analyses the experiences from Nazi Germany and points to a number of ways in which the Nazi analogy can be used in ethics, and a number of ways in which it cannot be used. He points out that the Nazi euthanasia programme and euthanasia as it is currently understood are by no means the same thing. He argues that within the area of reproductive choice we can none the less learn from the Nazi experience, especially when we discuss state control of reproduction. He concludes that basing decisions about the kind of children to be born on general social utility is a repugnant idea.

The next two chapters by Margaret Brazier and Marie Fox both look at the issue of reproductive choice from a feminist perspective. Brazier argues that although the law in the UK may seem to respect the reproductive rights of women this is, in reality, far from the case. She goes on to consider whether a right to reproduce or a right to have a child may not in the end be more constraining than liberating for women. Fox goes further and looks at the question of whether the rhetoric of the slogan 'a woman's right to choose' is now counter-productive in securing women real reproductive choice. She argues that focusing on rights in this way is risky because it can invite similar rights claims on behalf of fetuses or embryos, or on behalf of male partners.

Justine Burley considers whether or not society ought to pay for infertility services. Her analysis is based on Ronald Dworkin's theory of distributive justice. She concludes that in the end society has an obligation to pay for infertility services, since although children, on a Dworkinian analysis, fall within the class of goods which are characterized by being freely chosen, very expensive infertility must be considered a handicap compensatable according to the terms of the hypothetical insurance market.

Simone Bateman Novaes and Tania Salem take a French court case on the use of embryos after the male partner's death as their point of departure for a sociological analysis of how the embryo is embedded and constructed in the social debate. They argue convincingly that the status of the embryo is at present uncertain in public debate, and that a number of different interest groups try to influence the outcome of the dispute over this status. They conclude that 'The outcome of this social dispute will have crucial consequences, not only for the future of individual embryos, but also on definitions of their moral and legal status, as well as on institutional policies and practices. Arbitration necessarily involves deciding whose interpretation of the embryo's welfare must prevail. In this sense, the embryo's moral status and concrete destiny reveal, and will always reveal, arbitrary social choices.'

Bonnie Steinbock's contribution also takes a court case as its starting point for a discussion of the specific question of whether sperm can be said to be property. She argues that this way of asking the question is misconceived, and forced upon us by the legal context where sperm can only be bequeathed if it is property. Instead of looking intently at the category of property to discover whether sperm fits into this category, we should consider what may permissibly be done with sperm. She concludes that 'The arguments I have considered against permitting sperm to be bequeathed for reproductive purposes do not seem compelling.'

Charles Erin focuses on the issue of consent and considers the ethics of imposing reproductive choices on those who cannot consent. These may include the children to be born as a result of reproductive choices exercised by parents or indeed choices imposed on parents who are incapable of giving a valid consent. The use of ovarian tissue from aborted fetuses, or indeed from adult mothers who are dead as the law defines death, raises similar problems. As Erin shows, the ethics of decisions as to whether or not to proceed in the absence of consent in such cases can be difficult to establish.

The chapter by Søren Holm on pre-implantation diagnosis describes this new technique whereby the genetic make-up of eggs fertilized in IVF procedures can be analysed before they are implanted. He argues that this technique is not in principle different from traditional pre-natal diagnosis (amniocentesis, chorionic villus biopsy, etc.), but that it may have different social implications.

The chapter by Gamal Serour, Professor of Obstetrics and Gynaecology at Al-Azhar University in Cairo, gives an overview of the Islamic response to a range of new reproductive techniques. He demonstrates that Islamic scholars are able to make constructive use of their religious heritage in the assessment of these new possibilities for reproductive choice.

The chapter by Fleur Fisher and Ann Sommerville, and that of Guido de Wert, are both concerned with the problems of so-called 'post-menopausal pregnancy'. Developments in medical technology have now made it possible for women to become pregnant well into their sixties by combining *in vitro* fertilization with egg donation. This possibility has led to heated discussions in many countries. In most of these discussions an argument claiming that 'post-menopausal pregnancy is unnatural, and that it is therefore unethical' has been prevalent. This argument is discussed in both the chapter by Fisher and Sommerville and that by de Wert. Fisher and Sommerville point out that some women between 50 and 54 years of age do actually get pregnant and give birth to children the 'natural way', and that there are no good studies showing that older women have excessively high morbidity and mortality rates during pregnancy and childbirth. De Wert points out that any argument from the natural to the ethical is dubious, since most of medicine is aimed at subverting nature and preventing the natural (i.e. disease and death) from happening. He further considers the argument that it is problematic for children to have very old parents, and reaches the conclusion that 'there are compelling reasons not to treat couples over the age of 60'.

The last chapter by Inez de Beaufort takes the form of a letter from a mother to her daughter on the daughter's eighteenth birthday. Perhaps better than a rigorous philosophical analysis, it displays both the problems inherent in post-menopausal pregnancy, and the reasons why someone might choose the technique anyway.

J. H.
S. H.

1

Rights and Reproductive Choice

JOHN HARRIS

Introduction

Reproductive choice is an idea that is respected more in the breach than in the observance. It is when people, particularly women, actually want to exercise choice that the trouble starts. The trouble is well under way, particularly because technology is rapidly increasing the range and the nature of available choices. Recently a number of new possibilities have entered the market place of ideas, and some are already being offered in the bazaar, raising issues of market regulation, personal freedom, and fundamental ethics.

Headline writers have not been slow to exploit the dramatic possibilities of ideas like that of post-menopausal motherhood, egg donation between races, aborted fetuses themselves becoming 'mothers', and the infamous 'orphaned embryos opera' (more of which anon), but the exploitation has been largely to provoke public outrage. Instinctive and gut reactions to these possibilities have not been confined to the popular press and many arguments and claims of doubtful validity have been rapidly deployed to allay imagined disquiet[1] and in attempts to enforce a particular 'morality'.

In order to be clearer about what ought or ought not to constrain choice in reproduction this chapter attempts to resolve the outstanding ethical issues concerning the possible uses and abuses of fetal ovarian tissue and eggs, including one vexed question about cloning human eggs. We

I am grateful to Rebecca Bennett, Margaret Brazier, Justine Burley, and Charles Erin for helpful comments. Henrietta Wallace and I collaborated on an earlier draft of this chapter and I am greatly in her debt for many ideas and suggestions. For the sections on human cloning and on procreative autonomy I have drawn on my 'Goodbye Dolly? The Ethics of Human Cloning', *Journal of Medical Ethics*, 23 (Dec. 1997).

[1] See for example F. Anderson, A. Glasier, J. Ross, and D. T. Baird, 'Attitudes of Women to Fetal Tissue Research', *Journal of Medical Ethics*, 20 (1994), 36–40.

will also examine the issue of pre-natal and pre-implantation screening, testing, and experimentation and the question of the fate of spare or 'orphaned' embryos.

Eggs

There is a massive shortfall in the availability of donated eggs for the treatment of infertile women which is global in scope. In current medical practice, eggs are mainly donated by women who are undergoing sterilization or who have surplus eggs after fertility treatment. Some altruistic donations also take place, although the invasive and risky nature of the techniques involved means that few women will choose to undergo such procedures purely altruistically. There is commonly a three-year wait for egg donation and for certain ethnic groups the wait is even longer for same race eggs. Ovarian tissue or oocytes from all sources (women, cadavers, or fetuses) could be used to provide fertility treatment to women who are not able to produce eggs of their own. Some fertile women who are carriers of genetic diseases may also seek egg donation.

Fertility services are the only area of medicine in which health professionals are by law required to make social judgements about a person's suitability for treatment.[2] The legislation states that 'a woman shall not be provided with treatment services unless account has been taken of the welfare of any child who may be born as a result of the treatment (including the need of that child for a father) and of any other child who may be affected by the birth'.[3] This legislation constitutes prima-facie discrimination against infertile people since couples who can conceive naturally are not expected to demonstrate their potential fitness as parents. While it is argued by the BMA and others that, when health professionals become involved in helping people to bear children, they have special responsibilities to ensure that the resulting children will not be greatly disadvantaged,[4] they do not apply this reasoning to normal pre-natal care, for example, and so the apology rings hollow.

I have argued elsewhere that it is both unethical and impractical to require or even permit health professionals to make social judgements about an individual's suitability for treatment.[5] I will not rehearse these

---

[2] The Human Fertilisation and Embryology Act 1990.
[3] Ibid., s. 13 (5). I am grateful to Henrietta Wallace for pointing this out to me.
[4] BMA, *Medical Ethics Today: Its Practice and Philosophy* (London, 1993), 113.
[5] See John Harris, *The Value of Life* (London: Routledge & Kegan Paul, 1985), ch. 7.

arguments again here, but rest content with observing that there are no reliable tests for good parenting and no reliable evidence that single parents significantly disadvantage their children.[6] It seems invidious to require that people who need assistance with procreation meet tests to which those who need no such assistance are not subjected. If we are serious that people demonstrate their adequacy as parents *in advance* of being permitted to procreate, then we should license all parents. Since we are evidently not serious about this, we should not discriminate against those who need assistance with procreation.

Ethical Questions

The United Kingdom law on cadaveric donation is volatile. There have, for example, been recent and ill-considered eleventh-hour additions to the Criminal Justice and Public Order Act 1994 banning the use of fetal ovarian tissue. We should bear in mind that, whatever the law says, there is still a need to address independently the ethical issues arising from cadaveric ovarian tissue donation. These focus principally on consent, although one might legitimately ask whether donation of reproductive tissue is qualitatively different from other tissue donation, as some have suggested.[7]

The case of a woman agreeing in advance to ovarian tissue donation after death is arguably uncontentious. This would simply be another form of advance directive. If it is reasonable to permit women to donate eggs or ovarian tissue while alive (giving fully informed consent), then under the same conditions it seems reasonable that they be permitted to be cadaver donors. Thus if they sign a donor card, as is conventional in the United Kingdom, indicating that all their organs and tissue are available after death, this should be taken to include ovarian tissue also. If this seems problematic in view of the change it would represent, new cards could perhaps be printed making the permission to use ovarian tissue explicit.

In societies where an opting-out system rather than an opting-in system for tissue and organ donation is in operation, it is assumed that

---

[6] See for example Charles A. Erin and John Harris, 'Surrogacy', in W. A. W. Walters (ed.), *Human Reproduction: Current and Future Ethical Issues*, Baillière's Clinical Obstetrics and Gynaecology (London: Baillière Tindall, 1991), 631.

[7] See John Polkinghorne's suggestions in J. C. Polkinghorne, 'Law and Ethics of Transplanting Foetal Tissue', in Robert G. Edwards (ed.), *Foetal Tissue Transplants in Medicine* (Cambridge: Cambridge University Press, 1992), which are discussed below.

cadaver organs are available for transplant, unless there has been a clear notification to the contrary. In such a system, so long as the conventions of that society are understood to include eggs and ovarian tissue, there seems to be no reason why the consents should not be deemed to have been given if people have not specifically opted out.

But what if a woman has not made an advance declaration, and her wishes are unknown; should her ovarian tissue still be used? And on whose authority? In the case of a young girl, who has expressed no view either because she was not competent to do so or else had never considered the matter, is parental authority to tissue donation all that is needed? What if their consent is based on a desire to replace a child they have lost with a grandchild? Does this matter? We can answer this question at once.

In the case of a girl considered too young to be capable of giving informed consent, it seems reasonable to permit her mother to consent to posthumous donation on her behalf.[8] By hypothesis the daughter has no autonomous views on the matter and has probably expressed none. It is therefore no safer to assume she would have objected than to assume she would have been willing to donate. The principle that, other things being equal, it is better to do something good than to do nothing good thus applies, and it would argue in favour of donation. For other things are equal where there is no reason to suppose the daughter had views one way or another.

The issue of the desire of parents to replace a lost child with a grandchild is more complicated. If the donated eggs go to 'strangers' then, as in adoption, such parents would have no right to have access to their lost daughter's genes, present in their genetic step-grandchild. If the recipients of the eggs are thus protected, the motivation of the donors seems unimportant. It needs no more examination than the motives of a male medical student who donates sperm for artificial insemination by donor. He may like the idea of having lots of children in the world, but so what?

Of course, such parents might seek a surrogate host with a view to *themselves* becoming the parents of their grandchild. If there is no *other* objection to such parents employing a surrogate mother for a donated egg, and as long as relevant laws concerning consanguinity are observed, I again fail to see an objection. A mother might, of course, seek to have her daughter's egg fertilized and implanted in herself, perhaps using the

[8] In the absence of conventions for automatic cadaver donation of tissue and organs for which I have argued elsewhere. See my *Wonderwoman and Superman: The Ethics of Human Biotechnology* (Oxford: Oxford University Press, 1992) and *The Value of Life.*

technology which enables post-menopausal women to have children. This is the clearest case in which a woman might become, simultaneously in one sense at least, the parent and the grandparent of the same child. Again if consanguinity laws concerning the source of sperm are observed,[9] and in the absence of other independent reasons for denying this woman the right to have children, I see no obvious objection.[10] All too often the objection in a case like this is the incredulous repetition of the fact that the woman would be simultaneously a mother and grandmother of the same child, without any attempt to explain on what grounds this combination of *descriptions* (hardly of *roles*) is objectionable.

The other possible objection concerns the motivation of such a mother. It is obviously thought by some that to want to replace a lost child with that child's progeny is somehow discreditable, although it is never explained why this might be so. We do not normally criticize a grandmother when she takes on the mothering role for her orphaned grandchildren. Why should we object when she 'creates' the grandchildren her daughter never had? Many people have children, at least in part, to ensure the survival of their genes, and this is sometimes claimed to be the 'motivation' of the genes themselves.[11] Where this wish has been frustrated by the death of their child and where they genuinely want the new child for its own sake also, why should they not have another child related to themselves in this way if that is what they want?[12] If on the other hand she simply wishes to replace a beloved child with another child of her own who will also be connected with the child loved and lost, it is hard to imagine why this double bond with the new child would be objectionable.

One issue still requiring consideration is that of payment for gametes. There is a convention in the United Kingdom that women who give gametes are not paid for the donation, whereas men who donate sperm for artificial insemination by donor are usually paid, albeit a very small amount. There is thus certainly an anomaly and possibly an injustice as between men and women in the 'donation' of gametes. However, this is not an entirely accurate representation of what happens, since women who donate eggs prior to sterilization are very often paid in

---

[9] Assuming such laws to be morally and genetically defensible, a question that we do not have space to address here.

[10] See below.

[11] See Richard Dawkins, *The Selfish Gene* (Oxford: Oxford University Press, 1989).

[12] Indeed, if the desire is for the continuance of their genes, this desire could conceivably be genetically determined. Those who think this would make the desire 'natural', and hence acceptable, would have an added reason for approving.

kind. Sterilization, when part of the public health system in the United
Kingdom, often has a long waiting list, and women are frequently induced
to become egg donors in exchange for immediate sterilization, rather
than having to wait for protracted periods for the operation they seek.
For reasons explained elsewhere[13] it seems unreasonable not to pay women
for such services, but I shall not discuss the ethics of this here.

A number of new issues have arisen concerning eligibility for assisted
conception by women seeking egg donation which have sparked off some
controversy. One concerns the treatment of older, post-menopausal
women; another concerns egg donation between racial groups and the
issue of 'designer babies'.

Eggs and Ovarian Tissue from Fetuses

The use of fetal ovarian tissue has caused huge controversy in recent
years. Some of this controversy has to do with the nature of the consent which might be given for such donation, some of it has to do with
the nature of the donor herself, and some with the effects of such donation on the resulting child as it grows to maturity. We will look at each
of these in turn. To deal with the issue of consent we will consider the
proposals of the Polkinghorne Committee which reported to the United
Kingdom government on these matters.

Consent and the Pregnant 'Donor'

One of the key recommendations of the Polkinghorne code of practice[14]
was that a woman's decision to have an abortion should not be influenced by consideration of the possible uses which might be made of
the fetus and that the initiation or termination of a pregnancy in order
to provide suitable fetal material is unethical.[15] Many people, including
Dr John Polkinghorne, the chairman of the Committee which produced
the code of practice referred to, believe that people have a special interest in controlling the destiny of their own genetic material. They further
believe that because the gametes contain genetic material which will

[13] See Harris, *Wonderwoman and Superman*, chs. 5 and 6.
[14] *Review of the Guidance on the Research Use of Fetuses and Fetal Material* (London: HMSO, Cm. 762, 1989), Code para. 3.1.
[15] I have argued elsewhere that neither of these courses of action is necessarily unethical. See *Wonderwoman and Superman*, ch. 5.

be passed on indefinitely to future generations, any consent to the use of one's own genetic material in this way must be specific and must encompass the knowledge of its ultimate destiny.

For this reason, Polkinghorne has suggested that consent to the use of fetal ovarian tissue by the mother must be specific. However, the Polkinghorne code of practice insists that consent to the use of fetal tissue must, in general, be general, in order to avoid the possibility that women might be induced to have abortions in order to secure some specific outcome. If this is sound, the ethics of fetal ovarian donation are incompatible with the ethics of general fetal donation and it would consequently be unethical to use fetal ovarian tissue for transplant purposes.[16] Even if we grant[17] that women donors of fetal material should not be influenced by the possible uses of such material, it is completely unclear why a *specific* consent would be more influential than a general consent. Of course, if separation is to be maintained then one would have to ensure that the women who are asked to consent to the use of their fetal material after abortion are so asked only *after* they have finally determined to have an abortion, and have satisfied whatever the legal requirements are which entitle them to abortion. If this is done and if only then are they asked specifically whether they will consent to the fetal ovaries being used, there can surely be no question that they could be induced to have an abortion for that reason alone. An added security would be to deny such women any right to *direct* the particular destination of fetal ovarian tissue, but merely give specific consent as to the nature of its potential use.

Polkinghorne and others have further claimed that it would be unethical for the woman to delay the timing of her abortion until the fetus had developed to a point where certain tissue, including ovarian tissue, was usable for transplant purposes. Why this would be unethical has never been adequately explained. It is true that by delaying the abortion the woman puts herself under increased physical risk and mental strain, but if she does this freely, having been fully informed, it is surely her own decision to make. We must remember that, after the first trimester, giving birth is almost always more risky than abortion, and yet women are seldom criticized for deciding to continue a pregnancy.

---

[16] One cannot easily resist the conclusion that the insistence on specific consent for ovarian tissue transfer, in the face of a previous report demanding general consent for fetal tissue more generally, is designed to achieve a particular outcome—namely the impossibility of approving ovarian tissue transfer from fetuses.

[17] As I have indicated we would not.

Moreover, having decided on an abortion it might be a great comfort to the woman to know that although the fetus will be destroyed, its organs and tissue will be used for beneficial purposes to save life, restore health, and, in this case, allow another woman to have the child that she so desperately wants.

Doing Something Good is Better than Doing Nothing!

Here the principle that it is better to do something good than to do nothing good should be re-emphasized. Surely no one could believe that it could be better (more ethical) to allow the fetal material to go to waste than to use it for some good purpose? It must, logically, be better to do something good than to do nothing good; it must be better to make good use of something than to allow it to be wasted. It must surely be *more* ethical to help people than to help no one. This principle, that other things being equal it is better to do some good than no good, provides the woman with a good reason to delay an abortion so that these good outcomes may be achieved (given that she has already fully determined to have an abortion for reasons independent of the good outcome for others).[18]

We should note that the Polkinghorne report considers some of these points, but concludes that the arguments for not permitting a woman to vary the method and timing of her abortion so that fetal material will be available are 'of such ethical importance that they outweigh those for allowing the mother to make any direction regarding the use of her fetus or fetal tissue'. However the report nowhere states what these arguments are, nor how estimations of their importance are arrived at, and so we are not able to consider them.

In a more recent paper[19] John Polkinghorne has stated specifically, in the context of fetal ovarian tissue transfer, that since in such a case 'the fetus would be the genetic mother of the resulting child, and the mother providing the tissue[20] would be its genetic grandmother[, it] seems clear to this writer that it would be ethically wrong to allow the creation of a human person linked in this way with a family without the

---

[18] Those who disapprove of abortion would surely also welcome the possibility that, in postponing abortion, the woman has further time to reflect as to whether it is what she truly wants and therefore has time to change her mind.

[19] Polkinghorne, 'Law and Ethics of Transplanting Foetal Tissue'.

[20] This should surely read: 'the mother *consenting to the provision of* the tissue would be its genetic grandmother.'

explicit consent of the mother involved.'[21] It is difficult not to agree that specific consents should be required if consent is to be required at all. No consent which is not specific could be fully informed if the woman is not made aware of all the possible uses to which her fetus's tissue might be put. However, it cannot be for this reason that the creation of a genetically linked human person might be unethical, since this would give the mother, any mother, an effective veto on the production of grandchildren, whether those grandchildren were produced from the eggs of her dead fetus or from her live 25-year-old daughter.

To enable parents to veto the production of their grandchildren because their explicit consent for their children to have such grandchildren had not been given seems a trifle excessive. Moreover this insistence on the importance of *specific* consent to the transmission of genetic material sits oddly with Polkinghorne's insistence on denying donors of fetal ovarian tissue the right to direct where such material should go. Why not permit women to do this so long as they meet the qualification for abortion first?

The Effect on the Children

We must now consider briefly whether the long-term effects on the children who will be, or who may be, born as a result of the use of fetal ovarian tissue is such as to vitiate the whole process. One of the factors often cited is that the children produced by this method will have a mother who is an aborted fetus and that they will find this fact disturbing. They may also be disturbed by the idea that they were not wanted and valued by their mother and indeed that their mother was in turn not wanted and valued by her mother. The weight of guilt thus produced, so it is claimed, will be an unfair burden on such children.

Let's look first at the idea that such a child will be unwanted, and will know that it was unwanted, by its mother. This is surely a false and tendentious way of presenting things. Such a child could not fairly be described as 'unwanted'; somebody wanted it so badly that they were prepared to undergo the at present difficult search for such donated gametes and the difficult and problematic procedures to fertilize them and implant them and carry them successfully to term. The child is clearly

---

[21] Ibid. 328.

wanted, and wanted by its mother properly so called, the mother who will gestate it, bring it to birth, nurture it, look after it, and rear it.

It is difficult to know what effect the bare knowledge that its genetic 'mother' was an aborted fetus will have. It would of course be possible to conceal this knowledge from the child, and indeed to conceal it from the mother, by adopting the convention that the recipients of such donated gametes will simply be told that they have received donated gametes, without knowing whether these gametes result from live donation, cadaver donation, or fetal ovarian sources. The child would thus simply know that it was born as a result of gamete donation, a very common experience.

But let's not evade the issue by assuming that such conventions will, or should, be adopted. Suppose the child does know, or will come to know, that its origins involved fetal ovarian tissue transfer. Will this knowledge be so terrible that it would be better that no such children had ever been or were even born? It is difficult to be certain how to answer this question, but it is surely unlikely that the consequences would be unacceptably terrible. The only remotely relevant data are inconclusive.[22] One question we should ask is whether the act of producing such a child is in the overall interests of the individual who is thereby produced, or is wrongful for some other reason. In the expectation that it will live a normal lifespan and have a reasonably favourable balance of happiness over misery in its life, it is overwhelmingly likely that the individual will have what would be objectively judged[23] to be a worthwhile life. Its life will not be in any sense 'wrongful', such that it might have a legitimate claim that it was against its interests, harmful to it, or a wrong done to it to have been brought to birth in such circumstances.[24]

However, we should remember that no one suffers the wrong of not being brought into existence, and both responsible parents and a responsible society should ask whether, given the sort of life it will have to lead, it would be right to bring a child who will have to lead such a life into existence. The test should surely be to ask 'what a compas-

---

[22] See for example M. D. S. Ainsworth, M. C. Blehar, E. Waters, and S. Wall, *Patterns of Attachment: A Psychological Study of the Strange Situation* (Hillsdale, NJ: Erlbaum, 1978); J. Bowlby, *Attachment and Loss*, i: *Attachment* (London: Hogarth Press, 1969); id., *A Secure Base: Clinical Applications of Attachment Theory* (London: Routledge, 1980), and D. Baumrind, 'Rearing Competent Children', in W. Damon (ed.), *Child Development Today and Tomorrow* (San Francisco: Jossey-Bass, 1989).

[23] 'Objectively' here just means a life which others would judge to be worth living.

[24] See Harris, *Wonderwoman and Superman*, ch. 4, for a more detailed discussion of 'wrongful life'.

sionate parent ought to do or what a compassionate and moral society ought to think it right to have done'.[25] To be confident that neither compassionate parents nor a compassionate society would permit a child to come into being with particular prospects, those prospects would have to be both severely awful and highly probable, though not of such a high standard of awfulness as to trigger suggestions that the life was somehow wrongful or that it would be better all round that the child had never been born.

While the knowledge of the precise nature of its origins may be disturbing, it is surely unlikely to be so disturbing as to make it certain that no compassionate parent nor such a society would or should permit its birth. We should not prevent all less than optimal parenting or less than ideal circumstances into which to be born. One of the most reliable predictors of bad outcomes for children is poverty, but no one has yet suggested that the poor should not be permitted to reproduce. We should also remember that it is one thing to have reasons, or to believe one has reasons, for preferring not to create such a life, or not to live such a life oneself, but quite another to be justified in preventing others from so doing.

We may conclude that eggs and ovarian tissue from live donors, from cadavers, and from fetuses may be used in treatment if such use is not specifically ruled out by the donors or, in the case of fetal ovarian tissue, by the mother of the donor. This raises the issue as to whether the consent of both parents, the woman and her partner, is required. In many cases the identity of the father may not be known to the mother, or, if his identity is known, it may not be possible to trace him at the time consent is being considered. Indeed the mother may wish to have no further contact with him. Should the genetic father have the right to veto the donation of his genetic material present in the fetus he has engendered? The question is complicated, but I think the father's preferences must ultimately be ignored. To cut through complexities which are beyond the purview of this discussion, we can note that to give the father such a right would, as discussed above, give him an effective veto on the production of any grandchildren. Either he is entitled to control the destiny of his genes or he is not; if he is, then the intervening preferences of his daughter are irrelevant. The same is true, of course, of the mother. The reason the mother's specific consent is required, if it is, is not because she has a special interest in the destiny of her genes,

---

[25] As I argued in *The Value of Life*, 149.

but rather because of the special emotional ties of a mother to the fetus she has nurtured.

I have argued elsewhere[26] that all cadaver tissue and organs should automatically be available for transplant purposes irrespective of the wishes of the cadaver's former relations. I see no reason to regard the use of fetal ovarian tissue as a special case. Indeed if this practice were adopted there would be little question of a woman having an abortion for the specific purpose of obtaining material for donation or transplant, since she would have *no control at all* over the destination of such donated material. It would fall into the public domain and be available for transplant according to some fair principle of distribution.

Blood, Sperm, and Posthumous Parenting

This brings us to another recent 'hard case' on which to test the plausibility of the approach so far. On 6 February 1997 Mrs Diane Blood secured a landmark victory in the English Court of Appeal gaining the right to export her dead husband's sperm so that she could use it to have his baby despite firm opposition from the Human Fertilisation and Embryology Authority in the United Kingdom.[27]

Mr and Mrs Blood had been trying for a child when Mr Blood contracted meningitis and fell into a coma. Doctors removed his sperm and Mrs Blood wished to use it to have his baby. The Human Fertilisation and Embryology Authority (HFEA) refused permission and maintained that refusal despite repeated legal attempts by Mrs Blood to change their view and a media extravaganza on the issue. The four main grounds for the HFEA's refusal were:

1. the important requirements laid down by parliament that a sperm donor must have the opportunity of counselling and the chance to consider the implications of a posthumous birth;
2. the wrong of permitting United Kingdom law to be circumvented by the export of sperm;
3. that formal consent of the owner was required for the use of genetic material and that this consent should not be constructed from the evidence of another; and

---

[26] See *Wonderwoman and Superman* and *The Value of Life*.
[27] Reported in the *Guardian*, 7 Feb. 1997.

4. that Mr Blood had given neither consideration nor consent to the export of his sperm.[28]

We will leave aside for the moment the question as to whether these are sound as general rules. The question must be as to whether the circumstances of the case justify varying them. Almost all commentators concede sympathy for Mrs Blood and respect for her integrity.

These four reasons however really reduce to one on examination, namely an argument about what follows from the special nature of genetic material. For consent, while important, particularly where we know that it was emphatically withheld and where the agent is still alive and competent, seems less crucial here. One reason is that we are not talking of violating the clear will of a competent individual. There are many precedents for examining and using body products after death without consent, for example where a court orders a *post mortem* examination, or where bodies are disposed of in ways not governed by the specific request of the deceased. Why, for example, should letting body products go to waste be presumed to accord with consent when using them for beneficial purposes does not?

Moreover consent is often constructed from the reports and judgements of third parties where hugely important decisions are at stake, for example as to whether an individual would have wanted to be sustained alive in a persistent vegetative state or in some other problematic condition. In such cases relatives and friends often testify as to the sort of person the individual was before an accident or illness and whether they had ever expressed or implied views about what they would have wished to happen to them if they were ever in PVS or some other irreversible condition where their own views could no longer be consulted. For example in 1990 the Supreme Court of the United States upheld this principle in the landmark case of Nancy Cruzan.[29] Nancy Cruzan had been in coma for a number of years and the Supreme Court by a majority of five to four accepted evidence that Ms Cruzan would not have wished to be kept alive in such a state. While judgments of the United States Supreme Court are not binding in the United Kingdom it is significant that the principle of third-party evidence as to what an individual would have wanted is acceptable to the highest court in the United States in a case where that individual's very life turns on the outcome, but in the case of Mr Blood, where something comparatively trivial was at stake,

[28] Ibid.   [29] *Cruzan* v. *Missouri Department of Health 1990.*

the HFEA wished to insist on written consent, counselling, proper opportunity to consider the implications, and such consent given in clear and formal terms.

I have said that something comparatively trivial was at stake and this perhaps might be thought to be question begging. However, compared with life itself, the destiny of one's genes is surely *comparatively* trivial. Moreover, the idea that genetic material is of such fundamental importance that explicit informed consent as to its use is required, which we found in Polkinghorne, and in the statement of the HFEA's reasons for refusing Mrs Blood's request, is surely untenable. Genes are after all immortal.[30] Even if you grant people the right to determine the destiny of their genes in the first generation they inevitably lose all control thereafter. We may choose whether to have children (maybe) but not whether to have grandchildren.

Moreover this surely over-precious attitude to the destiny of male gametes is not one reflected in custom or practice. Men are notorious for leaving their gametes behind in all sorts of places, some of which may well result in the creation of life. They do so almost always without all these requirements for opportunities for counselling, formal consent, and time for reflection, and usually without missing them and without mishap without them. We normally accept that they have no say in the outcome one way or another. They cannot control their partners' use of contraception, nor insist on an abortion if they do not want their genes to survive in this way, or be mixed with those of this woman. It may be said that by consenting to intercourse (if they did) the men were also consenting to the possibility of producing a child. I doubt this, but let's grant it anyway. This consent is not formal, it is without benefit of counselling and so on, and (almost) nobody thinks that such men have had their fundamental rights infringed in any way. This of course is precisely Mrs Blood's case. She was married to Mr Blood, they were (no one disputes) trying to have a child, it is as reasonable to presume his consent dead as it would have been had he been alive, and she had conceived, and then he had turned round and said, 'I don't want her to have a child.'

Interestingly, Mrs Blood did not base her claim on the idea that the sperm she wanted was her husband's property. If sperm is or could be treated as property then presumably it would have become part of her husband's estate and, assuming Diane Blood to have been the

---

[30] Without of course implying that they cannot die.

beneficiary of the residual estate, it would lawfully have passed to her.[31] That it is lawful to sell sperm (unlike human eggs) in the United Kingdom might be some evidence that it is reasonable to think of it as property.

Of course underlying all of this is the attempt by the Human Fertil-isation and Embryology Act 1990 to impose notions of responsible par-enting for assisted reproduction when these are entirely absent from more usual parenting. The idea that Mr Blood had not had the opportunity to reflect on the desirability of fathering a child posthumously and that this is inherently undesirable is a common reaction.[32] As has been sug-gested, it seems unfair and burdensome to impose on those who require assistance with reproduction standards of parenting that are not required of the rest of the community.[33] This is particularly true when, so far from there being evidence that the reproductive choices of those who require such assistance constitute or presage poor parenting, such suggestions are the barest prejudice. As Wendy Savage commented: 'To suggest that the birth of a child in these circumstances would be a "tragedy" flies in the face of the available evidence (for example, how many fatherless children born after the first and second world wars would accept this view?), and is offensive to many women deserted by their partners once pregnancy was confirmed.'[34]

Post-menopausal Mums

In the cases of fertility treatment for older, post-menopausal women which were reviewed above, the major issues have been: unease about interference with natural boundaries to childbearing, the health of the mother, and the welfare of the resulting children.

The argument from what is or is not natural need not detain us long. Since the whole practice of medicine is unnatural (people naturally fall ill and die prematurely), if we were to accept an ethic which required us not to interfere with what was natural there would be little for medical

[31] I owe this suggestion to Margaret Brazier. See also Bonnie Steinbock, 'Sperm as Property', Ch. 8 below.

[32] That it was a tragedy was suggested by Martin Kettle and by Dr J. Stuart Horner, chairman of the British Medical Association's Ethics Committee in the *Guardian*, 23 Nov. 1996.

[33] See above and Harris, *The Value of Life*, ch. 7.

[34] Wendy Savage, letter in the *Guardian*, 25 Nov. 1996.

practitioners and medical scientists to do. The leading British obstetrician and gynaecologist Lord Winston, Professor of Fertility Studies at Hammersmith Hospital, London, has produced a novel twist to this argument for the moral importance of what is natural. He has said it is wrong 'to subvert a natural biological event. To do so seems to me to debase the value of the menopause.'[35] It is not explained why it is wrong to attempt to subvert natural biological events (like illness perhaps?). Nor does Winston explain what the value of the menopause actually is, nor how it might be debased in this case.[36] Many millions of women are now treated with hormone replacement therapy (HRT), which replaces hormones the lack of which causes the menopause. This therapy also undermines 'the value of the menopause', but it has met little opposition in medical circles. At least not for *this* reason.

The health of the mother, while of obvious concern, is of concern principally to the mother herself. If she feels it acceptable to risk her health in pursuance of her desire to have a child, or another child, that surely is a decision for her to take. It is, of course, a risk which all mothers always take, pregnancy and childbirth being risky at whatever age they are undertaken.

It is also claimed that post-menopausal women who are likely to be in their seventies when their children are teenagers would not be able to function adequately as parents. Robert Winston again: 'Children should reasonably expect that their parents should be young enough to play football in the park with them, or to have energy enough to indulge in the pursuits which are all part of growing up with their family.'[37]

This is a very disturbing claim by Winston, since it would debar many physically disabled parents from the right to procreate, an effect I am sure Winston would not have wished to defend. And as for having energy in other directions, it is now commonplace for people in their sixties and seventies to be looking after their very aged parents, who may be in their eighties and nineties. This is a task which society seems to expect more and more of older people and which is, by any standards, much more demanding than looking after children.

Finally we must consider the issue of whether or not the death of their parents, while they are still quite young, is a hardship to which children should not be condemned. While there is no doubt that the loss of parents whom one loves and on whom one depends is distressing and

---

[35] From the *Guardian*, 21 July 1993, p. 16.
[36] Why not 'exchanged' for something of greater value?
[37] Winston, *Guardian*, 21 July 1993.

problematic at any age, it is clearly likely to be the more so in children or adolescents. However, while there is some agreement in the literature[38] that such bereavement is a tragedy, the consensus seems to be that its harmful effects are manageable with care and support. We should also note that many of the bereaved do not come to psychiatric attention.[39] In any event, the question that must be pressed is: does such a bereavement even in childhood or adolescence make the entire life of that child so emphatically not worth living that it would be better had it never been born or make it wrongful in some way to have brought it into the world? Such an outcome is surely unlikely.[40]

Choosing the Racial Characteristics of Your Child

Many people seem to believe that parents ought to have children with broadly the same racial characteristics as themselves or at least with the racial characteristics that would probably result from their own union. Until recently in the United Kingdom it had been fairly standard practice to race-match children for adoption, although this practice is coming under increasing criticism.

Why do so many people firmly believe that children should be like their parents, particularly in terms of their general colour and racial characteristics? It is difficult not to view this desire, and attempts to implement it, as a form of 'ethnic cleansing'. It smacks very much of the pressure that so many societies and cultures have put upon their members not to 'marry out' or, to put it more bluntly, not to mate with somebody of another tribe or race. This has often taken the form of particular hostility to the resulting children, with pejorative terms like 'half-caste' being used to describe the children of a mixed race union. As with prejudice against inter-racial marriage, the therapy of choice is surely not to prevent people choosing their procreational partners according to their own preferences, but rather to try to eradicate the prejudice in society that makes people hostile to such unions and to the resulting children.

---

[38] See for example Dora Black, 'Psychological Reactions to Life-Threatening and Terminal Illness and Bereavement', in M. Rutter, E. Taylor, and L. Hersov (eds.), *Child Psychiatry: Modern Approaches* (London: Butterworth, 1994) and Rebecca Abrams, *When Parents Die* (London: Charles Letts, 1992).

[39] See Black, 'Psychological Reactions to Life-Threatening and Terminal Illness and Bereavement' and Abrams, *When Parents Die*.

[40] Jonathan Glover discusses these issues and makes this point in his *Fertility and the Family* (London: Fourth Estate, 1989).

Certainly, there is no genetic objection, as the English science journalist Tom Wilkie has remarked:[41]

It cannot be based in biology. Compared to most of the animal kingdom, humans are genetically remarkably homogeneous. There is less variation between human beings than among chimpanzees, for example, even though humans are incomparably more numerous. And to confound traditional views of how humanity is divided into 'families' or 'racial groups', geneticists have found that there is greater variation between individuals within one racial group than across the racial divide. To put it crudely, white men can differ more from each other than a white man from a black man. Differences between individuals such as skin colour or facial shape are probably controlled by only a very few of the human body's 100 000 or so genes.

Designer Children

Some people have objected that to choose the skin colour or racial features of children (in so far as these can be chosen—which is not very far) is an illicit form of parental preference. The phrase 'designer children' is often used pejoratively to describe the children of parents who are more concerned with fashion and pleasing themselves than with valuing children for the children's own sake. However, we should remember that choosing a same race or same race-mix child is also *designing* the child that you will have. This is no less an exercise of parental preference than is the case of choosing a different race or race mix, or, for that matter, colour. It is a truism that bears repeating, that once you have the capacity to choose and the awareness of that capacity, then choice is inevitable. It is not the less an exercise of choice because the choice is exercised in a traditional way, nor because the choice may involve doing nothing at all.

The best way both to avoid totalitarianism, and to escape the possibility of racial (or gender) prejudice, either individual or social, dictating what sort of children people have, is to permit free parental choice in these matters, and to do so whether that choice is exercised by choice of procreational partner or by choice of gametes or embryo, or by genetic engineering for that matter. For such choices are for the most part likely to be as diverse as are the people making them.

It is interesting that the Nuffield Council report on the ethics of genetic screening makes substantially the same point in drawing its distinction

---

[41] Tom Wilkie, 'Colours of Morality', *Independent on Sunday*, 2 Jan. 1994, p. 19.

between legitimate and illegitimate uses of genetic screening. It marks the boundary between legitimate choices and unacceptably eugenic choices precisely at the point at which 'the decisions of individuals [are] subjugated to those aims considered to be of benefit to the population or the state' (para. 8.21). By parity of reasoning it is legislation to prevent individual choice in race and gender, thus imposing the 'natural balance', which raises the spectre of eugenic control, allegedly in the public interest. It would have been instructive to know whether the members of the Nuffield Council working party would endorse opposition to legal interference with parental choice in race, gender, and other phenotypical traits, had they accepted these issues as part of their remit.[42]

It is sometimes said that parents who would want a child of a different race, or one which would be likely to look radically different from themselves in terms of colour or some other feature, must have discreditable motives, whether racist or of some other kind. It is, so the suggestion goes, wrong to allow such parents to have children at all and certainly wrong to allow them a choice born of suspect motives. I have criticized above the idea of scrutinizing social features, including motives, as a pre-condition for treatment and as a filter through which candidates for treatment must pass.

It is perhaps timely to press the question: why do we assume that the desire for a different-race child is racially motivated in some discreditable way, whereas the desire for a same-race child is not? If we are going to suspect people's motives, the desire for a child of the same race is surely as likely to be discreditable. It is after all societies which exclude different races that are assumed to be racist, not societies which welcome and celebrate diversity. Why should this not be true of families?

We should remember that the traditional way of producing children, namely by selecting a marriage (or less formally selected procreational) partner, is very often governed by prejudices or preferences, not only for a particular sort of partner, but for the particular sort of child that mating with that partner will produce. Many societies support and celebrate marriages within religious groups, or racial groups, or, for that matter, social or national groups, and apply intimidatory pressure on those who would 'marry out'. Such practices are usually regarded as either morally correct or at worst morally neutral; and yet they are as much a way of producing 'designer children' and indeed 'designer' societies as are the practices to which so many people so strongly object.

[42] See the Nuffield Council on Bioethics report *Genetic Screening: Ethical Issues*, pub. Dec. 1993.

Human Cloning

There are two rather different techniques available for cloning individuals. One is by nuclear substitution and the other by cell mass division. We will look at both of these in turn, starting with cell mass division because this is the only technique for cloning that has, as yet, been used in humans.

Cell mass division

Although the technique of cloning embryos by cell mass division has been used extensively in animal models, it was used as a way of multiplying human embryos for the first time in October 1993 when Jerry Hall and Robert Stillman at George Washington Medical Centre cloned human embryos by splitting early two- to eight-cell embryos into single embryo cells. Among other uses, cloning by cell mass division or embryo splitting could be used to provide a 'twin' embryo for biopsy, permitting an embryo undamaged by invasive procedures to be available for implantation following the result of the biopsy on its twin. We must now consider to what extent such a practice is ethically problematic. A number of objections have been made. There is the issue of how many multiples of a particular genetic constitution may be produced, the question as to whether identical siblings may be produced years apart, the issue (again) of 'designer children', and the question of the legitimacy of using one embryo to benefit another. Finally there are the questions of individuality and the effect on the variability of the gene pool.

Individuals, multiples, and genetic variation

First we should note that cloning does not produce identical copies of the same individual person. It can only produce identical copies of the same genotype. Our experience of identical twins demonstrates that each is a separate individual with his or her own character, preferences, and so on. Although there is some evidence of striking similarities with respect to these factors in twins, there is no question but that each twin is a distinct individual, independent and as free as is anyone else. To clone John Harris is not to create multiple John Harrises.[43] Artificial clones do not raise any difficulties not raised by the phenomenon of 'natural' twins.

---

[43] Not of course that that would necessarily be a bad thing.

If the objection to cloning is to the creation of identical individuals separated in time, then the sense in which the twins are identical, and the objection that such 'identicalness' might constitute, needs to be carefully understood. We should remember that such twins will be 'identical' in the sense that they will each have the same genotype, but they will never be identical in the more familiar sense of looking identical at the same moment in time. Each will be identical at birth, say, but since their birth days will be separated in time, the time at which each is identical to the other in appearance will (probably) be never! If we think of expected similarities in character, tastes, and so on, then the same is true. The further separated in time, the less likely they are to have similarities of *character* (the more different the environment, the more different environmental influence on individuality).

These considerations aside, however, the ethics of identical twins separated in time is surely no different from that of other 'twins'[44] thus separated—a problem that has been with us since it became possible to cryopreserve embryos. Nor is it greater than the 'problem' of having identical twins in the normal haphazard way. We do not normally think it objectionable when parents are delighted by their identical twins nor when they exacerbate possible identity problems by dressing their twins in the same clothes. I have seen no convincing objections to such temporal separation of siblings.

The issue of genetic variation need not detain us long. The numbers of twins produced by cloning will always be so small compared to the human gene pool in totality that the effect on the variation of the human gene pool will be vanishingly small.

Using siblings for the benefit of one another

We noted the possibility of using embryo splitting to allow genetic and other screening by embryo biopsy, where one embryo would be tested and then destroyed to ascertain the health and genetic status of the remaining clones. An objection often voiced to this is that 'one twin would be destroyed for the sake of another'.

This is a bizarre and misleading objection. In the first place it is ethically dubious to object to one embryo being sacrificed for the sake of another, but not to object to it being sacrificed for nothing. In *in vitro*

---

[44] The sense in which eggs harvested at the same time and fertilized even in the same Petri dish are 'twins' is of course highly problematic. Twins are, after all, in the 'everyday usage' sense, siblings born sequentially from the same womb having been gestated there at the same time.

fertilization, it is currently regarded as good practice to store spare embryos for future use by the mother or for disposal at her direction, either to other women, for research, or to be destroyed. It cannot be worse to use an embryo to provide information on its sibling than to use it for more abstract research or simply to destroy it. So long as early embryos may be used for research or simply destroyed, use for genetic and other health testing is surely permissible.

The crucial ethical issue here is whether it would be morally defensible, by outlawing the creation of clones by cell mass division, to deny a woman the chance to have the child she desperately seeks. If this procedure would enable a woman to create a sufficient number of embryos to give her a reasonable chance of successfully implanting one or two of them, then the objections would have to be weighty. If pre-implantation testing by cell biopsy might damage the embryo to be implanted, would it be defensible to prefer this to testing a clone, if technology permits such a clone to be created without damage, by separating a cell or two from the embryonic cell mass? On the other hand, if we assume each procedure to have been perfected and to be equally safe, we must ask what the ethical difference would be between taking a cell for cell biopsy and destroying it thereafter and taking a cell to create a clone, and then destroying the clone? The answer can only be that destroying the cloned embryo would constitute a waste of human potential; but this same potential is wasted whenever an embryo is not implanted.

We should note an odd tension between how we think of the ethics of the destruction of an individual embryo involving cell loss on the one hand, and destruction of an individual embryo without cell loss on the other. The process of embryo splitting also allows for recombination. The early cell mass (before the thirty-two-cell stage) may be split into a number of potentially viable embryos. Such embryos may also be recombined into one embryo again, which would remain equally potentially viable. Assuming this technique to be as safe as the creation of clones by cell mass division, if the embryos are recombined, a number of individual twins have been 'destroyed' without the destruction of a single cell. Is such a process more or less ethically problematic?

If, as seems likely, the reason why it is thought objectionable to recombine such clones is the loss of potential human beings, then perhaps it would be considered unethical *not* to split any embryo into as many twins as possible? By so doing we would, after all, maximize just that potential, the loss of which, supposedly, inhibits recombination. If all this has a dizzying effect, it is perhaps because the language that we use misleads us.

We are, as Wittgenstein was so fond of reminding us, often misled by the language we use. To think of these early clumps of cells as 'twins' deludes us into thinking of them as 'persons'.[45] Take an embryonic cell mass, split it into six clumps of cells. You have created six twin embryos. Take five away and destroy them or recombine them into one and you have done exactly the same thing in one sense, namely created a single potentially viable embryo. In another sense you have wasted potential experimental material or potentially viable embryos. Yet this latter action is done whenever a cell mass that could viably be divided is left undivided, or whenever an egg that could be fertilized is left unfertilized. What this shows, if it shows anything, is that we cannot logically *think* of the early human cell mass as if it were a person, whatever we choose to call it.

Nuclear substitution

This technique involves (crudely described) deleting the nucleus of an egg cell and substituting the nucleus taken from the cell of another individual. This can be done using cells from an adult. The first viable offspring produced from fetal and adult mammalian cells was reported from an Edinburgh-based group in *Nature* on 27 February 1997.[46] The resulting sheep was named 'Dolly'; she caused an international sensation, and was widely reported in the world press, with President Clinton of the United States calling for an investigation into the ethics of such procedures and announcing a moratorium on public spending on human cloning, the British Nobel prize winner Joseph Rotblat describing it as science out of control creating 'a means of mass destruction',[47] and the German newspaper *Die Welt* evoking the Third Reich, commenting: 'The cloning of human beings would fit precisely into Adolph Hitler's world view'.[48]

One major reason for developing this technique in animals is to permit the study of genetic diseases and indeed genetic development more

[45] We do not mean here to deny people the right to choose and use the vocabulary they find most compelling, and which is compatible with clear meaning or with the facts. We have no objection, for example, to people talking of the early embryo as an 'unborn child'. Our point here is that sometimes our choice of vocabulary can deceive us.

[46] Wilmut *et al.*, 'Viable Offspring Derived from Fetal and Adult Mammalian Cells', *Nature*, 27 Feb. 1997.

[47] *Guardian*, 26 Feb. 1997. [48] Reported in the *Guardian*, 28 Feb. 1997.

generally. The point of attempting such cloning techniques in humans is less obvious although it holds some prospect of preventing mitochondrial diseases and of providing tailor-made cells to prevent genetic defects. Moreover, for the moment to attempt to clone human embryos in the United Kingdom is widely thought to be illegal. Whether it would in fact be illegal might turn on whether it is plausible to regard such cloning as resulting from 'fertilization'. It is apparently only fertilized embryos that are covered by the Human Fertilisation and Embryology Act 1990.[49] The technique used in Edinburgh, which involves deleting the nucleus of an unfertilized egg and then substituting a cell nucleus from an existing individual, bypasses fertilization completely and may therefore turn out not to be covered by existing legislation.

Of course some vainglorious individuals might wish to have offspring not simply with their genes but with a matching genotype, but there is no way that could make such an individual a duplicate of themselves. So many years down the line the environmental influences would be radically different, and since every choice however insignificant causes a life-path to branch, the holy grail of duplication would be doomed to remain a fruitless quest. There has been some talk for example of using surviving tissue from the embalmed Lenin to create a clone of the revolutionary leader. A clone of Lenin, born into a world more than a century removed from his own birth, brought up by very different parents in a very different social, political, moral, and indeed epistemological climate, would bear little resemblance to the man who started life as Vladimir Ulyanov on 22 April 1870.

Whether we should legislate to prevent people reproducing not twenty-three but all forty-six chromosomes seems more problematic for reasons we have already examined, but we might have reason to be uncomfortable about the likely standards and effects of child rearing by those who would clone themselves. Their attempts to mould their child in their own image would be likely to be more pronounced than the average. Whether they are likely to be worse than normal attempts to duplicate race, religion, and culture might well depend on the character and constitution of the genotype donor.

Gender Selection

No discussion of the ethics of reproduction would be complete without a consideration of genetic screening and indeed pre-natal screening and

[49] Margaret Brazier alerted me to this possibility.

diagnosis more generally. However, having examined these issues in detail elsewhere I will consider them here only in so far as they relate to one of our present concerns, namely the question of designer children.[50]

We have already considered the ethics of a number of attempts to design children; let's turn for a moment to a very basic element of design, namely gender. The investigation will, however, have consequences for other morally neutral traits like hair and eye colour. I say 'morally neutral' because I assume no reasonable person thinks it could be *morally* better to have one colour of hair rather than another, nor for that matter to be one gender rather than another. The best I can do here is repeat a perhaps familiar thought, namely that although this is often taken to be a difficult question and indeed the idea of parents being able to choose such things very often causes outrage, I have found difficulty in seeing this question as problematic. It seems to me to come to this: either such traits as hair colour, eye colour, gender, and the like are important or they are not. If they are *not* important why not let people choose? And if they *are* important, can it be right to leave such important matters to chance?[51]

Of course the *manner of choosing* may be morally important. We might feel that abortion was not a reasonable way of determining such things; but if, for example, a litre of orange juice taken at a particular point in pregnancy could achieve the desired outcome, I doubt if any attempt to regulate its use would succeed or ought even to be attempted. At the moment a reliable method of gender determination in humans does not exist, but it is always important to decide principles in advance of practicalities.

Objections to the idea of gender selection and the like often turn on two forms of 'slippery slope' argument. Either it is claimed that a pattern of gender preference will emerge which will constitute a sort of 'slap in the face' to the gender discriminated against, an insult and humiliation, like a piece of racist graffiti perhaps. Or, it is suggested that the pattern of preference will be such as to create severe imbalance in the population of society with harmful social consequences. Plainly these are very different sorts of outcome.

We should note that a pattern of preference for one gender amongst those opting for gender selection would not necessarily be evidence

[50] See *Wonderwoman and Superman*, ch. 10. See also 'Sex Selection for Non-medical Reasons', Report of a Committee of the Health Council of the Netherlands, No. 1995/11E (The Hague, 16 June 1995).

[51] I have examined these questions at length on a previous occasion. See *Wonderwoman and Superman*, 158.

of sexist discrimination. There might be all sorts of respectable, non-prejudicial reasons for preferring one gender to another including just having a preference for sons or daughters. A preference for producing a child of a particular gender no more necessarily implies discrimination against members of the alternative gender than choosing to marry a co-religionist, a compatriot, or someone of the same race or even class implies discrimination against other religions, nations, races, or classes. Of course, if a pattern of preference in favour of one gender were to emerge it might have either or both of the effects we have noted and would certainly be cause for concern. However, it seems verging on hysteria simply to assume either that it would inevitably have these effects or that the effects would be so damaging as to warrant legislation to prevent the remotest risk of their occurring.

If we ask what level of 'risk' a society like the United Kingdom for example should be prepared to run in order to avoid the unnecessary imposition of legal restraint on choice and to see whether a pattern of preference emerged and if so whether or not it was a pattern of vicious preference, the answer is not clear.

A Modest Proposal for a Licensing Scheme

My own proposal would be that a society like ours, of about fifty-eight million people, could afford to license, say, one million procedures for gender selection over a ten-year period with options to revise the policy if severe imbalance seemed likely and was likely to prove significantly damaging to individuals or society. We could then see what patterns of selection and motivation emerged. Even if all choices went one way, the imbalance created would be relatively small before detection, and a halt could be called if this seemed justifiable. I doubt that the places allocated on such a programme would not be taken up (it would of course be self-financing and would not be part of the public health care system). It must be remembered that those who opted for gender selection would (with current technology) have to be very circumspect about their procreation and use sperm selection or pre-implantation testing as the method. This would not, I guess, be wildly attractive or indeed particularly reliable. For the foreseeable future the take-up will also be limited by the availability of clinics offering the service. In any event, the way forward for a tolerant society respectful of autonomy would surely be not to rush to prohibitive legislation, but rather to license the activity with regular monitoring and see whether anything so terrible that it required prohibitive legislation emerged.

Suppose that an unprecedented perturbation of the spheres, or other natural event, had caused a one-off increase in births of one gender, say by 1 per cent? Would the prospect of, even a million or so, more boys or girls than would otherwise have been expected throw society into a spin? Would anyone lose any sleep over it? Suppose we had to wake up to the fact that there *already was* a gender imbalance in our society in favour of girls? Suppose (perish the thought) that there were about 1.2 million more women than men already! In such a terrible eventuality perhaps we should hope that gender selection would predominantly favour males, and that some inroads into this adverse balance might thereby be made.[52]

In any event to say, as Ruth Deech, chair of the United Kingdom Human Fertilisation and Embryology Authority, did recently, that it was 'wrong to unbalance the level (of gender distribution) that nature gave us naturally' is surely counter-intuitive and supported by no plausible arguments.[53]

Genetic Screening and Testing

I assume (but shall not here argue the point)[54] that there is a strong moral obligation to prevent preventable harm and suffering and that this obligation applies equally to curing disease and injury and to preventing the avoidable creation of people who will have disease or injury. The strength of this obligation of course varies with the seriousness of the preventable harm, the costs of preventing it, and the likelihood of its occurring. I accept also that there are important differences between preventing such harm by deciding not to procreate, by declining to implant embryos following pre-implantation diagnosis, and by abortion following pre-natal screening. There is a massive danger in allowing attitudes to abortion to colour the issue of preventing the birth of children who will live in a significantly harmed condition.

---

[52] Taken from the home page of the Office for National Statistics on the World Wide Web: *The United Kingdom in Figures 1996*. The last figures available are for 1994.

[53] Interviewed on BBC Radio's *Today* programme, 26 Feb. 1997, about proposals to set up a gender selection clinic in Italy to avoid United Kingdom law.

[54] I argue at length for this in my *Wonderwoman and Superman*, and in my 'Should We Attempt to Eradicate Disability', *Public Understanding of Science*, 4 (1995), 233–42.

If there are six pre-implantation embryos awaiting transfer, and diagnosis reveals that three have genetic diseases and three are normal, which three should be implanted? Only those who think that it is legitimate to choose to implant the three with genetic illness believe there is no obligation to prevent preventable disease by making decisions as to whether or not babies with particular diseases should be brought into existence.[55] Now assume that we can tell that three are normal and three will have longer, healthier lives than the average. Is there a moral reason to prefer those with better prospects for a long healthy life? I believe so, but here the decision is tighter. In any event it seems improbable to conclude that it would be *unethical* to prefer the embryos with expectation of a longer healthier life than is normal for humans. Now assume something else, that there are another three embryos with superior intelligence genetically diagnosed prior to implantation. Again, for what it is worth, I would opt to implant the more intelligent. I can understand those who would not, but again it seems improbable that it could be *unethical* to implant those with predicted higher than normal intelligence.

Now assume that longer, healthier, more intelligent existence could be achieved by safe genetic manipulation of embryos. If it would not be unethical to capitalize on the chance 'blessings' of nature, if these could be diagnosed before implantation, what would make it unethical to confer such blessings if we had the technology to do so? I cannot think of a plausible answer to this question despite a sustained attempt to do so and I conclude that beneficial genetic manipulation (so-called genetic enhancement therapy), if we could be sure of its safety, would be legitimate.[56]

Pre-implantation Diagnosis and Abortion

In addressing the ethics of pre-implantation genetic diagnosis (PIGD) a comparison is sometimes made with abortion. The purpose of such a comparison is to suggest that PIGD must be justified using criteria comparably stringent with those required to justify abortion and that in particular a woman's motives for requesting PIGD must be minutely scrutinized. However, this comparison is seriously misleading if not

---

[55] I assume contrary to fact, that all have an equal chance of successful birth.
[56] See my *Wonderwoman and Superman*, ch. 7.

fallacious. The fallacy involved in the comparison is that a decision to abort must, in the United Kingdom, be endorsed by two medical practitioners and comply with the requirements of various Acts of parliament; and in most other jurisdictions the regulations governing qualification for abortion are equally stringent. On the other hand, a decision not to implant embryos requires no legal justification whatsoever. The decision not to implant embryos *in vitro* is within the unfettered discretion of any woman. This is certainly the case in the United Kingdom, and, I believe, in all other jurisdictions.

Since a woman cannot be forced to implant any embryos and is free to choose to decline to do so at any stage, we are entitled to ask what the justification is for examining the motives or the purposes of a mother before permitting her to do something that, in law, is within her unfettered discretion.

Now it might be objected that while she is entitled to refuse to implant any embryos, the decision to select between embryos is constrained by morality. She should not choose between them in ways which might constitute unfair discrimination, for example. However, choosing between embryos would only constitute *unfair* discrimination if the reasons for preferring some embryos to others focused on features which there could be no legitimate reasons to prefer. More likely, however, the features revealed by PIGD would either demonstrate a rational, ethically defensible basis for preference to implant some embryos over others or some before others or amount to a challenge to show why the proposed preference is discriminatory in some unjust way or unethical in some other way.

Moreover, we are entitled to ask why mothers or parents should be required to meet more stringent standards when deciding whether to permit implantation than is the government or other government-appointed supervisory bodies like, in the United Kingdom, the HFEA. The infamous 'orphaned embryo opera' which was played out in the summer of 1996, which culminated in the 'slaughter' of around 4,000 frozen embryos, was required by the provisions of the Human Fertilisation and Embryology Act 1990 which had permitted a maximum storage period of five years. Where then was the threshold of seriousness sought by those who compare PIGD with abortion? What justifications motivated the framers of the legislation which resulted in such profligate slaughter? If we seek for justification for the five-year limit which led to the slaughter it can only, I suggest, be found in a combination of two considerations:

1. vague fears, given form by the Act, that it was not safe to store frozen embryos beyond five years (fears that were demonstrably vague and ill-founded when, only six years after the Act and following the mass slaughter of embryos, the Human Fertilisation and Embryology (Statutory Storage Period for Embryos) Regulations 1996 were rushed through to extend the storage period from five to ten years); and

2. respect for the right of parents to determine the destiny of their genetic material.

While these may be adequate as justifications for killing frozen embryos, they neither of them surely come close to the level of seriousness of justifications required for abortion. We should not impose on individual women standards of justification more stringent than those which parliament sets for comparable consequences.

Procreative Autonomy

Throughout this chapter we have looked at the new reproductive technologies and asked two questions. Is their use unethical and should access to it, or use of it, be controlled by legislation and if so how? Our answers to these questions have on the whole indicated a tolerance of innovation and respect for individual choice. The spirit of such an approach has recently been defended by Ronald Dworkin. Indeed, he has argued that dimensions of it may even be protected in the United States by the Constitution and are, in any event, a vital feature of an essentially democratic approach to reproductive choices.

Dworkin talks in terms of a right to procreative autonomy and has defined this right as 'a right [of people] to control their own role in procreation unless the state has a compelling reason for denying them that control'.[57] Dworkin's discussion of this right largely centres on its manifestation in the abortion debate. For us, the more crucial question is whether or not it might legitimately be interpreted to include the right to reproduce with the genes we choose and to which we have legitimate access, or to reproduce in ways that express our reproductive choices and our vision for the sorts of people we think it right to create. Arguably, even freedom to clone one's own genes might also be defended as a

[57] Ronald Dworkin, *Life's Dominion* (London: HarperCollins, 1993), 148.

dimension of procreative autonomy. Many people and agencies have been attracted by the idea of the special nature of genes and the special relationship people have with their own genes. It was this special relationship, you will remember, which was the basis of the HFEA's objections to Mrs Blood's desire to use her husband's genetic material without his formal written consent.

Ronald Dworkin has suggested that 'procreative autonomy' is protected by both the First and the Fourteenth Amendments to the United States Constitution although, as far as I know, he has not applied his arguments specifically to our present concerns.[58]

The right of procreative autonomy follows from any competent interpretation of the due process clause and of the Supreme Court's past decisions applying it . . . The First Amendment prohibits government from establishing any religion, and it guarantees all citizens free exercise of their own religion. The Fourteenth Amendment, which incorporates the First Amendment, imposes the same prohibition and same responsibility on states. These provisions also guarantee the right of procreative autonomy.[59]

The point is that the sorts of freedoms which freedom of religion guarantees, freedom to choose one's own way of life and live according to one's most deeply held beliefs, are also at the heart of procreative choices. And this holds true even when the freedoms that people assert cause offence or are disturbing or even disgusting. A parallel with freedom of speech is instructive here. Dworkin suggests that free speech must be guaranteed even when it results in individuals being offended or insulted precisely because free speech plays a pivotal role in democratic theory—it is required to protect equality in a democratic society. As Dworkin argues:

Exactly because the moral environment in which we all live is in good part created by others, however, the question of who shall have the power to help shape that environment and how, is of fundamental importance, though it is often neglected in political theory. Only one answer is consistent with the ideals of political equality: that no one may be prevented from influencing the shared moral environment, through his own private choices, tastes, opinions, and example,

---

[58] See ibid. 160. See also R. Dworkin, *Freedom's Law* (Oxford: Oxford University Press, 1996), chs. 8, 9, and 10. I am indebted to Justine Burley for pointing these arguments out to me.

[59] Dworkin, *Life's Dominion*, 160.

just because these tastes or opinions disgust those who have the power to shut him up or lock him up.[60]

Thus it may be that we should be prepared to accept both some degree of offence and some social disadvantages as a price we should be willing to pay in order to protect freedom of choice in matters of procreation, and perhaps this applies to cloning and to the aspirations of Mrs Blood, as much as to more straightforward or usual procreative preferences.[61]

The nub of the argument is complex and abstract but it is worth stating at some length. I cannot improve upon Dworkin's formulation of it.

The right of procreative autonomy has an important place not only in the structure of the American Constitution but in Western political culture more generally. The most important feature of that culture is a belief in individual human dignity: that people have the moral right—and the moral responsibility—to confront the most fundamental questions about the meaning and value of their own lives for themselves, answering to their own consciences and convictions. That assumption was the engine of emancipation and of racial equality, for example. The most powerful arguments against slavery before the Civil War, and for equal protection after it, were framed in the language of dignity: for both religious and secular abolitionists, the cruellest aspect of slavery was its failure to recognise a slave's right to decide central issues of value for himself. Indeed, the most basic premise of Western democracy—that government should be republican rather than despotic—embodies a commitment to that conception of dignity. The principle of procreative autonomy, in a broad sense, is embedded in any genuinely democratic culture.[62]

In so far as decisions to reproduce in particular ways or even using particular technologies constitute decisions concerning central issues of value, then arguably the freedom to make them is guaranteed not only by the United States Constitution but by the constitution (written or not) of any democratic society, unless the state has a compelling reason for denying that control. To establish such a compelling reason the state would have to show that more was at stake than the fact that a majority found the ideas disturbing or even disgusting.

---

[60] Dworkin, *Freedom's Law*, 237–8. I am grateful to Justine Burley for pointing out this remark.

[61] Ronald Dworkin has produced an elegant account of the way the price we should be willing to pay for freedom might or might not be traded off against the costs. See his *Taking Rights Seriously* (London: Duckworth, 1977), ch. 10, and his *A Matter of Principle* (Cambridge, Mass.: Harvard University Press, 1985), ch. 17.

[62] Dworkin, *Life's Dominion*, 166–7.

Conclusion

I have covered extensive terrain and in doing so have tried to show the complexity of the legal, social, and philosophical dimensions of the reproductive choice issues raised by many of the new possibilities for using and testing eggs, ovarian tissue, and embryos. I have also attempted to expose the weaknesses of many of the arguments and claims which are so often made about the ethics of such use. What follows is not necessarily the slide from liberty to licence. There is no doubt that caution is indicated when considering the acceptability of scientific 'advance' and the use of new technology. Equally we must be cautious about needlessly denying ourselves the benefit of such advance and such technology, particularly when it offers much needed and much desired treatment or offers a legitimate extension of human choice.

The question, of course, is always whether or not such choices are legitimate. But if the arguments against free choice are as weak and flawed as many of those we have considered, the presumption should be against over-hasty prohibition. The way forward is perhaps through careful regulation and close monitoring, rather than baseless charges that the practices are 'unethical' and should therefore be banned. I have argued that the first of these claims is without foundation for very many of the new methods of exercising reproductive choice and that, for those same choices, the second (prohibition by legislation) neither follows from the first nor has been independently justified by any compelling considerations.

2

On the Concept of Pre-embryo: The Basis for a New 'Copernican Revolution' in the Current View about Human Reproduction

MAURIZIO MORI

The term 'pre-embryo' was introduced in the mid-1980s as a general word to denote the earliest stages of human life from fertilization up to a few days afterwards.[1] The upshot of such a proposal is a new partition of pre-natal life: instead of the usual twofold distinction between pre- and post-fertilization (with embryonic and fetal stage), now we have a threefold distinction: pre-fertilization, pre-embryonic stage, and post-pre-embryonic stage.

There is a heated controversy over the new proposal: 'pre-embryonists' (as I shall call them from now on) hold that it is required by a more accurate reflection on recent empirical data showing that in earlier stages after fertilization human life has some special features which make it significantly different from later stages. Fertilizationists (as I call the opponents) rejoin that the crucial event occurs at fertilization, and the new term therefore lacks any biological and logical bases, being only a semantic device introduced to justify experimentation on early stages of human life and its destruction. Pre-embryonists retort that lesser protection depends on the fact that the new distinction is well grounded in biology, and they charge fertilizationists with being wrong in claiming that questions concerning the beginning of life or personhood are 'questions of fact susceptible of straightforward answers . . . the answers to such questions in fact are complex amalgams of moral and factual

[1] I do not want to state precisely the end of the pre-embryonic stage (whether at six/seven days or fourteen/fifteen days after fertilization) because this is irrelevant to my argument. Moreover I know that many scientists are not enthusiastic about the new term 'pre-embryo' since they think that there are many more stages in a continuous process, so that 'pre-embryo' is too loose and general. However, I think it may be useful in order to denote some special features proper to earlier stages.

judgements'. Therefore, instead of considering the issue of the beginning of life, it is more convenient to go 'straight to the question of how it is right to treat the human embryo' and recognize that such an answer 'must necessarily be in terms of ethical or moral principles'.[2] However, to say that questions concerning the beginning of the person are 'are complex amalgams of moral and factual judgements' is not equivalent to saying that it is impossible to sort out the different aspects of the amalgam and assess them. In this sense the fertilizationists' claim cannot simply be dismissed but must be considered: it is possible to distinguish descriptive and evaluative parts showing possible mistakes in the argument and make clear which are the ethical principles involved in the matter. This is my major task in this chapter.

More specifically, I want to examine the controversy over the notion of 'pre-embryo' and distinguish different sorts of arguments. Focusing our attention on the descriptive one, we have to realize that the pre-embryo and the consequent new partition of pre-natal life shows a fundamental difficulty in the current 'conceptual framework' (more or less) implicitly used in discussing the issue. Therefore, the notion of 'pre-embryo' has a greater relevance than may appear at first, since in a sense it has a role analogous to that of Jupiter's satellites in the astronomical revolution: it compels us to admit that the current paradigm is unable to account for the new concept and we have to look for a new and more adequate conceptual frame. For this reason the notion of pre-embryo is the ground for a sort of new 'Copernican revolution' concerning the current view of human reproduction. The immediate effect of such a 'revolution' is a different description of relevant phenomena concerning pre-natal life and consequently new questions to be asked at the normative level. The new way of seeing the issue will also make it easier to understand why the answer to such a issue must be given in terms of ethical principles, and we will be able to individuate the relevant principles.

It is important to start by clarifying the general structure of the current debate over the issue. As already mentioned, fertilizationists usually do not draw a distinction between 'life' and 'personhood', and claim that the question concerning the beginning of a person can receive a straightforward answer so that the *descriptive* premise of the argument can be safely asserted. For them it is important to state that the crucial

---

[2] M. Warnock, *A Question of Life: The Warnock Report on Human Fertilisation and Embryology* (New York: Basil Blackwell, 1985), 11.5.

event happens at fertilization because from such a premiss they draw the *normative* conclusion that it is morally wrong to interfere with the newly fertilized egg (unless it is for its own good). If after fertilization there is no person—they say—there is no need of any protection; but if there is already a person, then—since in western societies persons have rights (and particularly the right to life)—even the newly fertilized egg is entitled to the same strong protection as any other person: any different solution would be an unjust and repugnant discrimination between persons. I am not sure that fertilizationists can really draw this practical conclusion, but here I will not deal with the inferential process, since I am interested in the *descriptive* premiss itself: I want to examine the arguments in favour of such a premiss. In this way we can identify the problems inherent in fertilizationism and why the notion of pre-embryo becomes relevant.

According to one version of fertilizationism the descriptive premiss can receive a straightforward answer, which is provided directly by biological sciences. A clear statement in this sense is that of Paul Ramsey, who wrote that 'microgenetics seems to have demonstrated what religion never could. The human individual comes into existence first as a minute informational speck,'[3] and this position seems to be accepted by the popular press and also among some scholars.[4] I think that this position holding that the descriptive premiss is a mere scientific statement is flawed in several senses. Here I mention only two. First, in order to know whether at fertilization there is or there is not a person we must presuppose a precise definition of 'person', and questions of definitions are never mere scientific questions nor mere questions of fact. A definition is like a piece of a large puzzle and its proposal presupposes a study of relationships with other pieces and a view of the whole picture; these are 'philosophical' tasks (and not merely scientific). Second,

---

[3] P. Ramsey, 'The Morality of Abortion', in D. H. Labby (ed.), *Life or Death: Ethics and Options* (Seattle: University of Washington Press, 1968), 61.

[4] For instance Teresa Iglesias writes that to solve the problem of the beginning of persons 'we must pay attention to the true description of the facts of early embryonic life. I believe that when these facts are adequately stated, the problems to which the early life of the human embryo is said to give rise disappear' (*IVF and Justice* (London: Linacre Centre for Health Care Ethics, 1990), 104). In this sense Iglesias says that authors such as Aristotle and Aquinas had different opinions on the origin of the person because they 'lacked biological information which is available to us today . . . in the light of our present biological information, we cannot avoid concluding that Aquinas *today* would have considered the human embryo from conception a *homo*, a being of human nature, a human bodily being endowed with a rational soul, "one of us", a human person' (pp. 106 and 109).

any definition of 'person' claiming to be adequate must consider that in western culture a person is a special entity endowed with an element which transcends mere physical nature: there are several ways to denote this special feature (symbolic capacity, rationality, etc.) and here I think it is convenient to use the old terminology and call it 'soul'. In this sense, we can say that a person is a special unity of body and a soul, and our difficulty becomes apparent: since science can say nothing on the soul, it cannot directly solve the controversy. So the straightforward answer we have examined is certainly wrong and misleading.

However, fertilizationists can refine their position and present a different formulation, which deserves attention.

According to this new version of fertilizationism, the descriptive premiss is not merely scientific, even if science is still most relevant in two different (and basic) senses:

1. it provides the empirical data to be interpreted in the light of some theoretical assumptions; and
2. at the same time it contributes to elaborate such theoretical assumptions.

More specifically science contributes to creating the interpretative paradigm, stating that the issue should be examined by means of a 'biological approach' which is 'biological' because it is grounded in a 'biological way of thinking'. In this sense, relevant data to be considered are those *internal* to the biological process, and sociological as well as psychological aspects concerning other people are to be disregarded. Moreover, the proper question to be asked is 'When does human life begin?', all other possible questions being irrelevant and arbitrary because they consider aspects which are *external* to the biological process. And even the whole issue concerning the 'person' must be set aside, since it is about something which transcends any mere biological process (and in a sense is 'external' to it). For this reason any distinction between 'human life' and 'human person' appears to be futile and arbitrary, and the real question to be answered is about the beginning of 'human life'.

I am aware that here we reach a crucial juncture of the argument and that the adoption of such a 'biological approach' as the specific interpretative frame can be challenged. So a critic can say that this approach is wrong since it leads to excluding the issue of personhood for methodological reasons, although this is the real problem to be examined.

However, fertilizationists may insist (and actually do insist) that questions concerning the spark of intellectual life are 'external' to biological processes and to biology's tasks and that for this reason they must be avoided. I am not sure that this move is acceptable, but I think that there is a sense in which it is true that problems about 'mind' and 'rationality' are not proper and specific topics for biological explanations. In any case, at least for argument's sake, I think it is interesting to accept the proposal of adopting the 'biological approach' outlined above, which I hope to have presented in a fairly impartial and acceptable way for fertilizationists themselves.

Having clarified the general features of the conceptual paradigm, we can now consider the allegedly relevant scientific facts in order to assess their interpretation. The claim is that at fertilization:

1. a new and unique genotype is formed;
2. the new entity is self-growing in an autonomous, co-ordinated, and continuous way.

When these facts are interpreted according to the biological approach —so the argument says—quite naturally we are led to the conclusion that fertilization is the crucial point for the beginning of a 'new human life'. There 'something' begins which is new, unique, autonomous, and self-growing, and this 'something' is continuous with the resulting person; therefore the natural conclusion is that it must already be a person from the beginning. Any further distinction is arbitrary because forced on the issue from without, as is any question other than 'When does human life begin?' In this sense fertilizationists holding this version of the argument can reach the same normative conclusion as those holding the former version without sharing the former mistakes. In this new argument the conclusion about a person's origin is not derived directly from science, but mediated by an 'interpretation' through a 'scientific conceptual framework'. In this sense this position seems to be 'formally' correct and at the same time can claim the authority of scientific thinking: for this reason this version of fertilizationism looks quite strong. It is therefore necessary to examine the interpretation of each of the allegedly relevant facts, and I shall start with the first one.

Uniqueness of genotype. It is true that at fertilization a unique and unrepeatable new genotype is formed, but we must emphasize that such a genotype is 'unique' in the sense that statistically it is very unlikely that the same combination of genes will ever occur again: the genetic lottery is so large that it is empirically quite impossible for the same combination to occur twice (even if logically it is possible). However, the genotype is not 'unique' in the sense that nobody else will ever have it, since monozygotic twins are possible: it is possible to have (and in fact we do have) several bodies with the same genetic (unique) endowment. Therefore, *genetic uniqueness* is not equivalent to *somatic* (or *bodily*) *uniqueness*, and we have to distinguish two different senses of 'uniqueness'. This descriptive distinction is important because usually we are spontaneously inclined to confer some special value on unique and unrepeatable events, or at least to think that uniqueness adds some value to them. But having distinguished two different senses of 'uniqueness', we need to know which sense is valuable: is it genetic uniqueness or somatic uniqueness that is precious? And is it intrinsically valuable, i.e. valuable in itself, or is it instrumentally valuable, i.e. valuable as a means to reach something else which has intrinsic value?

In order to hold its relevance, fertilizationists must say that genetic uniqueness is intrinsically valuable, because only from this claim can they draw the desired normative conclusion concerning the prohibition of any interference with the newly fertilized egg and any experimentation on it. However, this idea does not seem immediately self-evident and it is not clear to me how we can prove it. An attempt in this direction is Paul Ramsey's statement recalling that genetic uniqueness depends on randomness, and that genetic randomness 'is about as close as science is likely to come to the doctrine of creation ex nihilo', assuming that creation 'out of nothing' is clearly something of 'intrinsic value'. However, since sometimes genetic randomness is positively harmful to some newborns, it is not self-evident to me why it should be better (or even imperative) to let people come 'out of nothing'. Oliver O'Donovan seems to justify this conclusion saying that 'randomness is the inscrutable face which providence turns to us when we cannot trace its way or guess its purpose. To accept that face is to accept that we cannot program for the best as God plans for the best, and that we cannot read his plans before the day he declares them.'[5] But in this case, genetic uniqueness becomes an *instrumental* value, because we have to value it in order to show our belief in a providential plan. However, since we do not know (and according to O'Donovan we cannot know) such a plan, in this

---

[5] Oliver O'Donovan, *Begotten or Made?* (Oxford: Oxford University Press, 1984), 72. It might be interesting to remark that we can reach the same results even without resorting to the random doctrine, as witness Pope John Paul II when he says that 'no one comes into the world by chance, one is always the term of God's love'.

case this instrumental value seems to be (and can be considered to be) equivalent to intrinsic value, which is our desired conclusion.

It therefore seems as if fertilizationists can assert the intrinsic value of genetic uniqueness, even if with some difficulties. But a further premiss is necessary for the argument to hold, and since this premiss is theological it cannot be accepted as granted in a secular debate. The real problem, however, is not its theological nature but whether or not it is consistent with our assumed 'biological approach'. Those espousing a 'biological way of thinking' have no reason at all to hold that genetic uniqueness is intrinsically valuable. This viewpoint seems to lead to a vision more similar to that presented by Tennyson when he wrote that Nature 'so careful of the type she seems, so careless of the single life'. Therefore a unique genetic combination is to be seen just as one occurrence out of infinite possibilities in the natural lottery: not only newly fertilized eggs are 'unique', each gamete is unique, but this feature is not sufficient for conferring any special intrinsic value on gametes. In this sense, those defending the 'biological approach' cannot say that the 'uniqueness' of a genotype is in itself a relevant fact to be considered.

There is another way to reach the same result: fertilizationists claim the intrinsic value of genetic uniqueness because in this way they can justify a strong prohibition of any interference with newly fertilized eggs. And they are right in saying that an intrinsically valuable entity should not be destroyed, but for the same reason they also have to say that such an intrinsic value should be perpetuated as long as possible. In the case of genetic uniqueness this means that each human zygote should be interfered with and specifically split into two or more individuals in order to preserve the specimen and its genetic uniqueness. So even if it were true that genetic uniqueness is valuable in itself, a careful analysis of this idea would produce paradoxical consequences which are opposite to the fertilizationists' desired conclusion. This shows once more that genetic uniqueness is not a relevant fact for fertilizationism's main thesis.

Fertilizationists may however emphasize that the really relevant fact is the other one about autonomous growing, internal co-ordination, and continuity of the new entity formed at fertilization: there a 'substance' begins and this 'energy' is lasting up to the organism's death, and even if there are some changes during the process they are inessential to the moral status of the entity, as is being taller or shorter, fatter or slimmer, hairy or bald. In this sense fertilizationists claim that a correct interpretation of such a fact according to the 'biological approach' leads to the conclusion that after fertilization there is a human individual life with potentialities. As Angelo Serra writes, when the two sets of genetic information in the gametes unite,

there emerges . . . a *new project* and a *new programme*, which remain respectively delineated and inscribed in a stable manner in the genome of the zygote. It is precisely this new genetic constitution which *individualises* the zygote clearly and definitely, that is, it is constituted by a *subject* with its own independent existence and with its own characteristics, which distinguish it from any other. In a biological perspective this neo-conceptus is a new living being, which initiates its own existence, different and distinct from that of its progenitors. A new being rich in countless possibilities, which will become evident from later development, if it proceeds regularly without disturbance or obstacles.[6]

It is at this point that the pre-embryonists' criticism becomes most interesting. They share the same biological approach as the fertilizationists, and nevertheless they claim that the fertilizationists' twofold distinction (pre- and post-fertilization) is too simplistic, mainly because it does not explain the possibility of twinning which is a property of every newly fertilized egg, i.e. of pre-embryos. How can one say that there is already an 'individual', if it is still possible to have two individuals, i.e. two tokens of the same type? In order to explain the possibility of twinning we have to admit—so pre-embryonists say—that after fertilization the living process is still very flexible and indeterminate, and that this totipotentiality is a significant feature *internal* to the biological process. In this sense a careful analysis must lead to a further distinction: a pre-fertilization, pre-embryonic stage in which twinning is still possible, and proper 'individual human life'. As Norman Ford writes, 'we certainly cannot equate the expression "human life" with "human beings" ',[7] and he remarks that:

the zygote has the potential both to produce cells that will form extraembryonic structures that are not strictly constitutive parts of the future definitive embryo proper and fetus and other cells that will only form structures of the definitive embryo proper and fetus. Prior to this differentiation all the cells can give rise to both embryonic and extraembryonic structures. It is this indeterminate state

---

[6] A. Serra, 'The Human Embryo, Science and Medicine: Commentary on a Recent Document', in International Federation of Catholic Universities, *Human Life: Its Beginnings and Development. Bioethical Reflections by Catholic Scholars* (Louvain-la-Neuve: Ciaco Éditeur, 1988), 49.

[7] N. Ford, *When Did I Begin?* (New York: Cambridge University Press, 1988), 124 (emphasis mine).

of the zygote both in relation to the differentiation required for the formation of the definitive embryo proper and *the number of definitive embryos to be formed* that suggests the zygote is only potentially a human individual, but not yet an actual human individual.[8]

To face such a criticism fertilizationists must provide a different satisfactory explanation of twinning, and a typical answer is to observe that it is a rare phenomenon the origin of which is not yet well known, and probably its best account can be given in terms of an early birth: the first 'individual' gives rise to a second 'individual' as happens in agametic reproduction and parthenogenesis. A monozygotic twin is in a sense the child of the earlier cell, which is the 'progenitor' of the new one. As Serra writes:

it may be easier to understand how the phenomenon of twinning does not detract from the individuality of the embryo from which the twin is derived if we recall some simple facts. No-one would question, I think, that a bacterium is an individual, that is, a being which has its own existence distinct from that of any other. At the moment of its reproduction another cell is formed, similar to the original one, which remains for a while attached to the one it is derived from and then frees itself. Then this, an individual too, will be able to produce others with the same mechanism. It is obvious that the first cell does not lack its own individuality because it is capable of making another similar to itself. Something analogous happens wherever there is agametic reproduction. There is an individual, for example an hydra, constituted of few cells. At a given moment a cell is formed, the gemma, which, when it detaches itself, begins the formation of another hydra. The fact that it is the gemma from which another individual originates does not detract from the hydra's own individuality.[9]

According to Serra something similar may happen even within human reproduction. In this case usually reproduction occurs only after development of germinal cells, but this is not always so:

reproduction may occasionally happen at the beginning of the life cycle when, after having followed a certain road, one or more cells which still possess the potential to develop may detach themselves, in a way analogous to twinning and follow their own differentiation independent of the embryo from which they have been detached; a new individual is born, if we wish to put it that way. There has been a first, followed by one or more others. In conclusion: an accurate analysis of the phenomenon of twinning and a clear concept of what an 'individual' is do not seem to leave room for perplexity about the full individuality of the zygote.[10]

---

[8]   N. Ford, *When Did I Begin?*, 11.
[9]   Serra, 'The Human Embryo', 56.   [10] Ibid. 56–7.

Even if only implicitly, Serra's response seems to admit that twinning is possible because in its earlier stages the autonomous self-growing of a fertilized egg is different in kind from subsequent stages: the analogy with very simple organisms reproducing agametically shows that the newly fertilized egg grows in the sense of producing only exact copies of the original cell, with an increase in size and mass, but with little cellular differentiation and specialization. Only later does this self-growing become a proper development, i.e. that 'progression of changes, either quantitative or qualitative, that lead from an undifferentiated or immature state to a highly organized, specialized, and mature state'.[11] Similarly, we have to distinguish two different kinds of 'co-ordination', because in earlier stages the 'cluster of cells' is still undifferentiated and lacks proper specialization, and is in this way similar to lower forms of life.[12] This characteristic marks a fundamental discontinuity within the biological process after fertilization.

Fertilizationists may insist that the former remarks are irrelevant because even an adolescent grows fast and has special peculiarities not found in other stages of life, but this is not a reason to justify a *biological* discontinuity within the same individual's lifespan. But the pre-embryonists' answer is that any comparison between an adolescent's faster growth and the growth of a pre-embryo is misleading because in the first case there is a full body with an already differentiated and specialized life, while in the other case it is such a specialization which is lacking, and this makes a difference.

---

[11] B. Bogin, *Patterns of Human Growth*, (Cambridge: Cambridge University Press, 1988), 7. Bogin points out a useful terminological distinction between 'growth' and 'development' that is often disregarded: 'Though growth and development may occur simultaneously, they are distinct biological processes. *Growth* may be defined as a quantitative increase in size or mass. . . . *development* is defined as a progression of changes, either quantitative or qualitative, that lead from an undifferentiated or immature state to a highly organized, specialized, and mature state' (p. 7).

[12] Whilst we can and must say that the gametes, oocyte and spermatozoon, are potential human beings, that is, they are capable of becoming a human being at the moment when their fusion takes place, to affirm the same for the zygote would be a biological and logical error. The zygote is, in reality, a new human being, who activates, according to the general law of ontogenesis, the potentiality which it carries inscribed in its genome, and once it has expressed this, it gradually acquires the human form and figure with which we are more familiar. For this reason, and with no room for error, from the first moment when the zygote is formed until the completion of its life cycle, we are always dealing with the same subject. It is certainly correct to affirm that, from the moment when the zygote is constituted and during the whole embryonic and fetal period, we are in the presence of a 'human being' or 'an individual belonging to the human species who is in the first stages of development or is developing'. But this description in no way detracts from the intrinsic characteristic of being a human subject, a characteristic which must be ascribed to the zygote both from a biological and a *logical* point of view.

So we reach the basis of the controversy: we can now see that biological data are interpreted in two different ways because each contender presupposes a specific notion of 'individual'. More specifically, fertilizationists presuppose a common-sense notion of 'individual' according to which an individual is any spatio-temporal entity whose parts are contiguous and separated by sharp boundaries from the outer world. In this sense the boundaries are the essential condition of the individual itself, which comes into being rather instantaneously and completely when the boundaries are formed and is destroyed when the boundaries break down. On the other hand pre-embryonists presuppose a stronger concept, which seems to be needed in the biological context where there are 'individuals' constituted by many individuals: a cell is an individual, since it meets the common-sense requirement of spatio-temporal contiguity limited by sharp boundaries; but an organ (think of the heart) also meets such a condition, even if it is constituted by many individual cells. Obviously, a fully developed body is also an individual, even if it is formed by many individual organs and millions of individual cells; and finally even a species probably meets the requirement of spatio-temporal extension within the limits of a given territory, and therefore should be considered an individual formed by many individual bodies. For this reason, while for the common-sense notion the boundaries are the essential element, in the biological notion the *relations* occurring within different parts are more important: an 'individual' is something more than a 'cluster of cells' contiguously assembled within sharp boundaries, and in order to have a 'biological individual' (in the proper and here relevant sense) a special 'subordination' of parts to the whole is needed, so that each part is functional to the whole and cannot live independently from the whole.[13]

This distinction between the two notions of 'individual' facilitates our understanding of the controversy over the pre-embryo: fertilizationists espouse a common-sense concept and therefore insist on saying that a fertilized egg is already an individual, since it is a spatio-temporal entity delimited by sharp boundaries. Anything occurring afterwards within such boundaries is irrelevant to 'individuality', as irrelevant as being fatter or slimmer, and therefore the notion of 'pre-embryo' is a fictitious invention involving a logical mistake. Seen from this viewpoint, Serra's proposal of comparing a newly fertilized egg with lower forms of life is an attempt implicitly to reintroduce this common-sense notion of 'individual'.

---

[13] F. Raffaele, *L'individuo e la specie* (1905; Florence: Sansoni Edizioni, 1941).

On the other hand, pre-embryonists espouse the other, stricter, biological concept, and therefore are led to distinguish an earlier pre-embryonic stage in which the relation of strict subordination of the parts to the whole is lacking, and later stages meeting this requirement. In this sense they remind us that in lower forms of life there are entities like corals and worms which appear as individuals (in the common-sense meaning) because of sharp boundaries, but which in reality are a 'colony of many independent parts contiguously assembled' or an 'assemblance of cells', since they lack the necessary subordination of parts to the whole. For this reason, someone suggested that pre-embryos are 'pre-individuals' or 'sub-individuals', in order to make clear that they lack the required internal subordination of the parts to the whole.

It is now clear why the opponents charge one another with being illogical and why the controversy seems endless: starting from his own definition each one is right, and from our viewpoint this result is quite interesting. Fertilizationists claimed that the 'biological approach' could lead to a single question, 'When does human life begin?', and a single interpretation of biological data pointing at fertilization as the undoubtedly crucial event. But now we have to realize that the same 'biological approach' leads to at least two different questions: 'When does human life begin?' and 'When does human individual life begin?', and to two corresponding interpretations of the same biological data. I think that this is a sign of a fundamental difficulty within what I have called the 'biological approach' and its underlying conceptual paradigm. It is important to examine this new difficulty more closely.

Can we solve such a fundamental difficulty? A solution could be found by saying that one of the two different notions of 'individual' is clearly wrong. But this is not an easy way to go: on the one hand both notions are used in different areas of biology, and on the other hand, even if we say that the stronger one is more adequate (since we are dealing with mammalian life and not with lower levels such as algae), this notion presents at least one new problem: there are some relationships among parts that are a more basic feature of individuals than spatio-temporal contiguity within boundaries. The stronger notion of 'individual' emphasizes the distinction between 'contiguous assembled life' (pre-embryonic stage) and 'individual life': but what should we then say of the case in which there are some relations between living parts which are 'contiguous not-yet-assembled life'? So even the pre-embryonists' view does not appear fully adequate, and we are left with two irreconcilable responses, showing that our fundamental difficulty is deeper than it might seem at first sight.

Fertilizationists held that by means of a 'biological approach' to the issue it was possible to individuate a single question, whose answer could be given by means of biological data interpreted according to a unique (biological) conceptual framework. But now it is clear that there are at least two different conceptual frameworks and two corresponding questions, so that the same biological data lead to two different answers. Therefore, something must be wrong with our current 'biological approach', and our task is to detect such a mistake.

I think that its basic defect can be discovered if we look at the kind of questions suggested by holders of the current 'biological approach': 'When does human life begin?' or 'When does individual human life begin?' The first question looks very familiar, mainly because it fits with our common-sense view in which we usually deal with 'things' and 'objects' coming out of a mixture of other 'things': so a mixture of specific quantities of milk and flour gives origin to a cake, or a mixture of some atoms of oxygen and hydrogen gives origin to water. In this sense the boundaries are essential to the creation of a new 'object', which exists up to the breaking down of the boundaries themselves. Fertilizationism looks very appealing because 'life' is considered as any other 'object' and therefore this framework can rely on the support of such a familiar (commonsensical) view. In this sense, for example, fertilizationists can easily draw a clear distinction between prevention of the mixture of two objects (gametes) and consequent coming into being of a new 'object' (contraception), and proper destruction of the new 'object' itself (abortion).

The other question ('When does individual human life begin?') is similar in kind, even if it presupposes a stronger notion of 'individual' and therefore looks a bit odd. The reason for such oddity is that in our common-sense view we are not used to distinguishing between an 'object' and an 'individual object', since the two notions are usually equivalent. Even if it suggests a more refined notion, it shares with fertilizationism the same general common-sense view considering life as a 'common-sense object'. And it is exactly here that the current 'biological approach' goes astray: biology is not common sense, and a 'biological way of thinking' is not at all equivalent to the current 'commonsensical way of thinking'. There is a basic difference between the two ways of thinking, since in common sense we deal with 'things' mechanically combined, while in biology we deal with teleological processes and differently organized living entities, not with mere 'things'. In this sense the main defect of the current 'biological approach' is that it claims to adopt a 'biological way of thinking'[14] but in reality biological data are interpreted according to a common-sense framework. In other words, scientific data are smuggled into a commonsensical context, and it is for this reason that fertilizationism looks so strong.

But its strength is also (and at the same time) its weakness, since not every piece of the puzzle fits smoothly and the notion of 'pre-embryo' is one of these. This is its ultimate significance: the notion of pre-embryo shows a fundamental difficulty in the current 'biological approach', and compels us to a 'conceptual revolution' and to a change of our views concerning the issue. As always after a *Gestalt* switch we have to change not only our view of reality, but also our way of thinking as well as our basic questions and corresponding descriptions. This conceptual revolution may lead us to some results that are counter-intuitive seen from the point of view of common sense, but we should not be too worried about this, since even the classic astronomical revolution does not fit with common sense. We still ask: 'When does the sun rise?' even though we know that it is a metaphorical question, because literally speaking the sun never 'rises'. Analogously, we may continue to ask 'When does human life begin?', but we must be aware that it means something different. In fact the correct answer would be: 'Human life began once long ago in the past and since then it has been transmitted through sexuality.'

As soon as we adopt a real 'biological approach' (informed by a real 'biological way of thinking') we understand that the proper questions to be asked are: 'When does the process of life's transmission begin?' and 'When does it end?' As a preliminary I want here to devote some attention to the second question, whose answer shows a first important consequence of our conceptual revolution. I think that the correct answer is that the process of human life's transmission ends when a new person is born. In this sense, the new adequate 'biological approach' does not set aside the problem of the 'person', which is the completion of the process. While in the former misleading approach such a problem appeared to be external to the biological process, now it is simply its final stage, and I think that this is an important result, showing that the real scientific approach supports the idea that the crucial issue is the question about the person.

[14] M. Becker, *The Biological Way of Life* (Berkeley and Los Angeles: University of California Press, 1968).

However, here I will focus my attention on the other question, which is more directly relevant to our concerns, i.e. the one concerning the beginning of life's transmission process. Since we abandoned the 'object' mentality and started to think in terms of teleological processes it may be useful to summarize some features of the new correct 'biological way of thinking'. First of all, teleology and potentiality are mirror-concepts like convexity and concavity: potentiality denotes a process's intrinsic power to reach a certain goal, and teleology denotes the goal to be reached by a process having the corresponding potentiality. So, on the one hand potentiality is not to be confused with 'probability' of success, since there is potentiality even when the successful event is rare; and on the other hand we should remember that potentiality admits of several degrees: potentialities are more remote and indeterminate when the goal is more distant, and more proximate and determinate when the goal is nearer.[15]

Secondly, it is important to remember that transmission of human life occurs by means of sexuality and reproduction, which is a peculiar teleological process. As a matter of fact, reproductive organs are characterized by being functional to a peculiar goal, i.e. generation of new offspring. In this sense we can reformulate our original question as follows: 'When does the human reproductive process begin?' And our former remarks lead us to saying that this question is equivalent to: 'When can we say that there is a biological process directed toward the goal?' or 'When can we say that there are potentialities for a new offspring?'

Since human life is a continuous cycle it is not easy to state a fixed point, but I think that there are two reasons for saying that the right answer is the one pointing to sexual intercourse, i.e. when male gametes are brought into a woman's body. The first reason is that in the uninterrupted chain of life that act is freely chosen by the partners (or at least by one of them). Moreover, when human spermatozoa are liberated within a woman's body we have an active and autonomous process directed toward the birth of a new offspring: many are lost, but often a new birth occurs. In this sense even gametes in the proper environment are potential persons, since they are actively directed toward the goal: of course the process is as yet very indeterminate, but it has already begun. If fertilization occurs, the process becomes more determinate but not enough to constitute a proper 'individual life', and so for a certain period twinning is still possible. If everything goes smoothly, the process reaches

---

[15] This is quite important because it makes clear an important feature of biological process v. inorganic objects: the latter come into being immediately and abruptly, while the former need time

a new stage of proper 'individual life', and for some time it is a merely vegetative life, since there is no central nervous system. Later, such a system develops and we can assume a sentient life, and finally also an 'intellectual life'.

The outline of the process is not complete, but I wanted to give an idea of what a correct description given from an adequate 'biological way of thinking' would look like. As soon as we abandon the common-sense way of thinking implicit in the current 'biological approach' we realize that asking the single basic question 'When does human life begin?' is as misleading as asking a bachelor 'When did you last marry?' On the contrary we see that there are different stages of a process and this new description leads us to new problems concerning the normative level. I will examine some of these problems in the next section.

Our new approach presents a new question and now it is clear that the question 'When does human life begin?' is not relevant any more because we have different stages of 'human life'. Now this 'Copernican revolution' on a descriptive level has its counterpart on the evaluative level. Since our main question is 'When does the reproductive process begin?', the corresponding question will be 'What sort of protection is due to the human reproductive process?'

The answer seems to admit of three different solutions:

1. *An absolute duty of protection.* In this case human life in any stage is to be respected, and therefore it is intrinsically illicit to interfere with the reproductive process. One may then say that there are different degrees of responsibility, and that although all are illicit, some acts are graver than others. This seems to be the official Catholic position, and this explains the absolute prohibition of contraception.

2. *There is no duty at all toward the reproductive process.* In this case only persons must be protected and therefore the protection of pre-personal stages is at the discretion of the woman. This seems to be the 'abortion on demand' view.

3. *There is a prima-facie duty toward the reproductive process.* In this case duties are stronger according to the degree of determination of the process. So in the gametic stage—when we have 'contiguous not-yet-assembled life'—such a duty is so weak as to be practically non-existent, and later on it gets stronger and stronger. This suggestion has two important consequences: we can

easily explain the difference between respect due in the experimental context and in the abortion situation, and we can explain the distinction between 'prevention' of coming into life and 'destruction of life'.

In fact we can say that contraception destroys 'contiguous not-yet-assembled human life' and prevents the formation of 'contiguous assembled human life', i.e. prevents fertilization, which is an important step in the whole process. After fertilization the process becomes more determinate: now the boundaries are more precise and the 'object' is better determined, but still flexible enough to say that there is no 'individual human life'. This means that for instance IUDs destroy 'contiguous assembled human life' and prevent the formation of 'individual human life', since for a few days in the pre-embryonic stage there is no subordination of parts to the whole. Once the pre-embryonic stage is over, we have a human individual life, but for some time it is at a merely vegetative level since the central nervous system has not yet developed. After some time it will have developed further and the biological individual will be sentient as well, and finally there will be 'intellectual life'. There are thus different stages with a progressive passage from a more indeterminate stage to a more determinate one. I do not discuss here when we can say that the reproductive process ends, since this is a difficult problem which is not relevant at this stage. What is important here is the beginning, and I have shown that the new viewpoint is consistent and that it explains different phenomena in a coherent way: while the other had insoluble contradictions, here everything fits.

3

Eugenics: Some Lessons from the Nazi Experience

JONATHAN GLOVER

In one way, the existence of bioethics is very cheering. It is a fine thing
that in our time there is so much ethical discussion about what we should
do with the remarkable new developments in biology and medicine.
But it is also hard not to be struck by the feeling that much work in
bioethics is un-philosophical, in the sense of being unreflective on its
own methods.

In particular, much of bioethics seems uncritically Cartesian in
approach, in a way which makes the whole subject too easy. People
writing about certain practical issues, for instance in medical ethics, often
start off with principles which are taken to be self-evident. Or else there
is a perfunctory attempt to to explain why these are the appropriate
principles and then practical conclusions are simply derived from them.
Often the result is the mechanical application of some form of utilitarianism to various bioethical problems. Or, alternatively, there is a list
of several principles about autonomy, beneficence, and so on, which is
again mechanically applied.

What worries me about this approach is that it does not reflect real
ethical thinking, which is a two-way process. We do not just start off
with a set of axioms and apply them to particular cases. We also try to
learn from experience. There is something to be said for a more empirical approach to bioethics. This involves not only looking at principles
and thinking about what they imply. It involves also looking at particular experiences which, collectively, we have had, and seeing what
can be learnt from them. Perhaps from these experiences we can learn
something about the sorts of approach it would be a good idea to adopt.
Sometimes these historical experiences can teach us a different, but still
useful, lesson about the kinds of approach it would be a good idea not

to adopt. That is one of the reasons for looking at the Nazi experiment in eugenics.

Before talking about the Nazi episode, it is worth mentioning a quite different case which might also be described as, in one sense, a kind of eugenics. In thinking about the Nazis, it is important to bear in mind how very different their concerns were from the motives which sometimes make people these days want to be able to choose to have one kind of child rather than another.

A letter was published in an English newspaper, the *Guardian*, a few years ago. It was at a time when there was a move to try to lower the time limit for legal abortion. Part of the aim of this proposal was to restrict the possibility of so-called 'therapeutic abortion', since many of the tests for medical disorders would not give results by the proposed new time limit. Behind the proposal was an opposition to abortion on the 'eugenic' grounds of wanting a child without disability, as opposed to one who had a disability.

Two parents wrote to the *Guardian* in these terms:

In December 1986 our newly born daughter was diagnosed to be suffering from a genetically caused disease called Dystrophic epidermolysis Bullosa (EB). This is a disease in which the skin of the sufferer is lacking in certain essential fibres. As a result, any contact with her skin caused large blisters to form, which subsequently burst leaving raw open skin that only healed slowly and left terrible scarring. As EB is a genetically caused disease it is incurable and the form that our daughter suffered from usually causes death within the first six months of life. In our daughter's case the condition extended to her digestive and respiratory tracts and as a result of such internal blistering and scarring, she died after a painful and short life at the age of only 12 weeks.

Following our daughter's death we were told that if we wanted any more children, there was a one-in-four probability that any child we conceived would be affected by the disease but that it was possible to detect the disease ante-natally. In May 1987 we decided to restart our family only because we knew that such a test was available and that should we conceive an affected child the pregnancy could be terminated, such a decision is not taken lightly or easily . . .

We have had to watch our first child die slowly and painfully and we could not contemplate having another child if there was a risk that it too would have to die in the same way.

My reaction to this letter is one of complete sympathy with the parents' predicament and complete support for the decision that they took. Of course, this kind of decision raises very real questions. If you choose not to have a disabled child, there is a question about the impact on disabled people already alive, about what it does to the idea of equality of respect for the disabled. There is also an alarming slippery slope. How far should we go in choosing what kinds of people should be born? As soon as we start choosing at all, we enter a zone of great moral difficulty where there are important boundaries to be drawn.

But many people, when they think about this sort of issue, also have a feeling of horror and revulsion, linked in a vague way to the Nazi episode. Of course any morally serious person at our end of the twentieth century is bound to have reactions which are coloured by what the Nazis did. All the same, the Nazi episode is greatly misused in bioethics. People too readily reach for the argument that 'the Nazis did this' and that therefore we should not. It is a poor case for eating meat that Hitler was a vegetarian. It is necessary to look and see precisely what the Nazis did, and to look a bit harder than people usually do at exactly what was wrong with what they did.

In the case of the decision not to have another child with EB, there are two issues. First, is choosing not to have a child with EB in itself a 'eugenic' decision, in the objectionable way the Nazi policies were? Second, are we on a slippery slope, which may lead to objectionable Nazi-like policies?

It is worth making a brief mention of the parallel appeal to the Nazi example that is often made in the euthanasia debate. Here it is fairly obvious that the argument is used too crudely. The Nazi 'euthanasia' programme (as the quotation marks indicate) was extraordinarily different from anything that other advocates of euthanasia support. The Nazi euthanasia programme was itself bound up with their ideas about eugenics. It was driven by a highly distinctive ideology. For them, it was not at all important to consider the interests of the individual person whose life was in question. Their project was one of tidying up the world, in the interest of what they called 'racial hygiene'.

The Nazi theorists were concerned with Darwinian natural selection. They were afraid that the 'natural' selective pressures, which had functioned to ensure the survival of healthy and strong human beings, no longer functioned in modern society. Because of such things as medical care, and support for the disabled, people who in tougher times would have died were surviving to pass on their genes.

In the Nazi 'euthanasia' programme, 70,723 mental patients were killed by carbon monoxide gas. The thinking behind this is not a matter of acting on the patients' wishes. Nor is it a matter of asking whether someone's life is such a nightmare for them that it is in their own interests that they should die. The thinking does not try to see things from the perspective of the individual person at all.

The bible of the Nazi 'euthanasia' programme was a book by a lawyer, Karl Binding, and a psychiatrist, Alfred Hoche, called *Permission for the Destruction of Life Unworthy of Life*. In it, Karl Binding wrote: 'The relatives would of course feel the loss badly, but mankind loses so many of its members through mistakes that one more or less hardly matters.' That is very different from the agonized thought that goes into the decisions taken by doctors nowadays, when they wonder whether someone's life should be terminated. 'One more or less hardly matters' is not the thinking behind the moral case for euthanasia.

The impersonal approach characteristic of the Nazi programme was expressed in 1939 in Berlin. Victor Brack chaired a meeting about who should be killed. The minutes report his remarks: 'The number is arrived at through a calculation on the basis of a ratio of 1000 to 10 to 5 to 1. That means, out of 1000 people 10 require psychiatric treatment, of these 5 in residential form, and of these 1 patient will come out of the programme. If one applies this to the population of the Greater German Reich, then one must reckon with 65 to 75,000 cases. With this statement the question of who can be regarded as settled.'[1]

This impersonal approach went all the way through the Nazi programme. A nurse described one of the first transports from the asylum of Jestetten in Württemberg: 'The senior sister introduced the patients by name. But the transport leader replied that they did not operate on the basis of names but numbers. And in fact the patients who were to be transported then had numbers written in ink on their wrists, which had been previously dampened with a sponge. In other words the people were transported not as human beings but as cattle.'[2]

We all know how the later murder of the Jews was preceded by transport in cattle trucks. Many of the people who ran the Nazis' so-called euthanasia programme moved to Poland to work in the extermination camps there. The ideology behind the murder of the Jews was a mixture of race hatred and the same racial hygiene outlook found in the euthanasia programme.

The ideology was one of racial purity. There was the idea that genetic mixing with other races lowered the quality of people. One of the great fathers of the Nazi eugenics movement was Dr Eugen Fischer.

---

[1] Quoted in J. Noakes and G. Pridham, *Nazism, 1919–1945*, iii: *Foreign Policy, War and Racial Extermination: A Documentary Reader* (Exeter, 1988), 1010.
[2] Quoted ibid. 1023–4.

Many years before, he had been to South Africa and in 1913 had published a study of people who he called 'Rehobother bastards'. They were
children of mixed unions between Boers and Hottentots. He reached the
conclusion, on a supposedly scientific basis, that these children were, as
he put it, 'of lesser racial quality'. He wrote that 'We should provide
them with the minimum amount of protection which they require, for
survival as a race inferior to ourselves, and we should do this only as
long as they are useful to us. After this, free competition should prevail
and, in my opinion, this will lead to their decline and destruction.'[3]

In 1933 Dr Fischer was made the new Rector of Berlin University.
In his Rectoral Address he said: 'The new leadership, having only just
taken over the reins of power, is deliberately and forcefully intervening
in the course of history and in the life of the nation, precisely when this
intervention is most urgently, most decisively, and most immediately
needed . . . This intervention can be characterized as a biological population policy, biological in this context signifying the safeguarding by
the state of our hereditary endowment and our race.' Fischer in 1939
extended this line of thinking specifically to the Jews. He said: 'When
a people wants to preserve its own nature it must reject alien racial
elements. And when these have already insinuated themselves it must
suppress them and eliminate them. This is self-defence.'[4]

As well as belief in racial purity, there was the idea that in a given race
only the 'best people' should be encouraged to procreate. And the view
was that those who are not 'the best people' should be discouraged from
having children, or even prevented from doing so. In 1934, one of the
other fathers of the Nazi eugenics movement, Professor Fritz Lenz, said:
'As things are now, it is only a minority of our fellow citizens who are
so endowed that their unrestricted procreation is good for the race.'[5] Fisher
and Lenz, together with their colleagues, had perhaps more impact on
the world than any other academics in the twentieth century. In 1923,
Adolf Hitler, while confined in Landsberg prison, read their recently
published textbook *Outline of Human Genetics and Racial Hygiene*. He
incorporated some of its ideas in *Mein Kampf*.[6] These ideas influenced
the Sterilization Law brought in when Hitler came to power in 1933.

---

[3] Quoted in Benno Muller-Hill, *Murderous Science: Elimination by Scientific Selection of Jews, Gypsies, and Others, Germany 1933–1945*, trans. George R. Fraser (Oxford,
1988), 7–8.
[4] Quoted ibid. 10, 12.   [5] Quoted ibid. 10.
[6] Cf. Robert N. Proctor, *Racial Hygiene: Medicine under the Nazis* (Cambridge,
Mass.: Harvard University Press, 1988).

This made sterilization compulsory for people with conditions including schizophrenia, manic depression, and alcoholism.

This ideology is not one of the importance of the individual. There is a conception of the pure race and of the biologically desirable human being. Reproductive freedom and individual lives are to be sacrificed to these abstractions. One medical model had great influence on the Nazis. It is an appalling medical model: the idea that in treating people who are 'racially inferior', you are like the doctor who is dealing with a diseased organ in an otherwise healthy body. This analogy was put forward in a paper in 1940 by Konrad Lorenz, the very distinguished ethologist, now remembered for his work on aggression, and whose books on animals had an enormous charm. Lorenz wrote this:

> There is a certain similarity between the measures which need to be taken when we draw a broad biological analogy between bodies and malignant tumours, on the one hand, and a nation and individuals within it who have become asocial because of their defective constitution, on the other hand . . . Fortunately, the elimination of such elements is easier for the public health position and less dangerous for the supra-individual organism, than such an operation by a surgeon would be for the individual organism.[7]

The influence in practice of this thinking can be seen very clearly in Robert Jay Lifton's book on the Nazi doctors. He quotes a doctor called Fritz Klein. Dr Klein was asked how he would reconcile the appalling medical experiments he carried out in Auschwitz with his oath as a doctor. He replied: 'Of course I am a doctor and I want to preserve life. And out of respect for human life, I would remove a gangrenous appendix from a diseased body. The Jew is the gangrenous appendix in the body of mankind.'[8] This brings out the importance, not just of things people literally believe, but also of the imagery which colours their thinking. Dr Klein cannot literally have believed that Jews were a gangrenous appendix. It would be easier to think that the Nazis were all mad if they literally thought that.

The role of such imagery can be seen again in the way in which racism was given a biological justification. Appalling images likened Jews to vermin, or to dirt and disease. When all Jews were removed from an area, it was called 'Judenrein'—clean of Jews. Hans Frank, talking about the decline of a typhus epidemic, said that the removal of what he called

---

[7] Quoted in Muller-Hill, *Murderous Science*, 14.
[8] Quoted in Robert Jay Lifton, *The Nazi Doctors: A Study in the Psychology of Evil* (London, 1986), 16.

'the Jewish element' had contributed to better health in Europe. The Foreign Office Press Chief Schmidt said that the Jewish question was, as he put it, 'a question of political hygiene'.[9]

This kind of medical analogy was important in Nazi thinking. Hitler said, 'The discovery of the Jewish virus is one of the greatest revolutions that have taken place in the world. The battle in which we are engaged today is of the same sort as the battle waged during the last century by Pasteur and Koch. How many diseases have their origin in the Jewish virus! . . . We shall regain our health only by eliminating the Jew.'[10]

The medical analogies and the idea of racial hygiene were supplemented by the ideology of Social Darwinism. To study either Nazism or, further back, the origins of the First World War is to see how enormously more influential Social Darwinist ideas have been in our century than one would guess. Social Darwinist ideas were not confined to Germany. They originated in England. It would be unfair to blame Darwin, who was a very humane person, for these ideas. They were developed by people like Francis Galton and Karl Pearson. Before the First World War, Karl Pearson said that the nation should be kept up to a high pitch of external efficiency by contest, chiefly by way of war with inferior races. The influence of Social Darwinism in Germany was partly the result of the Englishman Houston Stewart Chamberlain, who became an adopted German nationalist, holding that the Germans were a superior race.

Social Darwinism fuelled the naval arms race between Germany and Britain, a contest which helped to cause the First World War. Admiral Tirpitz thought naval expansion was necessary because, if Germany did not join the biological struggle between races, it would go under. When the danger of the arms race was obvious, the British Foreign Secretary, Sir Edward Grey, proposed a naval moratorium on both sides. The German Chancellor, Bethmann-Hollweg, rejected Grey's proposal: 'The old saying still holds good that the weak will be the prey of the strong. When a people will not or cannot continue to spend enough on its armaments to be able to make its way in the world, then it falls back into the second rank . . . There will always be another and a stronger there who is ready to take the place in the world which it has vacated.'[11]

[9] Quoted in Raul Hilberg, *The Destruction of the European Jews*, student edn. (New York, 1985), 287.

[10] *Hitler's Table Talk, 1941–44*, introd. Hugh Trevor-Roper (Oxford, 1988), 332.

[11] Quoted in Michael Howard, 'The Edwardian Arms Race', in Michael Howard, *The Lessons of History* (Oxford, 1993).

Nazism emerged against this background of belief in life as a ruthless struggle for survival. According to Social Darwinism, victory goes to the strong, the tough, and the hard rather than to those who are gentle and co-operative. The Nazis took this up. They extolled struggle and the survival of the fittest. This led them to abandon traditional moral restraints. One Nazi physician, Dr Arthur Guett, said: 'The ill-conceived "love of thy neighbour" has to disappear . . . It is the supreme duty of the . . . state to grant life and livelihood only to the healthy and hereditarily sound portion of the population in order to secure . . . a hereditarily sound and racially pure people for all eternity.'[12]

The Nazis also extolled hardness, which they thought led to victory in the struggle for survival. Hitler was proud of his own hardness. He said, 'I am perhaps the hardest man this nation has had for 200 years.'[13] The belief in hardness came partly from Nietzsche. He was contemptuous of English biologists, and so was predictably cool about Darwin. Despite this, Nietzsche was in certain respects a Social Darwinist. He too thought compassion for the weak was sentimental nonsense, and advocated struggle and hardness.

Hitler, an admirer of the darker side of Nietzsche, was also a Social Darwinist. One day at lunch he said, 'As in everything, nature is the best instructor, even as regards selection. One couldn't imagine a better activity on nature's part than that which consists in deciding the supremacy of one creature over another by means of a constant struggle.' He went on to express disapproval of the way 'our upper classes give way to a feeling of compassion regarding the fate of the Jews who we claim the right to expel'.[14]

This outlook influenced the people who worked in the Nazi eugenic and 'euthanasia' programmes. They felt guilty about feelings of compassion, which they were taught were a weakness to overcome. One Nazi doctor involved in killing psychiatric patients as part of the 'euthanasia' programme expressed this in a letter to the director of the asylum where he worked, explaining his reluctance to take part in murdering the children there. He wrote,

I am very grateful for you willingly insisting that I should take time to think things over. The new measures are so convincing that I had hoped to be able to discard all personal considerations. But it is one thing to approve state

---

[12] Quoted in Lifton, *The Nazi Doctors.*
[13] Hitler, 8 Nov. 1940, quoted in J. P. Stren, *Hitler: The Fuhrer and the People*, 62.
[14] *Hitler's Table Talk*, 396–7.

measures with conviction and another to carry them out yourself down to their last consequences. I am thinking of the difference between a judge and an executioner. For this reason, despite my intellectual understanding and good will, I cannot help stating that I am temperamentally not fitted for this. As eager as I often am to correct the natural course of events, it is just as repugnant to me to do so systematically, after cold blooded consideration, according to the objective principles of science, without being affected by a doctor's feeling for his patient . . . I feel emotionally tied to the children as their medical guardian, and I think this emotional contact is not necessarily a weakness from the point of view of a National Socialist doctor . . . I prefer to see clearly and to recognise that I am too gentle for this work than to disappoint you later.[15]

This apology for his concern for his patients, his emotional tie to these children, as 'not necessarily a weakness in a National Socialist doctor', shows how deeply ingrained this ideology was.

What lessons can be drawn from this grim episode? Any conclusions from this more empirical approach to ethics have to be tentative. There is always the danger of the mistake attributed to generals and strategists, of preparing for the previous war. There will not be an exact rerun of the Nazi episode, so we have to be flexible in learning from it.

The Nazi episode is evil on such a grand scale that any conclusions drawn from it are likely to seem puny by comparison with the events themselves. But it is worth not being deterred by this, and, at the risk of banality, trying to focus on some of the things we should guard against.

One conclusion may be that it is a mistake to let any system of belief, including a system of ethics, become too abstract. There are dangers in getting too far away from ordinary human emotional responses to people. The worry behind 'racial hygiene', the worry about the consequences of removing 'natural' evolutionary selective pressures, was a thought you did not have to be a very evil person to have. We see it as a misguided thought, but it is still one a morally good person might have had. The danger is to get hooked on an idea, such as this one, and then to follow it ruthlessly, trampling on all the normal human feelings and responses to individual people in front of you. This is a general danger in ethics. Even a humane outlook such as utilitarianism can do great harm when applied with ruthless abstraction.

Another lesson, in our time fortunately a platitude, is that we should not be thinking in terms of racial purity and of lesser racial quality. It is not at all clear what these phrases mean. They are woolly and muddled

---

[15] Noakes and Pridham, *Nazism, 1919–1945*, iii. 1014–15.

ideas, which are manifestly incredibly dangerous. (I mention this platitude because sometimes what was once a platitude stops being one. Who, a few years ago, would have thought it worth stating that 'ethnic cleansing' should be utterly rejected?)

There is need for more thought about the answer to the claim about the necessity of replacing evolutionary selective pressures. All of us shudder when we see where this kind of thought led, but few do the thinking to find out exactly what is wrong with the arguments.

It is worth mentioning one thought about this. The fact that we can deal with some disorders, so that people with them are able to survive and have children who then may inherit the disorder, is supposed to be the problem. But, in the case of a disorder where people find their lives worth living, it is not a disaster if they pass on their genes. In the Stone Age, people with poor sight may have lost out in the evolutionary competition. Glasses and contact lenses are among the reasons why they now survive to have children. Their lives are not a disaster, and there is no reason why it is a disaster if their children inherit short-sightedness. To the extent that modern medicine makes possible, not just survival, but a decent quality of life, the supposed problem to which eugenics seemed to be the answer is not a real one.

Another lesson is the dangers of the group approach. The Nazis thought mainly in terms of nations and races. In decisions about who is to be born, decisions for instance about access to fertility treatment or about genetic screening, it is important to look first and foremost at those immediately involved: at the person who may be born and at the family. In the case of the kind of reproductive intervention where we are choosing the creation of one person rather than another, our central thought ought to be about what one kind of life or another would be like from the point of view of the person living it.

The case is like that of euthanasia. If we are to justify euthanasia at all, it has to be justified by saying either that a particular person wants not to go on living, or, where the person is past expressing any view, that their life must seem to them so terrible that it would be a kindness to kill them. We have to look at things from inside in taking these decisions. (Of course this is very difficult, which is a reason for extreme caution.)

It is utterly repugnant that 'euthanasia' should be defended for instance on grounds of general social utility, such as the cost of keeping certain people alive. Killing on those grounds is not euthanasia, despite the Nazi attempt to hijack the term for such policies. People now sometimes ignorantly misuse the Nazi policy as though it were a knock-down argument against genuine euthanasia. Those of us who study what the Nazis really did tend to dislike this propagandist move. As with the casual use of 'fascist' to describe political opponents, it makes light of something truly terrible, and leaves us without a vocabulary for the real thing. But the one place where the argument from Nazism really does apply is where killing the old or the sick or the insane to benefit other people is advocated.

In the same sort of way, I find repugnant the idea that decisions about the kind of children to be born should be made on grounds of general social utility.

Finally, there are issues about Social Darwinism. Rather few people these days hold Hitler's maniac racist views. But Social Darwinism may be a continuing danger. A crude interpretation of some claims in socio-biology could lend support to a renewed Social Darwinism. In mentioning this, I am not lending support to one crude reaction against sociobiology, a reaction which takes the form of denying any genetic contribution to the explanation of human behaviour. That sort of absolute denial is going to lose out in the intellectual debate. No doubt sometimes the evidence will suggest the existence of a genetic component. But, if people pro-pose social policies supposed to follow from this, we need to look very hard at the supporting arguments. Claims about simple links between biology and social policy are often backed by very dubious arguments. And it is not just that the thinking is poor. The Nazi experience sug-gests that the conclusions may also be dangerous. The victims of the Nazis were not killed just by gas but also by beliefs, which can be poisonous too.

4

Reproductive Rights: Feminism or Patriarchy?

MARGARET BRAZIER

Miraculous Technologies and Mothers

The popular perception of the new reproductive technologies is of a medical marvel offering untold blessings to womanhood. Media coverage of each new development to assist the infertile to have children of their own invariably includes photographs of ecstatic mothers and bouncing infants.[1] Assisted conception is vaunted as a vehicle for asserting women's reproductive rights. Feminists ought to applaud and claim the right to reproduce with science's aid as their own. Yet many feminists do not.[2] They appear downright ungrateful to their medical and scientific mentors. A brief excursion into some aspects of English law as it affects alleged reproductive rights may indicate why reproductive rights might be perceived by some women as patriarchy in disguise rather than feminism rampant.

Consider a little-known provision of the Human Fertilisation and Embryology Act 1990, section 29. Section 29 (4) provides:

In relation to England and Wales and Northern Ireland, nothing in the provision of section 27 (1) or 28 (2) to (4) read with this section, affects—

(a) the succession to any dignity or title of honour or renders any person capable of succeeding to or transmitting a right to succeed to any such dignity or title, or

---

[1] On the role of the media in relation to the debate on the new reproductive technologies see J. Van Dyck, *Manufacturing Babies and Public Consent* (Basingstoke: Macmillan, 1995).
[2] See, for example, P. Spallone and D. L. Steinberg, *Made to Order: The Myth* of *Reproductive and Genetic Progress* (New York: Pergamon, 1987); R. Arditt, R. D. Klein, and S. Minden (eds.), *Test-Tube Women: What Future for Motherhood?* (London: Pandora Press, 1989); R. Rowland, *Living Laboratories* (Bloomington: Indiana University Press, 1992); J. G. Raymond, *Women as Wombs* (San Francisco: Harper, 1993).

(b) the devolution of any property limited (expressly or not) to devolve . . .
along with any dignity or title on honour.

The practical impact of these pompous provisions of the Act is this.
The 1990 Act establishes in sections 27 and 28 that normally, where a
woman receives *in vitro* fertilization using donated eggs, she not the donor
(the genetic mother) will be in law the mother of any resulting child.[3]
Where a woman conceives as a result of artificial insemination by donor,
or *in vitro* treatment using donor sperm, then generally, if she has sought
treatment with a male partner, her partner, not the donor (the genetic
father), will be in law the father of any resulting child. The law seeks
to provide that the social parents are the legal parents of the child. Section
29 (4) and (5), however, creates an exception to that norm and ensures
that if a hereditary title, an earldom or whatever, is at stake, the normal
rules for ascertaining legal parenthood in cases of assisted conception
do not apply so as to allow transmission of the title to a genetically alien
heir. The bloodline must not be polluted. This is not perhaps a matter
of any great concern to very many of us, unless we move on from
the practical to the symbolic impact of these characteristically British
obsessions with heredity, and ask what they tell us about the nature and
purposes of the Human Fertilisation and Embryology Act and indeed
about the law's interest in reproduction more generally.

No one can deny that the birth of Louise Brown in 1978 was a technical marvel and brought hope to many couples who much regretted their
childlessness. In the twelve years it subsequently took parliament to
legislate to regulate infertility treatment and embryo research, much of
the debate on the consequences for society of the 'miraculous' medical
advances in reproductive medicine focused not on the rights of women
but on the status of the embryo.

The many embryologists and gynaecologists who fought to ensure
embryo research was permitted did address women's interests and rights
as they, and they were mostly male, perceived them. The public were
told that infertility was a disease. Infertile women were desperate for
a 'cure' and they had a right to health care.[4] Women, male scientists
asserted, enjoy a right to assisted reproduction. A woman who could

---

[3] The principles applicable to determine legal parenthood in the United Kingdom
where a child is born as a result of assisted conception are discussed fully in M. Brazier,
Medicine, Patients and the Law, 2nd edn. (Harmondsworth: Penguin, 1992), ch. 12; see
also J. K. Mason and A. McCall Smith, *Law and Medical Ethics*, 4th edn. (London:
Butterworths, 1994), ch. 3.
[4] On which see Raymond, *Women as Wombs*, 2–7.

not have a child considered herself to be a less than proper woman. She was denied her destiny.

Birke, Himmelweit, and Vines's excellent book *Tomorrow's Child* quotes an Australian woman. 'I felt a total lack of femininity. I reverted to a sort of neuter . . . I felt terribly spayed. It was quite loathsome . . . I did not really believe my body was there.'[5] Professor Robert Winston, and the test-tube fathers, Patrick Steptoe and Robert Edwards, all made impassioned pleas to parliament to legislate to provide for the future of IVF by allowing research, asking parliament to enact legislation which would thereby 'guarantee' a woman's fundamental right to reproduce.

More recently the Human Fertilisation and Embryology Authority established by the 1990 Act to regulate infertility treatment in Britain canvassed opinion on the ethics of culturing eggs from aborted female fetuses, there being an insufficient supply of donor eggs to treat women who fail to ovulate naturally.[6] Once again the needs, the rights, of the infertile woman were given centre stage by her male advocates. So should women hail the 1990 Act, and the structure created under that Act, as a victory for women, a recognition of a right to motherhood? I beg leave to doubt any such proposition.

The key provisions of the Act are these. The Act sanctions research on *in vitro* embryos up to fourteen days from fertilization. Section 3 requires any form of treatment necessitating the creation of an embryo *in vitro* or the storage of gametes to be licensed. Sections 27–33 clarify the legal relationships ensuing from treatment and provide the child with some limited access to her genetic heritage. But it is instructive to ask what the Act does not do. It does not (as we have seen) allow the rules it applies to you and me on parental relationships, should we seek assisted conception, to apply if titles of honour are in issue.

It sets in place a system (in section 31) which makes it nigh on impossible for a child to discover the identity of her genetic parents.[7] The Act does not apply at all to GIFT (gamete intra-uterine transfer) although GIFT is more likely than IVF to result in multiple pregnancy. It does not grant any women or men any *right of access* to assisted conception. Quite the opposite, it confers on the licence-holders, who provide treatment, a discretion about whom to treat. Indeed section 13 (5) expressly

---

[5] L. Birke, S. Himmelweit, and G. Vines, *Tomorrow's Child: Reproductive Technologies in the 90's* (London: Virago, 1990), at 63.

[6] See A. Plomer and N. Martin-Clement, 'The Limits of Beneficence: Egg Donation under the Human Fertilisation and Embryology Act 1990' (1995) 15 *Legal Studies* 434.

[7] Discussed by K. O'Donovan, 'What shall We Tell the Children?', in R. Lee and D. Morgan (eds.), *Birthrights* (London: Routledge, 1989).

provides 'A woman shall not be provided with treatment services unless account has been taken of the welfare of any child who may be born as a result of the treatment (including the need of that child for a father) and of any other child who may be affected by the birth.' And finally the enactment of the statute was not accompanied by any cash injection into the NHS to facilitate the provision of women's (or men's) rights to treatment.

If you scan Hansard to review the content of parliamentary debate, to see if parliament (whatever the dry language of the statute) saw the legislation as a feminist issue, the evidence in favour of such an opinion is scanty in the extreme. The majority of the contributions to debate concentrated on either the legitimacy of embryo research and/or attempts to ban any single woman from receiving treatment at all. An amendment which would have outlawed all fertility treatment for un-married women lost by one vote in the House of Lords. Their lordships also enjoyed some extensive discussion on section 29 (4) and (5), those fascinating provisions designed to protect aristocratic bloodlines.

The absence of any clear endorsement in the 1990 Act of women's rights to maternity should come as no surprise, nor should the provisions of the Act endorsing the primacy of certain bloodlines. There will be found in English law little evidence that the law recognizes or endorses such a right matched with a lively concern to ensure inheritance of property passes down the proper patriarchal line.[8]

Precious Organs?

More than twenty years ago, in 1976 in *Re D*,[9] one judge did unequivocally declare that a young girl should not be sterilized because that operation would infringe a basic human right, to bear a child. D was 11 years old and suffered from Soto's Syndrome, a congenital condition which caused her to reach puberty early. She was clumsy and physically unco-ordinated and suffered from moderate learning difficulties. At the time of the hearing, however, she was still developing intellectually. Her mother wanted to ensure that she did not become pregnant. She feared D's vulnerability to exploitation. A Sheffield doctor agreed to operate. It was D's headmaster and educational psychologist who successfully inter-vened to stop the operation. Mrs Justice Heilbron found that the girl

[8] On patriarchy and law more generally see C. Smart, *Law, Crime and Sexuality* (London: Sage, 1995), 130–45.
[9] *Re D (a minor) (wardship: sterilisation)* [1976] 1 All England Reports 326.

might well by 18 be quite capable of making choices on childbearing for herself. It was true that at 11 she was vulnerable but whose teenage daughter is not?

Later judgments from 1987 onwards have authorized non-consensual female sterilizations.[10] In most of these cases it must be conceded that the girls involved were considerably more intellectually impaired than D. But what has happened to the basic human right to reproduce asserted by Heilbron?

In *Re B*[11] (the Jeannette case) only two of their lordships considered the impact of any such right, declaring it existed only 'when reproduction is the result of informed choice of which this ward is incapable'.[12] A right to reproduce was a right 'of value only if accompanied by the ability to make a choice'.[13] Two years later, in *F* v. *West Berkshire Health Authority*[14] authorizing the sterilization of an adult woman of 35, the right to reproduce has shrunk yet further in the collective judicial consciousness. Lord Brandon, conceding that sterilization is a procedure which should be approached with caution, spoke of: 'the general irreversibility of the operation, the almost certain result of it will be to deprive the woman concerned of what is widely, and I think rightly, regarded as one of the fundamental rights of a woman, namely to bear children'.[15] Lord Goff came no closer to a right to reproduce than a passing reference to 'the fundamental nature of the patient's organs with which it is proposed irreversibly to interfere'.[16] In a judgment which found that there was no legal power to require that sterilization of adult women with intellectual disabilities at least receive judicial assent, albeit doctors should be advised to seek judicial sanction, the fundamental right to reproduce withers to recognition of some sort of special status for the reproductive organs.

If we pause and look back to review reproduction and the law in the context of English legal history, we should perhaps be less surprised to see women's rights figuring at best marginally. The only clear common law status accorded to the fetus in England outside laws prohibiting abortion was to be found until 1992[17] in the laws on succession. Where a fetus was *en ventre sa mère* at the time of a father or other relative's

[10] See generally Brazier, *Medicine, Patients and the Law*, chs. 15 and 17; Mason and McCall Smith, *Law and Medical Ethics*, ch. 4.
[11] *Re B (a minor) (wardship: sterilisation)* [1987] 2 All England Reports 206; HL.
[12] At p. 212 *per* Lord Hailsham.   [13] At p. 219 *per* Lord Oliver.
[14] [1989] 2 All England Reports 545.   [15] At p. 552.   [16] At p. 568.
[17] See *Burton* v. *Islington Health Authority* [1992] 3 All England Reports 933, CA.

decease the fetus, if safely born, could take any appropriate share of the deceased's estate. So if a widow were pregnant at the time of her husband's death, a child safely delivered could (and can) inherit from his father's estate. The provision was often crucial in relation to succession to great estates. Imagine the widowed mother of five daughters desperately awaiting the posthumous birth of a male heir to her husband's entailed estate.

Elaborate rules, which endured in large part until the Family Law Reform Acts of 1969 and 1987, sought to define legitimacy to ensure that where possible the wise father knew his own child. The primacy of the male bloodline and the need to protect patriarchal inheritance occupied a large space in the framework of property rules. However, at least the common law of England did countenance female succession to estates when the progenitors had not prudently created an entail limiting succession to males and there was no male child. Of course, even where female succession was a possibility, later-born males took priority over their sisters and as late as 1994 parliament threw out a bill to give first-born females the right to succeed to titles of honour. Should the Prince of Wales and his sons all be eliminated, his brothers, not their elder sister, would stand next in line for the crown.

If the reader moves from laws of property to laws of divorce maybe there is there a glimmer of an embryonic right to bear a child. When cruelty was one of the grounds of divorce, wilful refusal of sexual intercourse by a wife was almost inevitably designated cruelty depriving her spouse of his 'right' to conjugal relations. A similar refusal by a husband met an ambivalent response; after all, the poor chap could not be asked to perform on demand. A husband's deliberate and persistent refusal of procreative intercourse by insisting on contraception was however considered by some judges to be cruelty, denying the woman satisfaction of her natural maternal instinct, as long as there were no good grounds for accepting the husband's decision that children were inappropriate.[18]

A Brave New World?

Perhaps such musings should be dismissed as reflecting the bad old days. What a modern society should do is recognize and affirm women's reproductive rights and seek to ensure that in all subsequent legislative

---

[18] See generally Brazier, *Medicine, Patients and the Law*, 376–7.

responses to new reproductive techniques the woman's right to mother-hood takes centre stage. Hence should the provision of the Criminal Justice and Public Order Act outlawing the use of eggs from aborted fetuses in infertility treatment be wholeheartedly condemned? The amendment was described as 'irresponsible' by the chair of the Human Fertilisa-tion and Embryology Authority and as 'heartless' by leading infertility experts.[19] However, is such a ban truly a blow to women's rights? I have no definite answer but I am deeply cynical about the reality of the so-called right to reproduce.

Article 12 of the European Convention on Human Rights provides that men and women of marriageable age have the right to marry and found a family, though it is not clear whether the latter right to found a family is separate from, or dependent on, the former right to marry. But does or can such a right embrace the right to assistance to found a family and just what does it mean? Is it any more than a liberty to have a go at conception reinforced by a duty incumbent on the state not to interfere with that liberty?

Generally a right to *x* requires that there be a correlative duty on the part of some other person to supply *x*. Moreover, if a right to reproduce is a fundamental human right it must be gender-neutral. If women have a fundamental right to reproduce then so do men. Yet when rights to reproduce are debated in the context of assisted conception they are virtually always presented as exclusively female, even feminist, rights. Consideration of a right to reproduce as shared by men and demanding a correlative duty on the part of someone else may prompt hesitation on the desirability for *women* of any such right at all.

For nearly three centuries the common law of England declared that a man could not be guilty of raping his own wife. The recognition by the judiciary that marital rape is as much rape as any other rape, that wives retain control of their own bodies, was truly a much belated blow for women's rights.[20] What fuelled that long perversion of the law? There are judicial and extra-judicial pronouncements that a woman on marriage gave an irrevocable consent to sexual intercourse, com-plemented by statements that a wife must not be allowed to deny her husband an heir of his body. The husband's *right* to reproduce gen-erated her *duty* to reproduce.

[19] See Plomer and Martin-Clement, 'The Limits of Beneficence', 442.
[20] See *R.* v. *R.* [1991] 4 All England Reports 481, discussed in Mason and McCall Smith, *Law and Medical Ethics*, 33–5. And see K. O'Donovan, *Family Law Matters* (London: Pluto Press, 1993), ch. 1.

In other legal systems a wife's failure in her duty to reproduce was recognized as a legitimate ground for ending the marriage. Where barrenness was not expressly recognized as grounds for divorce, one husband at least, King Henry VIII, had to resort to wholesale religious conversion of the realm to get rid of his first wife, Catherine of Aragon, and execution for two further unfortunate wives, Anne Boleyn and Catherine Howard. And of course, as every schoolgirl knows, Henry VIII's inability to beget a male heir was his fault anyhow.

The modern world, we hope, is different. A right to reproduce can today, thanks to science, be enforced by more civilized means than marital rape or discarding an infertile partner. The self-same science has demonstrated to men that at least 40 per cent of infertility is a male problem. The woman with an infertile or unwilling partner (or no partner at all) can be helped to conceive with donor sperm. The woman who does not ovulate can have donor eggs. If we are only sensible, we can eventually ensure a sufficient supply of eggs from those aborted female fetuses. The couple where the woman cannot carry a child can find a surrogate. The man with an unwilling or no female partner can find a surrogate. If he has a fundamental right to reproduce that must follow. Any sort of restriction of his fundamental right must be strictly justified.

One common restriction requires that the welfare of any ensuing child be taken into consideration. Moral philosophers such as Jonathan Glover[21] and John Harris[22] argue that the speculative welfare of any infant resulting from treatment is no justification for infringing a right to reproduce, if applied in a discriminatory fashion. If we do not, as a society, judge that the interests of potential children should be weighed against the interests of potential parents where the potential parents are naturally fertile, we cannot impose those restrictions on those unfortunate enough to be infertile or lacking a suitable partner.

The right to reproduce (if acknowledged) must at the very least generate a duty on the state not to impede access to assisted conception. It is unethical, it is argued, to do nothing to stop me embarking on an unplanned and potentially disastrous pregnancy in a drunken chance encounter, yet in the interests of a hypothetical child deny a woman a few years older than me, and past the natural menopause, a child carefully

---

[21] See *What Sort of People Should There be?* (Harmondsworth: Pelican, 1984); *Fertility and the Family: The Glover Report on Reproductive Technologies to the European Commission* (London: Fourth Estate, 1989).

[22] See *The Value of Life* (London: Routledge, 1985), 150–6; *Wonderwoman and Superman* (Oxford: Oxford University Press, 1992), 73–8.

planned with her partner. Society should either impose contraception
via the water supply and license parenthood for all or allow free access
to every technique able to aid conception.

Jonathan Glover goes a stage further. Assume that society accepted
that discrimination between the fertile and infertile was unjustifiable and
in all instances parents should be banned from procreation not in the
interests of the child to be; then Glover argues it can only not be in
a child's interests to be born if his life is likely to be so dreadful that
non-existence is preferable to existence. The offspring of my drunken
one-night stand may have a difficult time with an elderly mother (presumably by now abandoned by her long-suffering spouse), an unknown
dad, and furious teenage sister, but his life is unlikely to be so bad
he wishes he had never been born. Almost anything goes and women's
reproductive rights flower. How could a feminist reject such a seductive
argument?

A Cynical Feminist

First, of course, even assisted by Glover and Harris, we have only reached
a position in which the right to reproduce prohibits impeding access to
assisted conception and outlaws current restrictions based on age, single
status, or which impede surrogacy arrangements. Access is liberal for
those who can pay. NHS provision of assisted conception remains limited. To facilitate a right to reproduce regardless of income a far, far
greater proportion of NHS resources would have to be earmarked for
infertility treatment. One woman's right to reproduce would have to be
weighed against her mother's right to preventive care to ensure breast
cancer is detected early enough, against her grandmother's need for a
hip-replacement, against perhaps her great grandmother's life itself.

Second, I find the language of the debate sometimes disturbing
and reminiscent all too often of earlier eras and out-dated visions of a
woman's role and identity. Suzanne Uniacke[23] and Robyn Rowland,[24]
among many others, have written powerfully of the inconsistencies in
many of the arguments promulgated by men about a woman's right to
a child. There is no doubt that many women do deeply desire a child

[23] 'Making Women Visible in the Embryo Experimentation Debate' (1987) 1 *Bioethics* 179.
[24] 'In Vitro Fertilisation and the Right to Reproduce' (1987) 1 *Bioethics* 241; and see her *Living Laboratories*.

and throughout history have suffered if that desire is unfulfilled. Can desire generate a right to its satisfaction? Women desire many things, success in their careers, beauty, scintillating partners, yet only the desire for a child becomes a right. Perhaps I fail to grasp the depth of that desire—and trivialize the pain of infertility; I hope not. Feminists raise pertinent questions about why that one desire is elevated above all others.[25] Is the pain of infertility perhaps exacerbated by society, is a private grief transformed into a public shame because the childless woman is somehow odd and unsatisfactory? Moreover, the more infertility treatment is trumpeted, the greater becomes the pressure to seek it, the harder the childless state becomes to accept. The supply of assisted conception in the private sector is plentiful and growing. Is the supply simply growing to meet demand? Or is the demand being fuelled by the potential profit in its supply? Reproductive medicine is big business.[26]

Infertility specialists are, I know, genuinely shocked and puzzled by any opposition from women to developments in infertility treatment. Ann Oakley[27] has written of women's apparent ingratitude, saying the true question should be not why do women want artificial modes of fertilization, but why they all do not. Doctors, she says, 'do not seem to understand that what they have to offer are not universally desired goods'. Perhaps they should reflect on two matters in particular.

Assisted conception remains a very unsuccessful treatment—with at best a 20 per cent or so success rate in the premier clinics for most procedures. Yet the number of women and couples having difficulty with conceiving is said to be reaching one in five. Women are perhaps rather more hard-headed than our brothers imagine. Seeing the chances of infertility for ourselves and our daughters rising dramatically and cash poured into a pretty feeble cure for the symptoms, do we perhaps wish more was done about the causes? Something like 30 per cent of candidates for IVF suffer from unexplained infertility diagnosed in some cases after six months to a year of trying. Are all the infertile truly infertile?[28]

In a debate on the use of eggs harvested from aborted fetuses, a distinguished doctor pleaded to be able to use such eggs 'for all those ladies who today delay conception to establish a career and thus risk

---

[25] See Birke, Himmelweit, and Vines, *Tomorrow's Child*, 61–5.

[26] See Raymond, *Women as Wombs*, ch. 4.

[27] See 'From Walking Wombs to Test-Tube Babies', in M. Stanworth (ed.), *Reproductive Technologies* (London: Polity Press, 1987), 54–5.

[28] See Raymond, *Women as Wombs*, 2–7.

by 35 or so having unviable eggs, or wish to avoid the risk of Downs' syndrome by resort to donor eggs'. He turned to me for support in linking women's rights to maternity to rights to a career. He seemed distressed at suggestions from the floor that what was wrong was that society all too often destroyed the careers of those who have children early.

The very emotive language with which women's reproductive rights have been promoted is all too often counter-productive. I return to my earlier quotation: 'I felt a total lack of femininity. I reverted to a sort of neuter—I felt . . . spayed.' Recall again Lord Goff's only reference to a right to reproduce as 'the fundamental nature' of the woman's organs. Such language reduces women to a uterus on legs. Whether it is intended or not the impression is given that a woman's primary function is to bear a child and failing in that function she is a failure, becoming a net burden on family and society. Throughout history women have all too often laboured under a duty to reproduce. Their reproductive interests have been subordinated to the interest of society in ensuring a suitable supply of the next generation and their partner's interest in ensuring the continuation of his bloodline. We must be very careful that under the banner of women's rights patriarchy does not triumph again.

5

A Woman's Right to Choose?
A Feminist Critique

MARIE FOX

Introduction

The 1990s have witnessed a number of developments in law and politics
which reflect a changing climate of thought on abortion throughout the
world, and have resulted in challenges to legal access to abortion. Many
former Communist states in eastern Europe have witnessed increased
conservatism on abortion issues, notably Poland. Even in the West abortion rights cannot be regarded as secure. This chapter focuses mainly
upon the present legal climate in Ireland, Britain, and North America.
In the United States the election of President Clinton engendered a feeling of complacency that the battle to secure the constitutional right to
abortion granted in *Roe* v. *Wade*[1] had been won, following concern at
the retirement of liberal justices from the US Supreme Court. However,
such complacency has been dispelled, as abortion has literally become
a battlefield following the murder of 'pro-choice' doctors and the fire
bombing of abortion clinics.[2] In Britain the 1967 Abortion Act, which
contains a number of exceptions to the prohibition on abortion in the
Offences Against the Person Act 1861, has been subjected to attack in
numerous private member's bills. Despite their failure to make the statute
book, these bills commanded significant support in parliament and significantly shifted the terms in which abortion is debated.[3] In both Irish

---

[1] (1973) 410 US 113.

[2] See R. Colker, 'Abortion and Public Violence', in *Pregnant Men: Practice, Theory
and the Law* (Bloomington: Indiana University Press, 1994); 'Special Report on Abortion'
Ms (May/June 1995) 42–66.

[3] For example, David Alton's private member's bill, which sought to reduce the time
limits within which abortion may lawfully be performed, received its second reading in
the House of Commons in 1988 and passed by a majority of 296 to 251. The bill ultimately failed through lack of time at the report stage. Yet Sally Sheldon argues that it
shifted the moral terrain in favour of 'pro-life' forces, who have now secured consensus

jurisdictions the Irish and British governments have lacked the conviction to legislate on abortion, so that women are only legally entitled to abortion in Ireland where their lives are endangered by pregnancy.[4] In all of these jurisdictions the 'pro-life' movement has had tremendous political impact. Recently the threat it poses to abortion rights has been coupled with the increased willingness of another political movement —the fathers' rights movement—to invade what had previously been seen as women's private domain, thus subjecting rights to abortion to a new political and legal assault. In this chapter it is my argument that we must begin to formulate new feminist strategies for responding to such threats. I wish to suggest that a necessary preliminary step is to jettison the language of choice, which has hitherto been the foundation for feminist campaigns to demand or defend the legal right to abortion. I seek to problematize the concept of choice from a feminist standpoint rooted in women's experiences.[5] Although the slogan 'a woman's right to choose' has been emblematic of claims for reproductive freedom and the right to control one's body which form the cornerstone of the women's movement, I argue that through time this slogan has come to be used unreflectively. In the wake of new threats to access to abortion, especially the emergence of new types of legal claims, the time has now come to reconsider whether this slogan does accurately capture our experiences and demands.

Choices in Law

From a legal perspective I would argue that the notion of a right to choose is problematic. I would contend that, just as others have argued

that abortion should not be available after viability and that the fetus is constructed as a separate individual in medical and scientific discourse—S. Sheldon, 'The Law of Abortion and the Politics of Medicalisation', in J. Bridgeman and S. Millns (eds.), *Law and Body Politics: Regulating the Female Body* (Aldershot: Dartmouth, 1995), 105–24. The increasing visibility of 'pro-life' activists was evidenced by the decision of the Pro-life Alliance Party to field at least fifty candidates in the 1997 election in seats where none of the existing candidates were identifiably 'pro-life'. See M. Freely, 'Is Abortion a Vote-Winner?', *Guardian*, 2 Jan. 1997.

[4] See N. Whitty, 'Law and the Regulation of Abortion in Ireland' (1993) 43 *University of Toronto Law Journal* 851; T. McGleenan, '*Bourne* Again? Abortion Law in Northern Ireland after *Re K* and *Re A*' (1994) 46 *Northern Ireland Legal Quarterly* 389.

[5] See, for instance, K. O'Donovan, 'Engendering Justice: Women's Perspectives and the Rule of Law' (1989) 39 *University of Toronto Law Journal* 127. In claiming to speak from such a position it is of course necessary to reflect carefully on what we mean in speaking of 'women's experiences' and to attempt to account for the diversity of those experiences.

of rights discourse,[6] the rhetoric of choice has not been productive in terms of tangible legal gains for women. Whilst the rhetoric of choice and rights has frequently been translated into law, which is part of its appeal,[7] this has not been true of our law on abortion. Irish, British, and American law all fail to endorse a woman's right to choose. In Britain the law is contained in the 1967 Abortion Act, as amended by the Human Fertilisation and Embryology Act 1990. As Linda Clarke has demonstrated, although the abortion debate is commonly couched in terms of the competing rights of the woman and fetus, English legislation actually bypasses this debate. It accords rights only to the doctor, who has the right to determine whether abortion should be granted according to the criteria laid down in section 1 of the 1967 Act.[8] The 1967 Act thus reflects the fact that, although this legislation was passed in the liberal atmosphere of the 1960s, it resulted more from pressure by the medical profession for clarification of the law than from any input from the embryonic women's liberation movement.[9] In both Irish jurisdictions the law remains unclear, as neither the Irish nor British governments have passed legislation to regulate abortion, although terminations are permitted to preserve the life of the pregnant woman.[10] Furthermore, in

---

[6] See E. Kingdom, in Bridgeman and Millns (eds.), *Law and Body Politics*; id., *What's Wrong with Rights: Problems for a Feminist Politics of Law* (Edinburgh: Edinburgh University Press, 1991); C. Smart, *Feminism and the Power of Law* (London: Routledge, 1989), 138–59; F. Olsen, 'Statutory Rape: A Feminist Critique of Rights Analysis' (1984) 63 *Texas Law Review* 387; id., 'Unravelling Compromise' (1989) 103 *Harvard Law Review* 104. However, all of the above writers recognize the political necessity of engaging with rights arguments on some level, given their powerful rhetorical appeal. For a defence of rights arguments from a feminist perspective see P. Williams, *The Alchemy of Race and Rights* (Cambridge, Mass.: Harvard University Press, 1991), and for an argument that rights discourse may be more flexible and adaptable than is suggested by the critique of rights see D. Herman, 'Beyond the Rights Debate' (1993) 2 *Social and Legal Studies* 25; K. O'Donovan, 'The Subject of Human Rights: Abstract or Embodied?' (1995) 46 *Northern Ireland Legal Quarterly* 353.

[7] See K. Karst, 'Woman's Constitution' [1984] *Duke Law Journal* 447.

[8] See L. Clarke, 'Abortion: A Rights Issue?' in R. Lee and D. Morgan (eds.), *Birthrights: Law and Ethics at the Beginnings of Life* (London: Routledge, 1989), 155–71. See also Sheldon, 'The Law of Abortion'. Similarly, in the United States, Lisa Bower refers to the 'legal fiction of "choice"' and suggests that '[p]arsed from the broader notion of the right of privacy, the U.S. Supreme Court [in *Roe* v. *Wade*] never suggested that women could make decisions about whether or not to bear a child independent of a state interest' —see L. C. Bower, 'The Trope of the Dark Continent in the Fetal Harm Debates: "Africanism" and the Right to Choice', in P. Boling (ed.), *Expecting Trouble: Surrogacy, Fetal Abuse and New Reproductive Technologies* (Boulder, Colo.: Westview Press, 1995), 143, 148.

[9] See T. Newburn, *Permission and Regulation: Law and Morals in Post-war Britain* (London: Routledge, 1992), 136–57. See also Sheldon, 'The Law of Abortion'.

[10] In the Republic of Ireland this was confirmed in *Attorney General* v. *X* [1992] ILRM 401. The controversy generated by that decision sparked a referendum in which a majority voted against a proposed amendment to the Constitution which would have

Ireland, abortion provision is even more tightly professionalized.[11] It will
be my argument below that this medicalization of abortion may actually
have helped secure women's right to abortion from attack more securely
than if the right had been framed in the preferred feminist language
of choice, notwithstanding the fact that it is problematic to rely on any
professional group to safeguard a woman's fundamental rights.[12] In the
United States the central premiss of the landmark 1973 Supreme Court
decision in *Roe* v. *Wade*—that the right of privacy enshrined in the
US Constitution is broad enough to encompass the woman's right to
terminate her pregnancy—remains intact, although as a result of the
decision in *Planned Parenthood of Pennsylvania* v. *Robert P. Casey*[13]
the state can now actively discourage abortions by placing conditions
upon women's choices. For example, it is now permissible to introduce
parental consent requirements for teenaged women, or waiting periods
for all women, or requirements that women receive information about
adoption before having an abortion, provided that such requirements
do not impose an 'undue burden' on women's right to abortion before
viability.[14] Thus, in each of these jurisdictions, only a limited number of

declared abortion lawful when performed to save the life of the pregnant woman. However, constitutional amendments permitting information about abortion services abroad to
be distributed in Ireland and guaranteeing freedom to travel to avail of such services were
passed. See Whitty, 'Law and the Regulation of Abortion'. That this is also the position
in the North of Ireland has been confirmed by a series of unreported cases between 1993
and 1995—*Re K*, *Re A*, and *Re SJB*. In both jurisdictions the law continues to suffer the
lack of clarity which was evident in English law prior to the passage of the 1967 Abortion
Act. Thus, both pregnant women and their doctors are continuously at risk of criminal
prosecution. Simon Lee has argued that this factor alone would justify legislation, regard-
less of differing moral opinions as to its desirability. See S. Lee, 'Abortion Law in Northern
Ireland: The Twilight Zone', Paper for the Standing Advisory Committee on Human Rights,
May 1993; 'An A to K to Z of Abortion Law in Northern Ireland', Paper for the Standing
Advisory Commission on Human Rights, June 1994 (reprinted in A. Furedi (ed.), *The
Abortion Law in Northern Ireland: Human Rights and Reproductive Choice* (Belfast:
Family Planning Association, 1995)).

[11] Since in *X* the vital determination that her life was in danger was made by an experienced clinical psychologist, rather than a doctor, it is possible that the diagnosis is not purely
medical. None the less, the decision is clearly one to be made by professionals rather than
entrusted to women—see M. Fox and T. Murphy, 'Irish Abortion: Seeking Refuge in a
Jurisprudence of Doubt and Delegation' (1992) 19 *Journal of Law and Society* 454.

[12] See, for example, A. Witz, *Professions and Patriarchy* (London: Routledge, 1992);
K. Luker, *Abortion and the Politics of Motherhood* (Berkeley and Los Angeles: University of California Press, 1984); Sheldon, 'The Law of Abortion'; K. McDonnell, *Not an
Easy Choice: A Feminist Re-examines Abortion* (Toronto: The Women's Press, 1984),
95–124.

[13] 112 S. Ct. 2791 (1992).

[14] See C. Bell, 'Case Note: *Planned Parenthood of Pennsylvania, et al.* v. *Robert
P. Casey, et al.*' (1993) 1 *Feminist Legal Studies* 91.

choices are endorsed by law. Furthermore, the law has not unequivocally ruled out the rights of others—such as putative fathers or, in the case of minors, their parents. As I discuss below, the possibility of actions by third parties poses a significant threat to women's reproductive liberty. Moreover, even if the law *had* unequivocally endorsed a woman's right to choose, it is my contention that such laws would have been vulnerable to competing legal claims couched in terms of a fetal right to life.

The Symbolism of Choice

The problems with legal endorsement of the right to choose are not simply a reflection of the law's inability to accommodate such a claim. In addition there is a theoretical problem inherent in such claims. To some extent all rights arguments are problematic for feminist theory and practice.[15] The assertion of rights arguments by feminists is generally defensive,[16] and they have a tendency to generate competing claims.[17] The discourse of rights stems from liberal imagery of autonomous individuals making choices in their own self-interest, and its one-dimensional nature means that it is difficult for this discourse to accommodate the pregnant woman. Reproductive rights arguments often seem to pit the rights of the woman against those of the fetus,[18] and also of the father or parents who seek to compel her to continue her pregnancy.[19] In this way, ironically, it is the father who appears more closely connected to the fetus—and it is his interests and those of the fetus which seem to coincide. Framing the right as one of *choice* simply compounds the problem inherent in rights arguments. The rhetoric of choice also stems from liberal imagery of autonomous individuals making choices in their own self(ish) interest(s) and thus facilitates the characterization of the woman

[15] See B. Brown, 'Bodily Oppositions/Controlling Fantasies', in *Body Politics: Control versus Freedom. The Role of Feminism in Women's Personal Autonomy*, Feminist Legal Research Unit, The University of Liverpool, Working Paper No. 1 (1993), 51–9, at 54, and n. 6 above.

[16] See Smart, *Feminism and the Power of Law*, 158.

[17] See ibid. 150, and L. Kingdom, 'Legal Recognition of a Woman's Right to Choose', in J. Brophy and C. Smart, *Women in Law: Explorations in Law, Family and Sexuality* (London: Routledge & Kegan Paul, 1985), 143–61.

[18] Most famously in Judith Jarvis Thompson's article 'A Defense of Abortion' (1971) 1 *Philosophy and Public Affairs*, repr. in P. Singer (ed.), *Applied Ethics* (Oxford: Oxford University Press, 1986), 37–58.

[19] See Olsen, 'Unravelling Compromise'.

who seeks abortion as selfish.[20] As Joan Williams points out, 'choice rhetoric [thus] fuels the right-to-life backlash by signalling that mothers —like other adults—should act as autonomous, self-interested adults'.[21] Moreover, pro-choice arguments often retain the anti-maternalist tendency which was evident in much second wave feminism, but is increasingly at odds with feminist theorizing about the complexity of motherhood.[22] The imagery of the selfish, amoral woman produced by choice discourse thus suggests the need for an alternative discourse in which to frame feminist demands.

Choices: Real or Illusory?

Yet the symbolism and rhetoric of a right to choose would be less troubling if the notion of choice reflected the reality of options available to women. An exploration of the choices open to many women demonstrates how limited such options are in practice. At the heart of this issue is the fact that women generally do not experience the decision to abort as one of choice. As Elizabeth Kingdom argues, the claim for a woman's right to choose glosses over the reality of women's lives where choice is, in fact, very restricted.[23] Indeed, it is unclear whether any woman would really choose to have an abortion—rather, most women who abort perceive termination as their only viable option.[24] Given a real choice, the vast majority of women who have an abortion would have preferred not to become pregnant; whilst those who abort on grounds of fetal handicap would have preferred to give birth to a healthy baby. Furthermore, Stoltenberg cites statistics from the National Center for Health

---

[20] See S. Sheldon, 'Who is the Mother to Make the Judgment? The Construction of Women in English Abortion Law' (1993) 1 *Feminist Legal Studies* 3, for a discussion of how parliamentary debates prior to the passage of the 1967 Act constructed women seeking abortions either as selfish or as victims.

[21] J. Williams, 'Gender Wars: Selfless Women in the Republic of Choice' (1991) 66 *New York University Law Review*, 1559, at 1574.

[22] R. B. Siegel, 'Abortion as a Sex Equality Right: Its Basis in Feminist Theory', in M. Fineman and I. Karpin (eds.), *Mothers in Law: Feminist Theory and the Legal Regulation of Motherhood* (New York: Columbia University Press, 1995), 43–72.

[23] See Kingdom, 'Legal Recognition of a Woman's Right to Choose', 153. She quotes the view of the Women's Reproductive Rights Campaign who state that ' "choice" means being able to pick from an ideal set of options'.

[24] For examples of how women reason on abortion, see C. Gilligan, *In a Different Voice* (Boston: Harvard University Press, 1982), 70–98; McDonnell, *Not an Easy Choice*, 27–41; R. Gregg, *Pregnancy in a High-Tech Age: Paradoxes of Choice* (New York: New York University Press, 1995), 110–20.

Statistics which suggest that one in five of the 14 million babies born in the United States would not have been born if mothers had given birth only to babies they wanted.[25] Although abortion rights have been framed in terms of the 'woman's right to choose', at best such choices have always been tightly circumscribed, if not rendered meaningless.[26] This is particularly true when women are not white, monied, educated, and assertive.

Choice may also be limited by the culture to which the woman belongs. An extensive US literature has demonstrated the lack of choice in the lives of young black women.[27] The same may well be true of young Irish women. The case of *Attorney-General* v. *X* is well known. A 14-year-old girl was raped by a friend of her family. When her parents decided to take her to England for an abortion they asked the Gardai whether genetic fingerprinting would assist in the prosecution of the rapist. The Gardai referred the matter to the Director of Public Prosecutions, who informed the Attorney-General, and on his application the Irish High Court granted an injunction (overturned on appeal) preventing the girl from procuring an abortion within or without the jurisdiction, or leaving the jurisdiction during her pregnancy. The Irish Supreme Court agreed that an abortion could be performed if it was proven that there was 'a real and substantial risk to the life, as distinct from the health of the mother, which can only be avoided by the termination'.[28] A less celebrated, but factually similar, decision was the unreported 1993 Northern Irish case of K. When the marriage of K's parents broke up she lived with her father, until he fell ill and was unable to control her. She was then taken into care by the local authority and lived in a children's home. She became pregnant in the wake of a number of incidents, including drunkenness and substance abuse. Given the prevailing climate in Northern Ireland, she almost certainly had no information on contraception.[29] Following K's threats to kill both herself and her 'unborn child', the medical experts and social workers concluded that in her

---

[25] See J. Stoltenberg, *Refusing to Be a Man* (Glasgow: Fontana/Collins, 1990).

[26] See R. P. Petchesky, *Abortion and Woman's Choice* (London: Verso, 1986).

[27] See, for example, ibid. 141–67; Bower, 'The Trope of the Dark Continent'; L. Ross, 'Raising our Voices', in M. Gerber Fried (ed.), *From Abortion to Reproductive Freedom: Transforming a Movement* (Boston: South End Press, 1990), 139–43; D. E. Roberts, 'Punishing Drug Addicts Who Have Babies' (1991) 104 *Harvard Law Review* 1419.

[28] *Attorney-General* v. *X* [1992] ILRM 401, at 425, per Finlay CJ.

[29] On the controversy occasioned by the decision to fund a Brook clinic in Belfast to advise young people about contraception, see Medico-legal Enquiry Group, *The Brook Clinic in Northern Ireland: An Agenda for Debate* (Belfast, 1992); 'Brook in Belfast: Why did it Take a Year' (1992) 1 (2) *Women's Choice* 27.

best interests the pregnancy should be terminated. The local authority sought an order from the Northern Irish High Court that she should be permitted to travel to England for abortion. Mr Justice Shiels granted the order sought, but in the process bravely clarified the legal position in Northern Ireland, stating that in the circumstances abortion would be lawful under Northern Irish law. In doing so he confirmed that the English decision *R. v. Bourne*[30] was applicable in Northern Ireland, so that abortion is lawful provided 'the doctor is of the opinion, on reasonable grounds and with adequate knowledge, that the probable consequence of the continuance of the pregnancy will be to make the woman a physical or mental wreck'.[31] However, no doctor could be found to perform the termination in Northern Ireland, so the court authorized the Northern Health and Social Services Board to arrange for the operation to be performed in Liverpool.

Given the lack of clarity in the law, the unwillingness of the medical profession to fulfil their responsibilities, the prohibitive cost of travelling to England, plus the absence of advice on contraception, what relevance does choice have in the lives of these young Irish women? Moreover, there are countless other women in Ireland, both North and South, who also experience limited choices given how their roles are constructed both in the legal Constitution of the Republic[32] and in the broader society they inhabit throughout Ireland.[33]

A related point is that, even where a woman does have access to abortion, characterizing her action as one of choosing fails to capture the complexity and ambivalence of women's responses to the experience of abortion. The slogan 'a woman's right to choose' risks masking women's problems with abortion—in particular the fact that abortion is not a complete solution to the problem of unwanted pregnancy. Yet, once a defensive impasse is reached, which may be inevitable once rights arguments are invoked, women are naturally reluctant to express ambivalence for fear of conceding ground to pro-life claims or appearing treacherous to the cause of reproductive freedom.[34] One place where women did have some place to express such feelings was in the pages

---

[30] [1939] 1 KB 687.   [31] Trial transcript at p. 12.

[32] See Fox and Murphy, 'Irish Abortion'.

[33] See A. Smyth (ed.), *The Abortion Papers, Ireland* (Dublin: Attic Press, 1992).

[34] This was the charge levelled at American writer Naomi Wolf when she questioned, in a *New Republic* article, the way in which feminists had approached the issue of abortion and expressed her own moral reservations about the practice. See 'Abortion: What Do You Think?', *Guardian*, 19 Oct. 1995.

of the now defunct British feminist magazine *Spare Rib*. In one issue Eileen Fairweather speculated on the reasons why the one in six women of reproductive age whom she claimed had had abortions did not publicly defend the right to abortion. In her article she sought to challenge the rationalist moral traditions which assert that, once a woman has made a 'rational decision' to have an abortion, she no longer has reason for all the difficult feelings of shame, regret, anger, longing, and sadness that might emerge:

> The women's movement was still very young when abortion first became a political football. We duly kicked back and, faced with the opposition's set of slogans, *defensively* [my emphasis] came up with our own. In our rush to do that, the complexity of abortion and its emotional significance for women somehow got lost . . . What we seem to forget is that women in their thousands won't come flocking to our demos when so many have never even *talked* to anyone of their own experience. The 'Antis' have 'God and right' on their side; we have a legacy of shame and secrecy, and often pain which goes so deep you can't even bear to think about it—much less fight back.[35]

I do not wish to universalize women's experiences of abortion as 'pro-lifers' are prone to do. Many women experience joy or relief after an abortion, but a sizeable number do feel shame and guilt, even when they know abortion was the right thing to do in the circumstances.[36] Although such negative feelings to some extent are culturally induced, that does not make the pain any less real, and these are emotions which feminists need to acknowledge. Space needs to be created for these women to discuss and come to terms with the impact of abortion and the violence which it involves in their lives.[37] This need for space is more acute

[35] E. Fairweather, 'The Feelings behind the Slogans', in M. Rowe (ed.), *Spare Rib Reader* (Harmondsworth: Penguin, 1982), 338–45, at 339.

[36] See L. B. Francke, *The Ambivalence of Abortion* (London: Allen Lane, 1979). It should however be noted that some feminist writers have criticized the emphasis on the altruism motivating many abortions, arguing that this keeps women on the defensive. See, for instance, L. Purdy, 'Abortion and the Argument from Convenience', in *Reproducing Persons* (Ithaca, NY: Cornell University Press, 1996), 143.

[37] Marie Asche argues that 'Pro-life advocates have accurately recognized in pro-choice discourse a practice of abstraction that tends to obliterate or erase the reality of bloodiness and violence attached to abortion. Women who consciously experience abortion become familiar with these realities and respond variously to them . . . [t]he failure of pro-choice discourse . . . to acknowledge the violence intrinsic to abortion . . . has constructed impediments to our speaking truly and deeply—and more variously—of what abortion means to us.' See M. Asche, 'Zig-zag Stitching and the Seamless Web: Thoughts on "Reproduction" and the Law' (1989) 13 *Nova Law Review* 335.

in the case of women whose voices have so far been absent from the pro-choice debate, which may hold little meaning for them.[38]

Once feminism has confronted the question of whether this slogan can capture the complexities of women's experiences and emotions, however, it is faced with an even tougher and more divisive issue. It involves questioning how far we, as feminists, are committed to the notion of choice. Certainly the law either disallows choice completely or confines it within tightly circumscribed parameters. Interestingly, this may reflect the wider social acceptability of abortion. Condit, in her analysis of the portrayal of abortion decisions on prime-time American television programmes, found support for abortion only when the decision fell within a limited range of circumstances.[39] It seems probable that her survey included some feminists, thus suggesting that not all of us may be absolutely committed to the choice of abortion in all circumstances.[40] The need to discuss this now is becoming more urgent because of the increasing intervention of fathers' rights groups in the debate. If we seek to deny men any legal rights in relation to what happens to a fetus (as I would suggest we should) we may need to explore whether women's choices should be absolutely without limit.

An example of possible limits to the acceptability of choice is provided by Tricia Greenhalgh—a London general practitioner and self-proclaimed feminist—who explained her reasons for refusing an abortion to one of her patients.[41] The patient in question was a 38-year-old married woman, with a large house and nanny for her three existing children, who had requested an abortion as her unplanned pregnancy would disrupt her skiing holiday. Even those who endorse legally sanctioned abortion are

[38] For instance, Loretta Ross, 'Raising our Voices', points out that the abortion debate, thus far, has largely been constructed between white women and white men, and those black voices which are given prominence tend to be 'pro-life'. Similarly debates on this side of the Atlantic have been conducted largely between women who are relatively empowered, and who rarely speak from personal experience of having or being denied abortion.

[39] See C. M. Condit, 'Prime-Time Abortion: Rhetoric and Popular Culture 1973–85', in *Decoding Abortion Rhetoric: Communicating Social Change* (Chicago: University of Illinois Press, 1990).

[40] Equally, it should be noted that 'pro-life' groups are not absolutely committed to the logic of their position. As Ronald Dworkin points out, many of those who are conservative on abortion would permit exceptions to save the pregnant woman's life, or in the case of rape or incest. He argues that '[t]he more such exceptions are allowed, the clearer it becomes that conservative opposition to abortion does not presume that a fetus is a person with a right to live'. See R. Dworkin, *Life's Dominion: An Argument about Abortion and Euthanasia* (London: HarperCollins, 1993), 32.

[41] T. Greenhalgh, 'The Doctor's Right to Choose' (1992) 305 *British Medical Journal* 371.

likely to have moral reservations about the acceptability of abortion for such a reason.[42] Yet, such abortions raise an important point about defining the reasons for termination as frivolous or convenient. It may prove difficult to draw a clear dividing line between a decision to have an abortion which would disrupt a holiday, and one which would interfere with a planned career move. The latter reason could equally be deemed frivolous by a doctor in circumstances where the woman was living with a man in paid employment. Obviously, feminists will disagree amongst themselves on where the lines should be drawn. This raises the issue of who should decide when abortions are permissible. Moreover, we must accept that there will always be rare cases of women who do choose abortions for frivolous reasons—any legal right is open to abuse. However, the existence of a small number of exceptional cases does not seem to me a sufficiently convincing reason to depart from a general position of trusting the pregnant woman to make the best decision for her fetus.[43] A further contentious 'choice' concerns abortions performed on the basis of fetal sex. Some feminists would claim it is indisputable that we should oppose terminations performed on this ground, which they argue can only contribute further to the cultural devaluation of women by treating gender as akin to disorder. Wertz and Fletcher point out:

Being born female is not a departure from the human norm. Any suffering that is attached to sex is suffering created by the family or society, not suffering created by nature. This suffering caused by society is indeed serious and needs to be removed; however, aborting fetuses of the sex that suffers more would be a rationale to reinforce and abet the conditions causing suffering, not one that would alleviate them.[44]

---

[42] See L. Hogan, 'Procreative Choice: A Feminist Theological Comment', in Smyth, *The Abortion Papers*. However, it should be noted that the reason which the pregnant woman gives to a doctor for seeking an abortion may not be the 'real' reason for her decision.

[43] See Gilligan, *In a Different Voice*; Brown, 'Bodily Oppositions/Controlling Fantasies', 54–5. Moreover, as Purdy points out, even if some abortion decisions may be rightly characterized as motivated by convenience, as a society we tolerate hundreds of thousands of deaths of living persons each year for reasons of convenience such as over-dependence upon motor cars—see Purdy 'Abortion and the Argument from Convenience', 145.

[44] D. C. Wertz and J. C. Fletcher, 'Sex Selection through Prenatal Diagnosis: A Feminist Critique', in H. B. Holmes and L. M. Purdy (eds.), *Feminist Perspectives in Medical Ethics* (Indianapolis: Indiana University Press, 1992), 240–53, at 245. See also H. B. Holmes, 'Choosing Children's Sex: Challenges to Feminist Ethics', in J. C. Callahan (ed.), *Reproduction, Ethics, and the Law: Feminist Perspectives* (Bloomington: Indiana University Press, 1995).

However, others, whose feminism is rooted more in actual experience than utopianism, would argue that this may only apply in an ideal society. In a less than ideal society we may wish to allow sex selection if it avoids repeated abortions and the trauma of abandoning children. My own position is undecided, but it does seem to me problematic that, under the guise of 'choice', even those doctors who oppose sex selection for social reasons may pressurize women into sex-selected abortions for medical reasons, such as haemophilia. This raises the much broader question of how much choice women really have in cases of fetal disability. Whilst the right to abortion is crucial, it is also important that women are protected from undue medical pressure to abort at a time when they may feel particularly vulnerable. A more common issue is that of second abortions. In Kristen Luker's study of attitudes to abortion, even amongst pro-choice advocates, support for the right to two or more abortions faded. She also found strong disapproval of using abortion as a method of contraception, notwithstanding the inadequacies of all existing methods of contraception.[45]

I am not advocating that we should devolve the power to law or medicine, as institutions of social control, to enforce such moral reservations, even when they are prompted by feminist concerns. It is necessary to concede to women the moral right to have abortions even if we personally might not decide to terminate in similar circumstances.[46] My argument is simply that proclaiming our belief in an absolute commitment to choice may overstate the position which many feminists hold. We need to discuss whether we can really claim to be committed to choice as a matter of principle, or whether we only support particular types of abortion. A crucial issue to be addressed is whether abortion is always a moral choice or whether it is really the choice of a lesser evil.

Men, Rights, and 'Choices'

These reasons to reconsider the language of choice and the issue of who decides have become more urgent in the light of new legal challenges to women's reproductive autonomy. Walters has referred to the assertion of rights by men who have shared responsibility for the pregnancy

---

[45] Luker, *Abortion and the Politics of Motherhood.*
[46] As Linda Clarke argues, 'Abortion: A Rights Issue?', 168, securing the legal right to abortion allows us the space to explore the morality of our decision.

as 'the next abortion issue'.[47] The assertion of men's claims in the context of abortion may take one of two forms—either to be *notified* when the woman makes the decision to abort, or to have a power to *veto* her decision. Such claims may be grounded either in the man's status as *father*, or in a *fetal right to life*, in which case the man is claiming a privileged status to protect that right, or in a *husband's right* to be consulted about any major decisions taken by the woman to whom he is married. Alternatively, state legislatures may attempt to make it mandatory for the woman to consult or obtain the consent of her spouse. In each case the motivation seems less concerned with protecting fetal life or promoting harmonious marital relationships (although that is the rhetoric in which it is usually couched) than with placing obstacles in the way of the woman who seeks an abortion. Yet, there is no doubt that denial of such claims by the legal system is provoking a sense of grievance, and in theoretical terms it may be difficult to contest them. As Kingdom points out: 'if feminists claim that a woman has the right to reproduce, there is no obvious reason why that right should not be claimed for men too, and on the traditional legal ground of equality it would be difficult to oppose that claim.'[48]

The point to be made in response concerns the blindness of traditional liberal theories to power differentials in gender relations, which entails that they discriminate against women. The staking of claims by putative fathers speaks volumes about contemporary female/male relations, especially over women's fertility and their power to control it. I would argue that the assertion of such rights affords an opportunity for feminist women to reconsider their relationship to both their sexual partners and their fetuses. Currently, it would appear that some men find it difficult to deal with the assertion of a woman's right to choose, and that this has produced what Stoltenberg terms a 'terribly embittered masculinity'. Masculine fears are most forcefully articulated in the work of George Gilder. In elaborating on the 'sexual dimensions of the abortion issue', he argues that opposition to abortion on demand stems not from a puritanical aversion to premarital sex, nor a religious belief that abortion is equivalent to murder, but from the fact that abortion symbolizes resistance to the erosion of male sexuality. He contends that the feminist demand

---

[47] M. Walters, 'Who Decides? The Next Abortion Issue: A Discussion of Father's Rights' (1988) 19 *West Virginia Law Review* 165.
[48] E. Kingdom, 'The Right to Reproduce' (1986) 32 *Medicine, Ethics and Law* 13th Annual Conference of Association for Legal and Social Philosophy 61 (quoted in Smart, *Feminism and the Power of Law*, 151).

for 'control over our own bodies' has been one of the most extreme claims of the women's movement. It

accentuated an unconscious recognition that *males have almost completely lost control of procreative activity* . . . A man's penis becomes an empty plaything unless a woman deliberately decides to admit a man's paternity . . . People [*sic*] resist legal abortion on demand out of a sense of justifiable conservatism towards continued changes in the sexual constitution.[49]

Whilst the rhetoric is different, both this claim and that of a right to choose appear to evoke similar responses. As Stoltenberg suggests: 'Men's individual feelings are diverse and complex, but they can be understood as having in common the fear that women will cease to sustain the sexual identities of men, and the fear that therefore masculinity will cease to exist.'[50]

Clearly women need spend little time agonizing over problems engendered by such male insecurities, but it is of concern that, in response to the assertion of women's rights, such men have the resources and willingness to use law to reaffirm their potency. In this article space precludes a detailed analysis of the legal response to such claims. However, the following general points may be noted. First, a reading of the cases betrays the extent to which men fail to take responsibility for birth control, and yet are prepared, by resorting to law if necessary, to compel a woman to continue an unwanted pregnancy, frequently after their relationship has ended, sometimes as a result of his violence.[51] Thus, such actions are frequently a punitive and vindictive assertion of rights through law, rather than an effort to secure justice. Secondly, there is a contrast between legal responses on both sides of the Atlantic. Both the US and Canadian Supreme Courts have considered and been unresponsive to such claims. In the US Supreme Court decision in *Casey* it is highly significant that a spousal notification requirement was the only part of a very restrictive Pennsylvanian statute on abortion to be struck down as unconstitutional. Despite noting the desirability of joint

---

[49] G. Gilder, *Men and Marriage* (Gretna, La.: Pelican, 1986), 106–7.

[50] See Stoltenberg, *Refusing to Be a Man*.

[51] For example, in *C* v. *S* [1987] 1 All ER 1230 the couple had unprotected sex, despite the man's strong anti-abortion views; in the Canadian case of *Tremblay* v. *Daigle* (1990) 62 DLR (4th) 634 the woman had been abused and coerced into discontinuing birth control. Moreover, John Stoltenberg cites a Planned Parenthood of Chicago research project which revealed that 70% of men under 25 surveyed thought that it was acceptable to use deception to obtain sex, 80% felt that contraception was not the man's responsibility, but almost 90% disagreed with abortion 'because it's wrong'. See Stoltenberg, *Refusing to Be a Man*.

decision-making, the majority acknowledged that it was 'an inescapable biological fact that state regulation with regard to the child [*sic*] the woman is carrying will have a far greater impact on the mother's liberty than on the father's'. The fact-intensive analysis of this clause, along the lines of the reasoning in *Planned Parenthood of Central Missouri* v. *Danforth*,[52] and the heavy reliance of the majority judgment upon expert testimony and academic writing on the effect of imposing such a requirement upon women, may be contrasted with the reasoning adopted elsewhere in the judgment.[53]

Similarly, although the fetus has been more successful in obtaining legal representation in Canada, this seems largely a reflection of the greater willingness of the Canadian courts to grant *locus standi* to interested parties, since the Canadian courts have generally been hostile to the assertion of substantive rights by the putative father.[54] The issue now appears closed in that jurisdiction, following *Tremblay* v. *Daigle* where the Supreme Court overturned an injunction granted to the father by the Quebec Court of Appeal preventing his ex-girlfriend from obtaining an abortion. The Supreme Court based its decision on existing Canadian law, which did not recognize the fetus as a person,[55] and summarily dismissed the argument grounded in fathers' rights:

> This argument would appear to be based on the proposition that the potential father's contribution to the act of conception gives him an equal say in what happens to the fetus . . . There does not appear to be any jurisprudential basis for this argument. No court in Quebec or elsewhere has ever accepted the argument that a father's interest in a fetus which he helped create could support a right to veto a woman's decision in respect of the fetus she is carrying . . . This lack of a legal basis is fatal to the argument about fathers' rights.[56]

In Europe, however, the prognosis appears more gloomy for those seeking to defend abortion rights, especially in central and eastern Europe where the trend is towards increasing conservatism on reproductive freedom. Hitherto, claims by putative fathers have rarely arisen before

---

[52] 428 US 52 (1976). This was the first post-*Roe* case to reach the Supreme Court, and it declared unconstitutional a Missouri statute which provided that a doctor could not perform an abortion within the first twelve weeks of the pregnancy without the written consent of the woman's spouse, unless the doctor was prepared to certify that her life was in danger.

[53] See Bell, 'Case Note'.

[54] See R. A. Mason and McCall-Smith, *Law and Medical Ethics*, 4th edn. (London: Butterworths, 1994), 119.

[55] *Borowski* v. *Attorney-General of Canada* (1987) 39 DLR (4th) 731 (Sask, CA).

[56] *Tremblay* v. *Daigle*, at 665.

the courts in Europe. Yet in many jurisdictions, such as Ireland, I would argue that there is considerable legal scope for the assertion of such claims.[57] Moreover, even countries with more liberal abortion laws, like Britain, may be vulnerable to legal challenges by fathers under the European Convention on Human Rights (ECHR). Although the issue has yet to be squarely confronted by the European Court of Human Rights,[58] in the past, some of its judges have indicated receptivity to claims by putative fathers seeking to protect the right to life of the fetus. In September 1992 the Court held that an injunction granted by the Irish Supreme Court restraining two counselling agencies in Ireland from providing information on the availability of abortion in Britain violated Article 10 of the ECHR (the right to impart and receive information). However, a number of the dissenting and separate judgments contained worrying dicta on the rights of third parties in relation to the abortion decision, most explicitly in the judgment delivered by Judge Matscher. He contended that interference with the right in question was necessary for the protection of morals (according to Irish standards) and added that, in his view, the rights of both the unborn child *and his father* should have been taken into account.[59] Other judgments in the case also specify that the rights of 'others' should have been considered under Article 10, without stating whether this encompasses putative fathers. Such pronouncements, in a case in which third-party rights were not directly in issue, give rise to serious concern for those who seek to protect the reproductive freedom of women.

First, the receptivity to the notion of fathers' rights on the part of Judge Matscher is illustrative of Carol Smart's point that courts seem readily to accept claims by men which are framed in the discourse of rights: 'Whilst the law has been slow in responding to equal rights claims by women, it appears to respond with alacrity to perceived inequalities in formal legal rights where fathers are concerned . . . men's wishes seem

---

[57] Certainly one consequence of the Supreme Court decision in *Attorney-General* v. *X* was to leave open the possibility that third-party interests could be taken into account by a court in deciding when abortion was justifiable under the Irish Constitution. See Fox and Murphy, 'Irish Abortion', 459–60.

[58] It did come before the European Commission in the case of *Paton* v. *UK* Application No. 8416/79 [1980] 3 EHRR, where the Commission disallowed a father's challenge to British abortion law which denied him a right to be consulted. However, the reasoning was somewhat ambiguous and based on narrow grounds. For criticism see P. van Dijk and G. van Hoof, *Theory and Practice of the European Convention of Human Rights*, 2nd edn. (Deventer: Kluwer, 1990), 386; M. Brazier, *Medicine, Patients and the Law*, 2nd edn. (London: Penguin, 1992), 309.

[59] *Open Door Counselling and Well Woman* v. *Ireland* (1992) EHRR 244.

to become law with remarkable speed.'[60] Smart's assertion rings particularly true in relation to child custody, where fathers have made substantial legal gains using the rhetoric of equality. As she points out, the fathers' rights movement has been based upon the strategy of securing the legitimacy that accompanies rights claims, whilst simultaneously occupying the terrain of children's welfare, arguing that, in principle, to protect fathers' rights is to protect children's welfare.[61] In reality, the agenda of such fathers (as in the case of abortion) may be more about controlling their estranged partners rather than caring for their children.[62] None the less they have successfully redefined children's rights as being predominantly a right of access to fathers.[63] Smart argues that, in the context of abortion, if men could similarly succeed in linking their claims to the welfare of their 'unborn children', they would stand a better chance of success before the courts. Instead, in the two British cases which address the issue, they have allowed the matter to be transposed into the medical domain. One case[64] turned on the issue of maternal health, and the other[65] on the point at which a fetus became viable, thus obscuring the substance of the claims on behalf of fathers. Unless fathers can shift the debate from the terrain of women's health, it seems that courts will lack the temerity to interfere with medical judgment. As Ken Mason remarks: 'so long as it is held that abortion is, effectively, only legal insofar as the pregnancy affects the health of the mother, it is clearly wrong that any third party should be able to come between a woman and her medical advisers . . . [a]s a result interventions effected by fathers have consistently failed.'[66] Ironically, therefore, despite the many valid reasons why women oppose the medicalization of abortion, one positive side-effect has been the ease with which it means that third-party claims can be ruled out.

[60] C. Smart, 'Power and the Politics of Child Custody', in C. Smart and S. Sevenhuijsen (eds.), *Child Custody and the Politics of Gender* (London: Routledge, 1989), 1–26, at 9.
[61] Smart, *Feminism and the Power of Law*, 155–6.
[62] For instance, in *Tremblay* v. *Daigle* the putative father confessed for the first time to doubts about his commitment to child care only after he had obtained an injunction to prevent the abortion in the Quebec Court of Appeal. He told the press he wanted 'to be a father but he didn't have the time right now', and later reasoned, 'I don't give milk. Women give milk. I guess the baby just needs his mother.' See J. Brodie, 'Choice and No-Choice in the House', in J. Brodie *et al.* (eds.), *The Politics of Abortion* (Toronto: Oxford University Press, 1992), 57–116, at 93.
[63] See Smart and Sevenhuijsen, *Child Custody and the Politics of Gender*.
[64] *Paton* v. *BPAS* [1978] 2 All ER 987.   [65] *C* v. *S*.
[66] K. Mason, 'Abortion and the Law', in S. McLean (ed.), *Legal Issues in Human Reproduction* (Aldershot: Gower, 1989), 45–79, at 58–60.

Secondly, it is unlikely that the courts will be able to evade an argument framed in terms of men protecting the welfare of their children for long. Just as men have invaded the 'feminine' domain of child care, so they may increasingly begin to assert rights in that other classically private sphere of reproduction. This seems to me the next logical focus for the men's rights movement, as it is an area where women have always retained a measure of power and control in resistance to attempts to medicalize it.[67] Furthermore, men have an added advantage in the sphere of abortion, as they can not only draw on the powerful rhetoric and imagery of protecting their unborn children, but can form a potent political alliance with pro-life groups. Despite their differing political agendas,[68] there is an obvious convergence of interest here.[69]

A third reason for women to take seriously the assertion of fathers' rights in the context of abortion stems from the combined fact that women's rights have never been fully accepted in the reproductive context,[70] and that the rhetoric of the fathers' rights movement seems to have penetrated the public consciousness. Such groups in Britain have consumed a disproportionate amount of media attention.[71] As the plethora of books purporting to 'defend the modern man'[72] testify, the fathers' rights movement seems to have tapped into some sort of *Zeitgeist*, which in turn fits into a much broader anti-feminist 'backlash'.[73] A combination of the contemporary crisis in masculinity which is linked to a perceived breakdown of traditional masculine authority in men's relationship with women and children,[74] allied to the other factors outlined above, makes a successful legal claim possible in Europe.

---

[67] See J. Wajcman, 'Reproductive Technology: Delivered into Men's Hands', in *Feminism Confronts Technology* (Cambridge: Polity Press, 1991), 54–80.

[68] See Smart, 'Power and the Politics of Child Custody', 17–19.

[69] As many of the Canadian cases demonstrate, men prepared to litigate in favour of these claims are often funded by pro-life groups.

[70] See Smart, *Feminism and the Power of Law*, 146–53.

[71] Recently not all of this has been favourable, but it is instructive to compare the attention devoted to fathers' campaigns against the Child Support Act with the lack of attention given to its much greater impact on the lives of women. See R. Collier, 'The Campaign against the Child Support Act: "Errant Fathers" and "Family Men"' [1994] *Family Law* 384.

[72] See, for example, N. Lyndon, *No More Sex War* (London: Sinclair Stevenson, 1992); D. Thomas, *Not Guilty* (London: Weidenfeld & Nicolson, 1993). As Collier comments, these books embody a particularly vituperative and bitter antifeminism—see R. Collier, *Masculinity, Law and the Family* (London: Routledge, 1995), 26.

[73] This is most cogently articulated in Susan Faludi's *Backlash: The Undeclared War against Women* (London: Chatto & Windus, 1992).

[74] See Collier, *Masculinity, Law and the Family*.

Hence, the crucial question becomes, how should feminists respond to such claims? One response to the staking of men's claims would be to fall back on the old assertion of a 'woman's right to choose', but it is one which I suggest should be avoided on the grounds that it is now outdated. As McDonnell points out, it is only in relation to abortion that feminists are still marching with the same slogans and much the same general position as we did in the 1970s.[75]

Choices, Language, and Limits

The aim of this chapter has been to explore the problematic aspects of the discourse of a right to choose. A further reason to jettison this discourse is that it would enable feminism to break free from the paradigm of the current debate which has been singularly unproductive. At present, there exist two polarized camps—one labelled 'pro-life' and the other 'pro-choice'—which are resolutely opposed and allow no common ground on which to debate. This has caused some feminists to advocate the need for dialogue to break the impasse.[76] Attempts at dialogue might be facilitated by abandoning the traditional polarized discourse of choice versus life, in which the moral high ground is implicitly conceded to the 'pro-life' camp. Moreover, the current polarization around abortion may facilitate the division of women and men into oppositional camps by placing men on the defensive and inhibiting dialogue between the sexes. We need to be as wary of essentializing the responses of all men as we do when discussing women's various responses to abortion. Many men do not exhibit the vituperative response to abortion decisions evidenced in the reported cases, but wish instead to be supportive to a partner considering whether or not to abort. It is conceivable, as Neustatter has suggested, that the assertion of a woman's right to choose may inhibit men from expressing their views on abortion, even where they would seek to be supportive of a woman personally or the right to abortion publicly.[77] Clearly in such a situation we would wish to facilitate communication between the parties, especially if this would result in men assuming more responsibility in the decision to beget and

---

[75] See McDonnell, *Not an Easy Choice*, 23.

[76] See R. Colker, *Abortion and Dialogue: Pro-Choice, Pro-Life and American Law* (Indianapolis: Indiana University Press, 1992).

[77] See A. Neustatter (with G. Newson), *Mixed Feelings: The Experiences of Abortion* (London: Pluto Press, 1986).

care for children. As McDonnell argues, in every other area of reproduction we are urging men to take more responsibility, but in relation to abortion we have never worked out a position on their role.[78] Unless we seek to negotiate such a role for men, we risk the courts imposing a decision which would permit men to control our decisions.

There is one final reason why this may be a particularly opportune moment to reconsider our strategy on abortion. This relates to the shifting terrain of the battle for reproductive rights. Cynthia Daniels argues that in the last decade or so:

A new kind of reproductive politics has emerged on the American political stage. In the past the focus was on either reproductive choice (the beginning of pregnancy) or the politics of motherhood (the aftermath of pregnancy)...
The new politics of fetal rights focuses on the politics of pregnancy itself—on mediating and regulating what some now characterise as the *social relationship* between the pregnant woman and the fetus.[79]

Her thesis is that, ironically, the assertion of a right framed in terms of choice has affirmed the state's right to regulate and control a woman's pregnancy. 'Pro-life' forces may argue that once a woman chooses to proceed with a pregnancy she assumes an obligation to her fetus which the state may enforce.[80] Moreover, such arguments are not the exclusive preserve of sexual conservatives. She cites Alan Dershowitz, a liberal Harvard law professor, who argues:

I believe that a pregnant woman should have the right to choose between giving birth or having an abortion. But... I believe that no woman who has chosen to give birth should have the right to neglect or injure that child by abusing their collective body during pregnancy... Your right to abuse your own body stops at the border of your womb.[81]

Therefore, as the focus shifts to pregnancy we have an additional reason to seek a new language in which to frame our interests, or else risk the language of choice being co-opted by those who seek to control the pregnant woman in the interests of her fetus. The language of choice is

---

[78]   See McDonnell, *Not an Easy Choice*, 61.

[79]   C. Daniels, *At Women's Expense: State Power and the Politics of Fetal Rights* (Cambridge, Mass.: Harvard University Press, 1993), 2.

[80]   Ibid. 24–6.

[81]   A similar analysis is implicit in Ronald Dworkin's theorizing on abortion, when he argues that 'If a woman smokes during her pregnancy, a human being may later exist whose interests will have been seriously damaged by her behavior; but if she aborts, no one will exist whose interests her behavior will have damaged.' See Dworkin, *Life's Dominion*, 19.

also being co-opted and used against women's interests in other contexts. As Margaret Brazier argues, it is under the guise of choice, and feminism, that new reproductive technologies have been introduced.[82] The discourse of choice has also been invoked in favour of other controversial developments, such as the choice to be a surrogate mother,[83] to harvest eggs from aborted fetuses, to buy or sell gametes, or to engage in potentially dangerous forms of self-abortion.[84] In this way the whole language of choice becomes debased. As Janice Raymond argues:

The reproductive liberals—the technologists and doctors, the surrogate brokers, the lawyers—have been adept at manipulating pro-choice philosophy and politics, knowing that many will accept the rhetoric without questioning the reality of what is promoted as choice . . . Choice is increasingly allied with consumption in contemporary society; the right to choose has effectively become the right to consume.[85]

In this context there are grounds for concern that the slogan 'a right to choose' may be debased, and that, divorced from its roots in the women's liberation movement, it may be utilized against the interests of many women.

Abandoning Choice: Affirming Reality

For all the reasons outlined above, it seems to me that we have reached a point when we should abandon the language of choice, grounded as it is in an individualistic Rawlsian conception of justice. To secure justice for the pregnant woman we should seek to reframe our demands to match her experiences, and in a language which is accessible and meaningful to women who may not experience choice and control in their lives. However, we must do so with awareness of the dangers of allowing the discourse of choice to fade from feminist debate. Some feminists would assert that if the real problem is that women lack choice, a feminist politics should aim to enhance their power to choose. However, this fails to recognize how debased the notion of choice has become and how

[82] See M. Brazier, 'Reproductive Rights: Feminism or Patriarchy?', Ch. 4 above; and also P. B. Richard, 'The Tailor-Made Child: Implications for Women and the State', in Boling, *Expecting Trouble*.

[83] See L. Purdy, 'Surrogate Mothering: Exploitation or Empowerment?' (1989) 3 *Bioethics* 18.

[84] See R. Chalker, 'The Whats, Hows and Whys of Menstrual Extraction', 26 *On the Issues* (Spring 1993) 42–7.

[85] J. G. Raymond, *Women as Wombs: Reproductive Technologies and the Battle over Women's Freedom* (San Francisco: HarperSanFrancisco, 1993).

it potentially can be used against the pregnant woman. Moreover, given the power of rhetoric the symbolism of words in this context is highly significant. Continuing to adopt the language of choice too easily allows abortion to be depicted as a matter of women's convenience which is counter-posed to the taking of an unborn child's life, which fits in neatly to an anti-feminist backlash.[86] A consequence of forsaking such language will be the loss of a sense of opposition, whilst a further risk is that feminists may make concessions in the interests of dialogue and progress while no ground will be conceded by sexual conservatives such as Pat Buchanan and George Gilder. Nevertheless, such a scenario could also offer the opportunity to marginalize the more extreme elements of the anti-abortion movement, and sketch out a feminist position to those whom we currently fail to reach. McDonnell suggests that the middle ground of people are currently not addressed in the abortion debate: 'the great middle ground of people . . . are not the confirmed anti-abortionists, but people who simply feel that abortion does have a moral dimension that they don't see being addressed in the feminist stance.'[87]

As I have suggested above it is the language of choice which obscures the complex moral reasoning of most women who have abortions. If the complexity of this moral reasoning process could be rendered visible, the 'middle ground' to which Mc Donnell refers may be moved to support the right to legal abortion through appreciation of the moral dimensions of such decisions.

However, if we do abandon the rhetoric of choice, the way forward in asserting and defending the legal right to abortion is unclear. This is necessarily the case since a new and more woman-centred vision and language must emerge from a dialogue within feminism. Various ways forward have been tentatively proposed. One emerges from the writings of Ronald Dworkin, who commends a search for common ground on the basis that both sides to the abortion debate value the sanctity of life.[88] This position has been adopted by some feminist organizations, such

[86] See K. Pollitt, 'Children of Choice', in *Reasonable Creatures: Essays on Women and Feminism* (London: Vintage, 1995), 11–15, at 12; Purdy, 'Abortion and the Argument from Convenience'.

[87] See McDonnell, *Not an Easy Choice*, 24. See also B. W. Harrison, 'The Morality of Procreative Choice', in *Our Right to Choose: Toward a New Ethic of Abortion* (Boston: Beacon Press, 1983), 32–56.

[88] See Dworkin, *Life's Dominion*. A similar search for consensus is evident in the work of Lawrence Tribe, who concludes that 'In a democracy, voting and persuasion are all we have.' See L. H. Tribe, *Abortion: The Clash of Absolutes* (New York: W. H. Norton & Co., 1990), 240.

as the US group Planned Parenthood which been a significant player in US abortion cases. Since Clinton's election and under the direction of its own new president Pamela Maraldo, the organization has moved away from a rhetoric of feminist sexual politics towards a focus on health care reform, and a concern with reclaiming the moral high ground from the anti-abortion camp. Maraldo has contended, 'We *can* begin again to inculcate America with our values. We are the *real* pro-life force in America. I want to take the moral high ground.'[89] This stance has been controversial and does run the risk that in such a debate the pro-abortion forces will always lose out, given the association between the anti-abortion movement and the protection of life. Rosalind Petchesky has suggested, more persuasively, that we should abandon the rhetoric of choice in favour of one rooted in women's needs.[90] Although Smart points out that this risks depicting the woman who seeks abortion as a victim,[91] it may have the advantage of more accurately reflecting the situation of women like the young Irish women discussed above, and also of being more meaningful for them, given their limited opportunities to exercise choice. Moreover, focusing on needs may help us to frame a vision of justice founded in the needs and realities of women's lives as a building block towards a meaningful vision of equality.

Indeed, some of the most powerful feminist work on abortion has argued that claims for a legal right to abortion should be explicitly rooted in the feminist demand for equality. As Catherine McKinnon argues, 'Many of the social disadvantages to which women have been subjected have been predicated upon their capacity for and role in childbearing . . . short of achieving sexual and social equality—short of changing the context—abortion has offered the only way out.'[92] Recently this equality analysis has also been adopted by those who would move away from the traditional concept of women's right to choose, or control their own bodies, towards a strategy which emphasizes instead the notion of women's reproductive health.[93] This tactic has the advantage

[89] See J. Warner, 'Mixed Messages: Where is Pamela Maraldo Taking Planned Parenthood?', *Ms* (Nov.–Dec. 1993) 20–5.

[90] Petchesky, *Abortion and Woman's Choice*, 384–5.

[91] Smart, *Feminism and the Power of Law*, 153.

[92] C. MacKinnon, 'Reflections on Sex Equality under Law' (1991) 100 *Yale Law Journal* 1281–328, at 1308, 1317. She also cautions, at p. 1318, that reproduction is a much larger and more diverse experience in the life of women than the focus on abortion permits. See also Siegel, 'Abortion as a Sex Equality Right'.

[93] Such a concept would need to be a broad one, but a promising formulation is provided by the definition contained in the Programme of Action of the 1994 International Conference on Population and Development in Cairo, albeit one which does not escape

of potentially acting as a powerful lever on the state, especially in claiming resources. Furthermore, as Noel Whitty argues:

[the] introduction of the concept of 'women's health' into international human rights discourse is valuable, not only because it situates abortion in a very recognizable social context, but because it might provide a departure from the dominance of an (arguably unhelpful) individualistic civil and political rights discourse in this area.[94]

Again this strategy entails risks—most obviously that it will entrench still further the dominance of medical control of abortion,[95] and bury explicit references to both feminism and abortion. As will be apparent from this range of alternative strategies, if choice is purged from the rhetoric of feminist demands on abortion, dialogue is only beginning on which discourse should be adopted and how it can be turned into reality. The task is daunting, and all the alternatives are risky, but feminism must be prepared to abandon its sacred cows, instead of remaining wedded to a language and way of thinking which has now served its purpose.

---

the language of choice: '7.2 Reproductive health is a state of complete physical, mental and social well-being and not merely the absence of disease or infirmity, in all matters relating to the reproductive system and to its functions and processes. Reproductive health therefore implies that people are able to have a satisfying and safe sex life and that they have the capability to reproduce and the freedom to decide if, when and how often to do so. Implicit in this last condition is the right of men and women to be informed and to have access to safe, effective, affordable and acceptable methods of family planning of their choice.' Programme of Action, in Report of the ICPD, UN Doc A/CONI, 171/13 7.2 (18 Oct. 1994), quoted in S. Coliver, 'The Right to Information Necessary for Reproductive Health and Choice under International Law', in S. Coliver (ed.), *The Right to Know: Human Rights and Access to Reproductive Health Information* (Pittsburgh: University of Pennsylvania Press, 1995).

[94] N. Whitty, 'The Mind, the Body, and Reproductive Health Information' (1996) 18 *Human Rights Quarterly* 224–39.

[95] Such fears lead McDonnell to suggest instead the need to reclaim abortion from medical professionals by establishing women-only clinics and exploring the possibilities of self-abortion—see McDonnell, *Not an Easy Choice*, 135–9.

6

Embedding the Embryo

SIMONE BATEMAN NOVAES AND TANIA SALEM

Questions about embryos are rarely addressed to social scientists: the fact that they tend to contextualize issues rather than inquire into their universal logical and moral properties may seem to circumvent essential discussions about life, individualization, humanness, and personhood that appear crucial to the solution of problems involving embryos. A social science approach may none the less provide a distinctive perspective on how, when, where, and why such discussions arise and, above all, on who are engaged in these discussions—possibly a useful step in better identifying and framing the immediate implications of the questions we ask ourselves.

Our chapter is an attempt to submit questions about embryos to a social science perspective, in which we explore concrete situations involving conflict over particular embryos. We have chosen, as a way of illustrating our approach, a case study: a widely publicized dispute which ended up in court. The case brings together actors who disagree as to the best way to proceed in deciding what is to be done about *in vitro* fertilized embryos being held in frozen storage. The impasse in the attempt to resolve the question among the actors themselves leads to an attempt to seek ethical and ultimately legal arbitration. We have approached our case study, not as a question about the legal status of the human embryo or as a philosophical question concerning when the human embryo becomes a person or an individual human life whose rights or interests require protection, but as an attempt to identify who the actors involved by an embryo's destiny are and how they go about trying to decide what is to be done. Because, as social scientists, we are considering a concrete situation, it must be remembered that the case

A first draft of this paper was presented at the second plenary conference of the European Commission Research Project, Fertility, Infertility and the Human Embryo, Barcelona, 21–3 Oct. 1994.

occurred in France, in the context of French legal precedents and cultural background.

In December 1990, a 37-year-old woman expecting twins after six earlier unsuccessful *in vitro* fertilization (IVF) procedures suffered a miscarriage during her ninth week of pregnancy. While hospitalized for a curettage in a large city near her home, she lost her husband, killed in a car accident on his way to visit her. The woman nevertheless wanted to make a final attempt to become a mother and requested the transfer of two remaining frozen embryos, several weeks after her miscarriage and her husband's death.

The attending physician was reluctant to comply with her wishes: in fact, the couple had signed a document accepting the hospital's policy that the embryos would only be transferred in the presence of both spouses and that, in the eventuality of 'dissolution of the couple' (meaning either separation and divorce or death of one or both partners), storage would be terminated and the embryos left to perish. The physician nevertheless decided to consult the other members of his staff, including a psychiatrist to whom the widow was referred for consultation. In view of the diverging opinions, he also solicited a statement from the local ethics committee. The overall balance was negative and, in March 1992, the hospital formally refused to comply with the widow's request and informed her that, putting into effect the terms of the signed document, the embryos would be destroyed. In response, the widow decided to take her case to court.

During the first proceedings on 7 October 1992, a temporary agreement was concluded according to which storage of the embryos would continue until a decision on the substantive content of the case was reached by a competent jurisdiction. For in fact one of the key points in the lawsuit, touching upon the status and the validity of the document that had been signed, was deciding whether it concerned a disagreement over an administrative act between a hospital and one of its patients or whether it raised issues pertaining to a 'fundamental right to procreate and to be born', as expressed by the plaintiff's lawyer in an interview to the press (*Le Quotidien de Paris*, 8 October 1992).

On 11 May 1993 (Jugement du 11 mai 1993, Tribunal de Grande Instance de Toulouse, Première Chambre)—despite the fact that the latter interpretation of the case had been chosen—the court ultimately ruled that the widow did not have a valid suit against the hospital. The court based its judgment on terms similar to those of the 'bioethics' bill being voted by parliament (and finally promulgated on 29 July 1994), restricting the use of assisted conception to heterosexual couples with infertility problems and stating that both partners must be alive and give their consent at the moment of transfer or insemination. According to the court, the conditions under which the hospital had been providing treatment to the plaintiff were perfectly legitimate: physicians had been merely attempting to remedy the infertility problem of a socially recognized heterosexual partnership, limiting their intervention to an 'imitation of natural procreation'. However, now that one of the partners had died, the situation justifying medical intervention no longer existed; the hospital therefore had no further obligation to provide treatment. This ruling was later confirmed by a court of appeal on 18 April 1994 (Arrêt du 18 avril 1994, Tribunal de Grande Instance de Toulouse, Première Chambre), which also decided that the frozen embryos, originally destined exclusively for infertility treatment and possessing in their present state no statutory rights by law, were to be left to perish, following a court order to this end. This last legal procedure, however, has (to our knowledge) not yet been carried out.[1]

The sudden appearance of this unusual case in the public arena, known as that of the widow of Toulouse and widely covered by the French press, can be said to result from the rapid advances in assisted conception and cryopreservation techniques, making it possible to fertilize eggs in a Petri dish and then store the resulting embryos in a suspended state of animation outside a woman's body. The immediate legal and philosophical question raised by the lawsuit is whether or not a woman has a right to pursue infertility treatment in the form of an embryo transfer after the death of her husband, which of course leads to discussion as to the consequences of a positive or a negative response to such requests. Embedded in this discussion, however, are social issues of a more general scope, which transform the widow's personal request into a 'case': for in fact this woman's legal plaint unexpectedly challenges—and thus highlights—dominant social values regarding an ideal model of the family, according to which the presence of both a mother and a father is deemed necessary for a child's welfare and well-being. Moreover, acceptance of the woman's request for embryo transfer, if pregnancy and childbirth were to ensue, would also create a dilemma concerning the legitimacy of paternal filiation: French law states that a child

---

[1] This procedure probably requires that the hospital request authorization to terminate storage. The new bioethics bill (Loi du 29 juillet 1994) stipulates that storage must end if the embryos have not been used after five years. This five-year limit has not yet expired for the widow's embryos.

born more than 300 days after the legal severing of marital ties through divorce or death of the woman's spouse is to be considered born of an unknown father (Article 315 du Code Civil). Both of these problems are mentioned by the attending physician, who thus expressed his opinion to the press: 'It is not good knowingly to bring to life orphaned children who will never bear their father's name' ('il n'est pas bon de créer sciemment des enfants orphelins qui ne porteront jamais le nom de leur père', Prof. Jean Parinaud, responsible for the IVF centre of La Grave Hospital, Toulouse, cited in *Le Parisien*, 7 October 1992). His statement, in turn, also raises a more general question regarding an appropriate medical approach to situations in which 'treatment' means impregnation.

Even if the case we are considering—precisely because of its exceptional character—raises questions specific to the situation, it also uncovers dilemmas which are not peculiar to it. As with most extraordinary occurrences, the widow's case renders visible latent issues and tensions which, far from being aberrations or exceptions in the practice of assisted conception, are its constitutive elements. The widow's case can therefore be analytically approached as a paradigm, that is, as an example of a situation that gives access to key elements and to the underlying structure of a more general social problem.

The case we are analysing outlines a dispute over the destiny of two frozen embryos, opposing a woman having contributed her eggs for fertilization with the sperm of her husband, since deceased, and a hospital service responsible for the fertilization procedure and for the frozen storage of 'excess' embryos. It highlights the fact that, in cases involving assisted conception, any alleged or apparent right of the genitors (that is, the contributors of gametes) to control over the use and disposal of their stored embryos will be subject to substantial limitations.

At first glance, such restrictions would seem to apply only to special situations, although not exceptional ones: many official documents and reports, both in France and elsewhere, now frequently backed by new laws, place responsibility for appropriate action regarding frozen embryos in the hands of the storage authority, whenever it is confronted with disagreement in the couple, a lack of explicit directives, or termination of their union. Otherwise, these documents usually provide that the couple themselves should decide as to how embryo(s), stored for their own future use, will be disposed of in various situations where the partners have ceased to pursue treatment. In other words, it is implied that genitors are given priority in deciding 'their' embryos' destiny.

This principle notwithstanding, a couple who seek treatment through assisted conception—even in non-problematic situations—must accept the decisions and policies of the clinic offering these services. The genitors' rights over 'their' embryos are, therefore, automatically subject to restrictions: the terms of the document signed by the widow and her late husband illustrate this point. It must also be noted that, in order to justify access to treatment, the couple must usually possess certain social and psychological characteristics, as required and evaluated by the clinical staff. This fact reveals that, contrary to usual reproductive situations, persons seeking assisted conception must be authorized by a third party to become parents and, under certain circumstances, may have to quarrel with other protagonists over decisions which are normally considered to be of a private and intimate nature.[2]

We therefore posit that, despite apparent consensus over statements of principle, controversy over situations of assisted conception—of which the widow's case can be seen as a paradigmatic example—raises in the most radical way questions as to who has ultimate authority in deciding what is to be done with frozen-stored embryos. We hypothesize that this dilemma is an effect of the displacement of the reproductive act from the private sphere to a laboratory situation, which results both in the increased complexity of the network of actors surrounding embryos and in renewed questioning as to the way in which network participants and/or their respective arguments should be ranked. As we discuss the elements bringing about this change in the fertilization scenario, we will be taking as a point of reference, both for the network of actors involved and for the principles which underlie decision-making about embryos, the abortion situation as it is dealt with by French law (Loi du 17 janvier 1975, reconduite le 1 janvier 1980). We will argue that assisted conception redistributes power among the principal protagonists in a way significantly different from the one established by the abortion law.

First of all, what do we mean by increased complexity of the network surrounding embryos in situations of assisted conception? The quantitative increase in the number of participants is the first obvious dimension of this phenomenon, which nevertheless needs to be qualified. For in situations involving a normal pregnancy, even in societies where the

---

[2] This is why, in examining British legislation in the area of assisted conception, Stern concludes that 'although at first glance it appears that the balance of control over donated and stored reproductive materials lies in favour of gametic contributors, in practice it will often be the clinic which holds the upper hand' (Kristin Stern, 'The Regulation of Assisted Conception in England', *European Journal of Medical Law*, 1/1 (1994), 11).

nuclear family thrives as a value and as a fact, the woman and her partner are necessarily immersed in a wider network of relatives.[3] Despite
the fact that a young couple may plan and define the arrival of their first
child as an 'event for two', the presence of close relatives in their daily
life during pregnancy, and particularly after the arrival of the newborn
baby, is the prevailing social trend.[4]

At the start, therefore, the embryo's network already includes a large
number of protagonists. However, with assisted conception, it is the number of actors directly involved in *conceiving* the embryo that increases.
Moreover, by separating fertilization from sexual intercourse and thus
segmenting procreative roles, reproductive technology introduces not
only more but also unprecedented protagonists into the network: along
with the couple (or the woman) and their respective relatives, there are
physicians, biologists, and sometimes even donors contributing genetic
material or physical processes. Each of these protagonists puts forward
different criteria—not necessarily comparable—to justify and thus establish his or her relationship to the embryo. The infertile couple can invoke
a genetic link, and the woman in particular: her bodily implication in
the embryo's coming to life. Physicians responsible for fertilization
procedures may argue that their intervention is decisive to its very existence. When donors intervene, they may contend that they provide the
biological material without which the embryo would not exist. Infertile
couples, whose treatment requires the contribution of donors and who
are therefore unable to justify their claim genetically, can always insist
on their desire and decision to have a child.

Furthermore, in certain situations—as exemplified in the widow's
case—protagonists may use their respective arguments to compete for
prevalence in deciding an embryo's fate, thus ultimately quarrelling over
which of them is best qualified to speak on its behalf. Once again, this
scenario in itself is not new. In the first place, under usual reproductive
circumstances, occasions for conflict between the mother-to-be and
other relatives do exist, as the latter also feel concerned about the child
to come. They may therefore try to influence or control the mother's
behaviour (for example, to keep her from smoking, drinking, taking drugs,

---

[3] It is interesting to note that, during the trial, any alleged right of the widow of Toulouse
to 'her' embryo was contested by members of her deceased husband's family (Jugement
du 11 mai 1993, Tribunal de Grand Instance de Toulouse).

[4] T. Salem, 'O "casal grávido": Incurso em um universo ético' (On the 'pregnant
couple': an incursion into an ethical universe) (Ph.D. thesis in social anthropology, Universidade Federal do Rio de Janeiro, 1987).

or from having an abortion); in other words, they will attempt to set up some form of indirect access to the fetus through the mother, alleging its welfare. Questions concerning who should decide the embryo's fate have also pervaded the abortion debate. None the less, with respect to situations of assisted conception, the answers seem to require that other facts or variables be taken into consideration: who are the actors claiming a right to make decisions concerning an embryo and what normative justifications do they invoke? What are the bases of their competing claims in vying for precedence in decision-making and what are the underlying premises of the solutions they propose? What are the social stakes of the different possible outcomes of conflict over an embryo's fortune?

A second dimension of the increasing complexity of the network surrounding embryos is the presence of members representing a social sphere different from that of the family, that is, the medical institution. Complexity ensues from the fact that these participants—biologists and especially physicians—introduce into the procreative sphere norms and values specific to their own institutional activity which do not necessarily coincide with those of the family. Physicians are not new members of the network, and have progressively imposed their expertise in the management of sexual and reproductive matters during the last two centuries. Novelty nevertheless derives from their unprecedented involvement in fertilization and in the storage and transferring of embryos —a medicalization of impregnation which seems to be affecting the social forms of their participation in the network. As physicians redefine their professional obligations and responsibilities with respect to this new approach to conception and pregnancy, they are radically changing the bases for claims to precedence in decision-making—at least for situations in which the embryo is outside the woman's body.

This is why the other important effect of the physical dislocation of conception from a woman's body to a laboratory is renewed questioning as to the ranking of network participants and of their respective arguments: technical access to embryos and fetuses by physicians has, in fact, offered new premises for a reappraisal of the criteria giving certain actors the power to make choices. In any particular situation, uncertainty as to priorities may create conflict between the protagonists and, as illustrated by the widow's case, tension and dispute may oppose family members to the medical institution. But the change in locus of the reproductive act also affects the relationship to embryos of those within the private family sphere, in particular that of the future parents.

In other words, increased technical mastery of the conditions for fertilization and embryo storage is changing the way responsibility for decision-making is being granted or redistributed among three of the most important protagonists in an embryo's network: the woman, her partner, and the medical staff. By focusing on the changes produced by assisted conception in each protagonist's position with respect to the embryo, we will break down the phenomenon we have designated as the 'increased complexity of the network'.[5]

Why, however, compare the way in which the widow's case was argued and decided with the legal dispositions for handling cases of abortion in France during the first trimester of pregnancy? This way of proceeding follows, at least, two orders of reasoning. In the first place, the abortion law may be considered as an established normative reference in determining who is entitled to make decisions about an embryo's fate—a question which, as we have already pointed out, also characterizes the case of the widow of Toulouse. The dispositions of the abortion law thus appear applicable to this particular case. Of course, from a situational and social standpoint, the action being considered in each case is quite different. In one case, the woman wishes to be rid of an embryo that she is carrying, because she does not wish or feel that it is possible to become a mother (or its mother) under her present circumstances. In the other, a woman demands that embryos which are not in her immediate possession be transferred to her womb, because she perceives them as children both emotionally and physically related to her. None the less, both situations require third-party technical co-operation (in most cases a physician) for the request to be fulfilled and, even more important, both action and non-action provide a response to the question as to who is considered to have ultimate authority in deciding an embryo's fate. This coincidence of fundamental parameters in the two situations justifies a comparison between them.

Secondly, the dispositions of the abortion law for first trimester pregnancies may be taken as a contrasting reference in understanding the widow's case: whereas the abortion law refers to a situation in which the embryo is inside a woman's womb, the widow's request and the

---

[5] A more extensive analysis of network complexity and of the redistribution of responsibilities in decision-making regarding embryos would, of course, lead us to consider other protagonists, such as donors of gametes or other physical processes not involving the couple. We have not done so in this article, because these actors do not appear in the case of the widow of Toulouse.

reactions it provokes revolve around embryos which are outside her body (and thus also beyond her control). The opposition inside/outside a woman's body summarizes those changes which have recently transformed reproductive circumstances and, in a sense, can be considered as the main reason for reappraisal of each actor's position in the network. In fact, as we shall try to argue, each situation points to significantly different ways of delegating and (re)distributing responsibility to actors vying for precedence in deciding their fate.

Societies do expect minimal survival of their social agreements—a particularly acute problem in pluralist or complex societies where consensus is difficult to come by. Although a working consensus does not cancel the possibility of conflict and dissent, it does make it legitimate to ask: do the dispositions and the premisses of the abortion law apply to the new situations created by reproductive technologies? Is the political compromise reached in 1975 and expressed in the abortion law an adequate reflection of the way legal or social institutions are currently dealing with situations such as that of the widow of Toulouse? Referral to the abortion law in analysing the widow's case may enlighten us, at least partially, as to the way in which a society uses existing normative references when dealing with novel social dilemmas.

Let us begin our analysis by examining the way in which the relationship between the woman and the embryo has been affected by technology intervening in reproductive processes, especially IVF. The promotion of technical access to the woman's body, and thus to the embryo and the fetus, is certainly not historically a new phenomenon. Ever since the invention of the forceps in the eighteenth century, and more particularly in recent times, diagnostic and surgical techniques designed to assist or control reproductive processes have given physicians unprecedented access to the contents of the pregnant womb. This has altered —and is still altering—scientific perceptions as well as social and moral definitions of the embryo and the fetus, with evident implications both for reasoning and decision-making with regard to pregnancy and for the way in which the relationship between women and these entities is being socially defined.

In fact, several authors have recently stressed that ultrasound, amniocentesis, and fetal surgery are promoting representations of the embryo and the fetus as individualized or separate beings, distinguishable from the pregnant woman's body in such a way that, even when inside her womb, they are already medically perceived as 'second patients' for

monitoring and eventual therapy.[6] As advanced by Rothman, 'the technology of pregnancy that we as a civilization have developed is a technology of separation and individuation—the technology is geared to
recognizing the fetus as separate from the mother'.[7] In virtue of this new
clinical attitude, certain problematic pregnancies calling for medical
intervention—such as Caesarean sections or fetal surgery—have already
been a source of uncertainty and conflict. Usually framed as a disagreement between the pregnant woman and the physician over treatment,
the key issue in numerous recent cases has been the physician's right
to override the woman's refusal to consent to a procedure when access
to the fetus appears medically justified. Underlying this issue are antagonistic perspectives on what the mother's and the fetus's best interests
and rights are and how they should be ranked. In addition, these situations reveal that there is a conflict as to who—woman or physician—
is best entitled to speak on the fetus's behalf.[8] Put in different terms,
difficulty in deciding what action should be taken lies, at least in part,
in uncertainty as to whether a pregnant woman should be treated as one
or two discrete entities, and the priorities that, in the latter case, each
may have.

These considerations suggest that increased access by third parties
to the embryo or the fetus *inside* the woman's body has promoted new
forms of individualization,[9] that is, possibilities for discourse and action

[6] Janet Gallagher, 'Eggs, Embryos and Fetuses: Anxiety and the Law', in M. Stanworth
(ed.), *Reproductive Technologies: Gender, Motherhood and Medicine* (Cambridge: Polity Press, 1987), 139–50; Rosalind P. Petchesky, 'Foetal Images: The Power of Visual
Culture in the Politics of Reproduction', in Stanworth (ed.), *Reproductive Technologies*,
57–80; Barbara Katz Rothman, *The Tentative Pregnancy: Prenatal Diagnosis and the
Future of Motherhood* (New York: Penguin, 1987); Evelyne Aziza-Shuster, 'Le Traitement "in utero": Les Libertés individuelles en question', in *Éthique médicale et droits de
l'homme*, La Fabrique du corps humain (Paris: Actes Sud et Inserm, 1988), 85–92; Frances
Price, 'The Management of Uncertainty in Obstetric Practice: Ultrasonography, *In Vitro*
Fertilization and Embryo Transfer', in Maureen McNeil, Ian Varcoe, and Steven Yearley
(eds.), *The New Reproductive Technologies* (New York: St Martin's Press, 1990), 123–
53; Michéle Fellous, *La Première Image: Enquête sur l'échographie obstétricale* (Paris:
Nathan, 1991).
[7] Rothman, *The Tentative Pregnancy*, 114.
[8] This statement is based on the consideration of recent lawsuits which, although rare
and highly controversial, appear as significant events. In the United States, women have
been forced to undergo Caesarean deliveries or to submit to surgery while pregnant in
order to correct a fetal anomaly, because physicians have been able to convince judges
that these procedures, which the women had originally refused, were necessary for the
health or survival of the fetus (Gallagher, 'Eggs, Embryos and Fetuses'; Aziza-Shuster,
'Le Traitement "in utero" ').
[9] On the theme of individualization, its different stages and forms in contemporary
world-views, see Tania Salem, 'O "individualismo libertário" no imaginário social dos

which treat these entities as separate and distinct from the mother. This is precisely what creates the possibility of a *perception* of conflict between the two. However, from a certain point of view, such individualization is only apparent: third parties cannot deny, despite technical access, a *de facto* biological inseparability of the embryo and the non-viable fetus from the woman's body for survival.

In vitro fertilization has none the less opened to reassessment some facts and premisses which, until very recently, were taken for granted. First, in the context of what we have termed the medicalization of impregnation, the woman's body is no longer the privileged locus of conception. Secondly, IVF undermines the concept of biological inseparability between an embryo and a woman's womb: at least in its first stages of development, the embryo may now more convincingly be presented as a physically discrete unit, existing independently of its eventual implantation in a woman's womb. In this sense, it is not exaggerated to state that IVF introduces a qualitative breach with regard to other kinds of technical access.

We should not dismiss the feminist critique which insists that one of the effects of assisted conception—especially *in vitro* fertilization—is the eclipsing of the pregnant woman's part in childbearing. As pointed out by Stanworth, the phrase 'test-tube baby' conjures up the odd image of a fetus growing independently of a woman's body.[10] In analysing recent imagery concerning the fetus, Petchesky stresses that it is always presented in a biased manner as a 'disconnected', 'solitary', and 'autonomous' entity, whereas the pregnant woman is simply 'absent' or 'peripheral',[11] or, to put it in Rothman's words, 'an empty space'.[12] Taking this into account, some feminists have insisted on the need to restore women to a central place in pregnancy by creating new images that 'recontextualize' the fetus—in other words, that clearly locate it in the uterus, embodied by a woman situated in social space.[13]

From a certain perspective, the pertinence of these observations is indisputable: even outside the woman's body, the embryo can only

anos 60' ('Libertarian individualism' in the social imagery of the 1960s), *Physis: Revista de saúde coletiva*, 1/2 (1991), 59–75, and 'A "despossessão subjetiva": Dos paradoxos do individualismo' ('Subjective dispossession': on the paradoxes of individualism), *Revista brasileira de ciências sociais*, 7/18 (1992), 61–77.

[10] Michelle Stanworth, 'Reproductive Technologies and the Deconstruction of Motherhood', in Stanworth (ed.), *Reproductive Technologies*, 26.

[11] Petchesky, 'Foetal Images', 61–3.

[12] Rothman, *The Tentative Pregnancy*, 114.

[13] Petchesky, 'Foetal Images', 78–9.

survive under certain conditions which suspend its development. Under any circumstances, in fact, the image of a 'free-floating entity'[14] is quite obviously distorted: even if we were to suppose that we are on the verge of an era in which the fetus will develop entirely in an artificial womb, independently of its genetic mother, this still would be—as stressed by Harris[15]—a form of dependence comparable to that on the mother. Sociologically speaking, the technical possibility of gestation in an artificial womb would render the embryo's existence dependent on appropriate care from medical staff.

Nevertheless, we must admit that the widow's request and other such cases involving *in vitro* fertilization lead us to a situation which is rich with meaning and implications for the future: an embryo need no longer be conceived inside the woman's body and can now, under certain conditions, survive outside it—and thus independently of it. This remarkable achievement appears to raise questions as to whether a woman, as mother-to-be, should in fact be considered as the principal protagonist responsible in determining an embryo's fate—at least while it is located outside her body. In other words, whether fairly or not, this unique state of events seems to be undermining one of women's major grounds for claiming absolute pre-eminence over 'their' embryos—that is, the biological tie, through pregnancy, to the female body. Women in these novel and exceptional situations—as is the case more generally for their male counterparts—are reduced to claiming their contribution of gametes and their expression of intent to become a parent (a 'demande parentale', according to the new French law) as grounds for establishing relatedness to an embryo.[16] From this follows the question as to how much decisional autonomy a woman should have over embryos conceived with her gametes: must she be given priority over other actors in a conflictual situation and why? This dilemma—exemplified by the

---

[14] This term is not uncommon in the literature on assisted conception. For example, it was used by the Warnock Committee to designate the embryo before implantation in the uterine walls—in other words, the recently baptized 'pre-embryo' (Mary Warnock, *A Question of Life: The Warnock Report on Human Fertilisation and Embryology* (Oxford: Blackwell, 1985), 58). We are using this expression, given that, according to Petchesky and others, the image of a 'free-floating entity' has also been used to characterize not only embryos after implantation, but fetuses in general.

[15] John Harris, 'Embryos and Hedgehogs: On the Moral Status of the Embryo', in A. Dyson and J. Harris (ed.), *Experiments on Embryos* (London: Routledge, 1991), 75.

[16] Even so, arguments based on intentionality must be advanced by persons in a socially recognized and legitimate partnership. Although the form of this partnership may vary from one culture to another, the important point is that intentionality in this context must not be understood as the expression of a personal choice or will, but as a socially sanctioned request.

case of the widow of Toulouse—reflects uncertainty as to what defines
the social and moral relationship between the woman and the embryo,
usually intimately associated by pregnancy but, at least at the moment
of the dispute, not physically linked to one another.

Transformations induced by novel fertilization techniques in the
position of women *vis-à-vis* embryos and other actors involved in the
reproductive act are even more striking, when compared to the premisses
underlying pro-choice arguments during the French abortion movement
in the 1970s and the legal dispositions of the 'voluntary interruption
of pregnancy' Act of 1975. In these ideological and legal contexts, a
woman was deemed the primary social actor in deciding an embryo's
fate and, at least in part, this was justified by the fact that her body
encompassed it.[17] During the abortion debate in the 1970s, French feminists insisted on a woman's right 'to dispose freely of her own body'
in making major life decisions ('la liberté de disposer de son corps'),
and by thus defending a woman's right to abortion, they were asserting that the embryo was a part of that body over which a woman had
a right to decide.[18] This position apparently denies the embryo status as
an independent human entity while expressing, in a paradigmatic way,
a representation of woman as a self-defined individual, with absolute
moral autonomy of decision over her body and whatever happens to
it. Other less radical supporters of this position granted woman moral
precedence over the embryo, in that she is a person in the full sense of
the term—involved in the reality of human relationships for which she
must assume responsibility—in contrast, therefore, with embryos and
fetuses deemed to be 'persons *in potentia*' or 'the potential to become
full human beings'.[19] Although not equivalent, both assertions share an
essential premiss of the pro-choice argument: not only the 'interests'
and/or the rights of embryos, but also those of other actors must be clearly
subordinated to those of women.

Most abortion laws have had to come to terms, to some extent, with
this proposition. If we focus on the French case, it must be emphasized

[17] Another important moral argument in favour of giving priority to women in the abortion decision—often raised by feminists and others—is the fact that they are primarily
responsible for the day-to-day care of children.
[18] Simone Novaes, 'La Grossesse accidentelle et la demande d'avortement', *L'Année
sociologique*, 30 (1979–80), 219–41; Simone Novaes, 'Les Récidivistes', *Revue française
de sociologie*, 23/3 (1982), 473–85.
[19] Paul Ladrière, 'Religion, morale et politique', *Revue française de sociologie*, 23/3
(1982), 417–54; Paul Ladrière, 'Personne humaine potentielle et procréation', *Cahiers STS
no. 11: Éthique et biologie* (Paris: Édn. du CNRS, 1986), 95–107.

that the 1975 abortion law does not grant a woman a right to abort on demand, nor does it accord to any particular person a statutory right to decide an embryo's destiny. Abortion in France remains a criminal offence, except under the circumstances specified by law: up to the tenth week of pregnancy, a woman may request that a physician perform an abortion, if her pregnancy is a cause of 'personal distress'. It does not oblige the physician to comply with this request if he is morally opposed to abortion;[20] however, it does imply (but not specifically oblige) that he should refer the woman to another colleague who accepts the practice. Physicians may also propose and perform an abortion at any time during a pregnancy, if they deem that such action is medically justified; nevertheless, the woman must request or agree to the termination of her pregnancy.

These restrictions notwithstanding, when we focus on the terms of the law concerning the first three months of pregnancy, they undeniably grant the pregnant woman 'in a state of distress' significant decisional autonomy over an embryo's destiny. The only limitations she is subjected to are *time*—the abortion must be performed by the end of the tenth week of pregnancy—and *procedure*—the abortion must be performed by a physician in a public or private hospital. The central position conferred on the pregnant woman by the law is patently evident in two other ways. First of all, the significance and suggestive quality of the expression '*voluntary* interruption of pregnancy' should not be underestimated: not only does the term 'voluntary' distinguish the woman's situation from that of the loss of an embryo or fetus caused by factors beyond her control, it also explicitly designates, when associated to the first ten weeks after conception, 'the period of *freedom* to abort' ('la période de la *liberté* de l'IVG'),[21] as opposed to abortions performed subsequently which require a 'therapeutic indication'. Secondly, the notion of a woman's distress ('détresse') appears as a key element in understanding the law, in that it constitutes the major argument for legal access to abortion during the first trimester. It must be emphasized that distress may only be invoked by the woman herself: she is the sole judge of what in her life constitutes a situation of distress and thus a reason (or reasons) to 'interrupt' her pregnancy. In contrast with the medical approval required for the termination of pregnancy after ten weeks, no

---

[20] Clause in the 1975 French abortion law, allowing individual physicians morally opposed to abortion the right to refuse to perform them.

[21] Dr Escoffier-Lambiotte, 'La Détresse et le médecin', *Le Monde*, 30 Nov. 1974 (our emphasis).

third party representing society's interests is asked to intervene during this initial phase, whether it be to confirm her distressed condition or to countersign her decision. She is required to undergo an interview with a social worker, so as to consider the other options she might have, and to respect a seven-day period of reflection, after making her first request. None the less, the pregnant woman is the one who ultimately decides the fate of the embryo she is carrying, even in the case of a medically justified abortion.

These considerations lead us to the conclusion that the abortion law treats the woman's deliberation over an unexpected pregnancy as a personal moral dilemma: the state intervenes to regulate the practice of abortion, but it does not interfere with her decision—at least during the initial period of pregnancy. The underlying premiss seems to be that society's interests are not directly at stake, or at least not sufficiently so, to justify overriding the woman's personal response to her dilemma. In fact, the law does not even bring to bear any considerations regarding the woman's partner, family, or the future child on her decision to abort. Even though behind the notion of 'personal distress' may lie a woman's concern regarding the adequacy of her family relationships and/ or of her relationship with her partner in accommodating the arrival of a child,[22] this issue is not explicitly addressed by the law. The woman's spouse or partner is not mentioned at all and the 'couple' only once, regarding their joint participation ('when possible') in a consultation with a social worker. 'Parental authority' is also cited once, in reference to the abortion of minors, which requires the consent of parents. In sum, the accent placed by the law on 'personal distress', and, conversely, the almost total absence of legal dispositions regarding other family members in the abortion decision, is major evidence that women (with the exception of minors) are acknowledged, in the context defined by French law for abortion during the first ten weeks of pregnancy, as the most important protagonists in deciding an embryo's fate.

Were these premisses applied in treating the widow's case? Apparently not. Despite the fact that the widow's case also involves an embryo, her state of emotional distress was of no use to her as an argument to sustain her claim. On the contrary: whereas the woman's request for an abortion is accepted because she maintains that her pregnancy is a source of distress, the widow's demand for a transfer of the frozen embryos is refused precisely because she is deemed—by others—already

---

[22] Novaes, 'La Grossesse accidentelle' and 'Les Récidivistes'.

sufficiently distressed by the death of her husband. Indeed, this was one of the main reasons given by the psychiatrist to whom the widow was referred for consultation justifying refusal to comply with her request: the psychiatrist—and others—felt that her desire to have the embryos transferred was directly related to her being in mourning over her husband's death. Consequently, from the point of view of the criteria set by the abortion law—that is, a situation in which there is an embryo (or embryos) and a woman in distress—there is apparent inconsistency between the two decisions.

Furthermore, in contrast with the abortion situation, the case of the widow of Toulouse illustrates quite vividly that, excepting an opinion of the French National Ethics Committee (Comité Consultatif National d'Éthique, 1993), the prevailing assumption in France is that the question of how to dispose of frozen embryos after the death of one of the partners is not a matter to be left to personal moral judgement. This is revealed in several ways. The very fact that a physician believed he had valid, justifiable grounds to refuse to comply with the widow's demand for transfer of 'her' embryos is, in itself, a first obvious indication. In addition, third parties called upon to give their opinion on the legitimacy of the request and arbitrate the conflict between physicians and the widow represent more than individual points of view: psychiatrists and the medical staff personify, and ethics committees and courts embody, an authorized expression of society's interests. In evaluating and judging the widow's request, solicited arbiters, as well as physicians, brought to bear on the situation a professionally or legally sanctioned account of society's concern for other protagonists affected by her decision—in this case, essentially the child. They referred, for example, to the probable negative effects on the child's development that could be expected from the widow's emotional distress and from the abnormal family situation into which the child would be born, in particular the absence of a father—a disadvantage accentuated by the legal impossibility of establishing paternal filiation. By expressing apprehension for the child's future, arbiters seemed, in fact, to be voicing their concern with the long-term social consequences of acquiescence to such a request. If, in principle, the genitors may be given the right to specify the way in which their 'excess' embryos should be disposed of, not all possible solutions are to be considered equally valid: some may present consequences so awesome for collective interests that they must be excluded outright.

An issue common to both the abortion decision and the debate surrounding the widow's request therefore seems to be: what are acceptable conditions for bringing a child into the world? In each situation, however, the question is not being asked by the same persons or for the same reasons. In the case of abortion, it is the pregnant woman who considers her personal life conditions to be momentarily (or permanently) inadequate to make it possible for her to have a child. Her questioning stems from the responsibility she feels she must assume for the outcome of her pregnancy. The widow, on the contrary, asks no such questions, as she is already fully involved in treatment to have a child; that her embryos should be transferred and her pregnancy come to term seems self-evident. Other actors nevertheless intervene and raise these questions, countering the widow's intentions, because they deem both the child's welfare and society's interests to be at stake.

From the preceding considerations we can conclude that, in terms of the part women play in the reproductive drama, the two situations we are analysing present a clear contrast. In the case of an abortion, the law gives women during the first ten weeks of pregnancy moral, social, and legal priority over other actors in deciding whether or not to pursue their pregnancy—thus determining the destiny of the embryo. The widow's case, on the other hand, clearly illustrates that a woman, having contributed with her gametes to an assisted conception procedure, is not to be allowed unconditional autonomy in settling the fate of the resulting embryos. On the contrary, her wishes and moral reasoning may even be overridden by other actors who invoke different criteria to impose their point of view. Rothman's statement that 'technology which makes the baby/fetus more "visible" renders the woman invisible'[23] seems perfectly adequate in describing the widow's situation, as opposed to that of any woman requesting an abortion.

How might we explain the differences between the two situations? In the first place, the fact that the legitimacy of paternal filiation for the future child is at stake in the widow's request must not be dismissed: this gives her personal dilemma a fundamentally social dimension requiring legal measures. However, this legal question, although important, does not seem to be the main or the real issue at stake. In an earlier similar case, in which a widow requested and obtained the transfer of her embryos after the death of her husband, the court of Angers ruled

---

[23] Rothman, *The Tentative Pregnancy*, 113.

that the child, born more than nine months after his genitor's death, was legitimate. The child received the name of his dead father, and the court ultimately justified its decision by stating that a child should be granted legitimate filiation 'whenever it appears to be in his/her interest' ('à chaque fois qu'il va de son intérêt', Jugement du 10 novembre 1992, Tribunal de Grande Instance d'Angers, Première Chambre).

Secondly, although abortion may raise the very difficult philosophical and moral question of ending potential life, it does not entail, in terms of social relationships, a change in the status of the woman requesting the termination of her pregnancy: she is in fact requesting a return to her status quo ante, thus also maintaining the whole network of family relations intact. In the case of the widow, she is making a claim to widowed parenthood, which has many social and legal implications for the whole family network into which the child would come to be born. Her request is, from this point of view, more radical in the sense that a positive response to her personal distress would ultimately have an effect on the situation of many more people, including the child eventually born from the procedure, the status of her dead husband, and, more generally, attitudes in the population as to what is socially and morally acceptable in terms of reproductive options and choices. 'Distress' in these two cases therefore does not refer to equivalent social, legal, and moral dilemmas.

Last but not least, the fact that the embryo is, in the first situation, inside the woman's body, and in the other outside it, is also an important variable, clarifying differences in the way the question of the disposal of embryos is being dealt with in each circumstance. Although both types of events bring up decisions concerning embryos, in the context of *in vitro* fertilization, actors other than the woman—especially physicians—have leverage to oppose her wishes, precisely because she is not yet pregnant: the embryo is in their possession and not in her body. As stated earlier, it is this unprecedented scenario which allows for questioning concerning the limits of a woman's rights, *vis-à-vis* the claims of other actors, over her frozen embryos.

Doubts concerning a woman's priority in making decisions about embryos and eventual alterations of her privileged status are necessarily linked to changes in the priority ranking of other network participants. To explore this phenomenon more fully, let us focus on another protagonist, whose genetic contribution is essential to the embryo's coming into existence: the woman's partner.

In a situation involving abortion, the woman's spouse or sexual partner, although alive, is legally 'invisible'. As we have already pointed out, he is not mentioned by the French abortion law and, in this sense, he has no legal voice in the decision to terminate or to pursue a pregnancy. This may partially reflect the fact that, in some cases, the woman may not be able to locate or even to identify the partner who is the genitor and who might be considered to have a voice as the future father: the pregnancy may be the result of a passing sexual encounter, or the woman may have had several partners in the immediately preceding weeks. A married woman may also have conceived through sexual relations with a man other than her husband, in which case both the lover and the husband may find themselves emotionally and legally concerned by the woman's pregnancy and the paternity issues that arise from the situation. None of these problems is explicitly addressed by the law: deciding the outcome of her pregnancy, whatever relational difficulties this may entail, is considered the woman's dilemma, responsibility, and prerogative.

In contrast, the absence of the widow's husband by virtue of his death is not only noted but taken into account as an argument by those opposing compliance with her request: the very absence of his voice and will is presented as a major problem, to the point that it is the key element triggering conflict. This state of affairs can be considered, to a certain extent, as a sign or a consequence of a more central role accorded to the male partner in situations of assisted conception in general. Most French practitioners, now backed by the recent 'bioethics' law, have in fact always required that assisted conception be provided only to heterosexual couples with infertility problems: *both* the woman and the man had to consent to insemination or embryo transfer, as well as provide instructions for dispositions regarding any 'excess' embryos. Whether or not the man himself contributes the gametes for fertilization, as the woman's husband or socially recognized partner he is considered the future father and entitled, as such, to a voice in decisions concerning the procedure and its outcome.[24]

The contrast in the male partner's position in each case is striking: whereas the recently promulgated 'bioethics' law now explicitly states

---

[24] This does not mean that, in the case we are analysing, knowledge of the deceased partner's opinion would have mattered or even resolved the situation. In the first judgment pronounced on the case of the widow of Toulouse, the judge stated that, were it to be established that the deceased spouse had wanted his wife to bear his children posthumously, this still would have no legal effect: the clause in the 'bioethics bill' (which had not yet been definitively voted and promulgated) requiring the presence of both spouses for embryo transfer must be considered as 'a rule necessary to public order, and a way of registering the partner's intention only to procreate while alive' (Jugement du 11 mai 1993, Tribunal de Grande Instance de Toulouse, Première Chambre).

that the husband or partner must also express his opinion and give consent to all procedures involving 'his' embryos, the 1975 abortion law makes no reference to the partner's situation or wishes. One might say therefore that the abortion law is anchored on the premiss that there is an inherent asymmetry between genders in their respective relations to an embryo's destiny (with evident pre-eminence accorded to the pregnant woman), whereas the 'bioethics' law, by imposing consent from both genitors as a requirement at the time of replacement, expresses a more egalitarian conception of the couple.[25] This apparent situation of gender equality with respect to reproduction can, at least partially, be attributed to the 'ironing out' of the differences in the body ties which men and women hold with respect to the embryo in situations involving *in vitro* fertilization. This phenomenon seems to be leading, in turn, not only to changes in the woman's position, but also to at least nominal reconsideration of the role traditionally played by her partner in reproductive scenarios, in particular with respect to the weight of his opinions and decisions in problematic situations involving an embryo's destiny.[26]

Furthermore, one might also remark that, whereas the abortion law avoids some of the complex paternity issues raised by unexpected pregnancies (given that, after an abortion, they are legally if not emotionally irrelevant), the 'bioethics' law can be said to anticipate them and settle them in advance. By limiting access to medical reproductive procedures to stable heterosexual couples, the law not only tries to ensure that the child will be born into a 'normal' family environment, with both a mother and a father, but apparently seeks, in so doing, to avoid opening reproductive procedures to any confusion as to the respective place and importance of each of the protagonists. This legal approach has led some to the illusory conclusion that further events during the procedure would no longer lead to doubts about how to proceed and about who should be making decisions: it conceptualizes the embryo as primarily related to the couple.

And yet another party has increasingly asserted itself as a significant other in the embryo's network, even though it can claim no genetic

[25] Salem, 'O "casal grávido" '; ead., 'O casal igualitário: Princípios e impasses' (The egalitarian couple: principles and impasses), *Revista brasileira de ciências sociais*, 3/9 (1989), 24–37.

[26] On equality as a value in contemporary ideology and in the construction of present-day conjugal relations, as well as the predicaments it entails, see Salem, 'O casal igualitário' and 'O "individualismo libertário" '.

ties: this is most obviously the medical staff, in particular physicians. Their unprecedented status in the network derives from the fact that, by providing a novel form of infertility treatment, they have displaced the locus of conception to the medical arena and become directly involved in fertilization and impregnation. As medical practitioners submitted to legal constraints and to a professional code of ethics, they are expected to refer their decisions and actions to norms and values pertaining to the quality, the security, and the efficacy of medical acts. A physician's dispositions and choices in treatment situations may also be influenced by more personal or immediate concerns related to the internal dynamics and logistics of his or her professional activities. Medical attitudes regarding appropriate action in dealing with infertility may therefore sometimes be quite different from those which guide members of a family in their reproductive choices.

Privileged technical access to embryos, supported by a peculiar status in the network as professionals, has given physicians more concrete foundations on which to claim a right to speak on the embryo's behalf. This is particularly evident in situations involving external fertilization and the storage of frozen embryos. One might say metaphorically that, under these circumstances, the embryos are—at least temporarily—located within the physician's own body; they are, in any case, within his or her institutional domain and, consequently, physical possession and custody. This exceptional situation necessarily implies a new power arrangement among the different actors with respect to the embryo.

Evidence of this fact is the way in which physicians introduce the notion of professional responsibility to justify prevalence in decision-making.[27] This does not cancel or neutralize the power of traditional yardsticks based on both biological and social ties that a couple (or, in our paradigmatic case, the widow) may claim to maintain with the embryo. Nevertheless, as physicians increasingly affirm their technical capacities to produce, store, and eventually treat embryos, they expand the basis of their decision-making power in the network by claiming a responsibility invested in them as social agents accountable to society for issues concerning public health. In certain circumstances, they may thus be able to challenge successfully the force and the pertinence of traditional criteria in establishing a priority to decide an embryo's fate.

[27] Simone Novaes, 'Éthique et débat publique: De la responsabilité médicale en matière de procréation assistée', in *Raisons pratiques: Épistémologie, sociologie, théorie sociale*, iii: *Pouvoir et légitimité: Figures de l'espace public* (Paris: Éditions EHESS, 1992), 155–76.

Physicians have always attempted to devise and impose professional standards and guidelines for problem-solving: as professionals, they are, in fact, held legally—and morally—responsible for providing their patients with adequate treatment under satisfactory conditions. Although, under most circumstances, physicians are not held legally accountable if treatment does not provide the desired result, most of them feel morally obligated to ensure that their actions will have the best possible outcome. By invoking the importance both of their expertise and of professional responsibility for their actions, physicians significantly contribute to shaping and defining these new reproductive situations and thus set the conditions under which occasional conflicts will have to be resolved.

Questions about medical responsibility usually arise in situations which involve risk-taking, and protagonists may hold differing views of what constitutes an acceptable risk in the light of expected benefits.[28] In reproductive procedures, eventual risks first concern the woman's health as she is always the patient: because the purpose of treatment is to induce a pregnancy, it is always on her body that the physician intervenes—even when the cause for a couple's barrenness is attributed to the husband. Many of the questions deriving from antagonistic conceptions of an acceptable risk do not differ essentially from those ordinarily raised in a traditional therapeutic situation. However, what complicates matters is that the direct purpose of these procedures is ultimately the birth of a child. As such, they are not immediately vital to any woman's physical health and may even expose her to certain risks, even though she is otherwise in good health. The woman or the couple may still feel that failure to provide assisted conception will result in serious personal distress. Doctors' concern with the best possible outcome will none the less often tend to include what they perceive as the primary interests of the unconceived child and the interests of society therewith involved.

Should professional responsibility be guided by the endeavour to do anything more than simply avoid procedures harmful to the woman's health and life? Some physicians feel that, as social agents responsible for the health of patients under their care, they are justified in refusing access to a reproductive procedure, if the quality of life of the future child is at stake. As physicians, they feel they must assume some professional responsibility for the risk of a serious disorder that might afflict

---

[28] Simone Novaes, 'Éthique et débat publique'; ead., *Les Passeurs de gamètes* (Nancy: Presses Universitaires de Nancy, 1994), esp. ch. 4.

the child to be born.[29] Even though the birth of a healthy child can never be guaranteed, physicians claim they can and must attempt to maintain the risks incurred by a procedure at a limit defined as acceptable by the standards of their profession.

However, the criteria they invoke to assert their position when disagreement does arise may often not be based exclusively on claims of a medical nature: by the very fact that reproductive procedures entail fertilization and impregnation, it is not surprising to see physicians' personal moral views about life, death, sexuality, and the family come into play. The case of the widow of Toulouse is, once again, an illuminating example. The reasons advanced by the medical staff to justify their opposition to embryo transfer are centred fundamentally on value judgements of a social and moral nature: the woman has not finished mourning the death of her husband; she should not parent by herself (in other words, a child needs a father); legal complications with paternal filiation would ensue from eventual acceptance of her request. In sum, physicians seem reluctant to provide infertility treatment to patients in unconventional family situations, because they feel concerned about the *social consequences* of an act which their professional knowledge and skills have made technically possible. This observation confirms a fact which, although not new, is of the greatest relevance: through innovative practices which subvert our common notions of personhood and individuality, of time and finitude, of the natural and the normal, of family ties and medical treatment, physicians have become increasingly involved in predicaments whose solution often lies beyond competence on medical questions, and which ultimately require public debate and negotiation.[30]

The medical setting for new forms of technical access to the contents of the pregnant body also necessarily affects the nature and the framework of conflicts which are perceived to oppose the mother and the embryo (or the fetus). Objectively speaking, there is no reason to state that a woman's interests are always compatible with those of the child she bears throughout the pregnancy. A woman is constantly making choices between her own immediate interests and her long-term interests regarding the child she is going to have, between what she might prefer and what she is willing to do—despite opposite inclinations—on behalf of

[29] P. Jalbert *et al.*, 'Genetic Aspects of Artificial Insemination with Donor Semen: The French CECOS Federation Guidelines', *American Journal of Medical Genetics*, 33 (1989), 269–75.

[30] Novaes, 'Éthique et débat public'.

her child. Taking into account the fact that it is women who bear children and who for the most part assume day-to-day responsibility for their care, women are, at least in some western societies, given legal and moral priority in making decisions about abortion, as exemplified by the 1975 French law. In other words, a decision to abort depends on the formulation by the woman herself of such a conflict of interests.

But as medical access to the embryo and the fetus becomes more concrete and direct, defining a situation between mother and future child as conflictual may become the prerogative of protagonists other than the woman, her partner, and other family members. We have already mentioned this possibility when the embryo or the fetus is encompassed by a woman's womb: physicians—particularly those who consider the fetus or even the embryo as their primary patient—may try to override a pregnant woman's decision to refuse treatment, by alleging a conflict between her own interests and those of the embryo, derived from the fact that refusal of treatment endangers the embryo's or fetus's welfare or survival. When embryos are located outside a woman's body, this way of proceeding may appear as more strongly justified, given that pregnancy has not yet begun; this also avoids, among other dilemmas, violating the woman's body to achieve a desired purpose.

The widow's case constitutes a typical example of such proceedings. The woman sees no contradiction between her own interests and those of the frozen embryos: in the same way that she wishes to have children and perceives herself as having a right to procreate, her embryos have, in her understanding, a right to this chance to be born. The physicians responsible for the storage of the embryo do not perceive the situation in the same way. It would nevertheless be incorrect to conclude that they intervene as arbiters to resolve a conflict of interests between one of the genitors and the embryos; on the contrary, it is their interpretation of the possible evolution of the situation which prompts them to 'denounce' an incompatibility of interests between the two parties and call for third-party arbitration. This, in fact, provokes a situation of conflict between the woman and the physician over the way her request and its consequences should be understood.

The direct involvement of physicians in the very act of conception has therefore done far more than impose their presence in a reproductive network: it has clearly altered the weight and significance of their contribution *vis-à-vis* other protagonists. If we refer, once again, to the abortion situation, we note that physicians in general (although not, given the 'clause de conscience', each physician in particular) must defer to

Embedding the Embryo   125

a woman's decision concerning the outcome of her pregnancy during the first ten weeks. This observation also partially applies in circumstances referring to a medically justified abortion after this period: for even if a woman may not determine alone the termination of her pregnancy at that stage, she can—if she so wishes—pursue it, despite expert opinion and indication to the contrary. Pre-eminence in decision-making is therefore conferred on pregnant women, over both their partners and their physicians.

This clear-cut hierarchical ranking of priorities seems to be undergoing major changes in the context of IVF. In fact, representations of the situation surrounding the widow's case suggest not only that the woman's role in conception has been reduced to that of a gamete contributor but also, and even more important, that her 'donation' of germinal cells for fertilization is considered as 'simply materializing the expression of *one of the three necessary wills* [concurring to create an embryo]' ('ce don . . . matérialise seulement l'expression de l'une des trois volontés nécessaires [concourant à sa création]', Jugement du 18 avril 1994, Tribunal de Grande Instance de Toulouse, Première Chambre, our emphasis). In short, from a situation where there is an unequivocal hierarchy between the three protagonists—the woman, her partner, and the medical staff, with an indisputable priority granted to the first—we seem to be headed, at least on the level of discourse, towards another characterized by an assumed equivalence between gamete donors and physicians responsible for fertilization and impregnation.

There has been, over the last few years in France, more than one request for embryo transfer after a partner's death. Each case was handled differently, appealed to different sorts of arbitration, and had different outcomes (*Le Monde*, 13 May 1993). We might say that discussion of normative references regarding the best line of conduct for moral dilemmas involving embryos usually arises from concrete situations characterized by conflict in the network of actors involved in an embryo's existence. Physicians in particular have significantly contributed to a blurring of the boundaries between the medical and the family worlds, by mediating through technology the relationship between mother, fetus, and other family members. This has resulted in a lack of clarity as to the appropriate normative references for problem-solving in these situations, which explains why each case was handled differently and why arbitration arrived at contrasting outcomes.

Despite the existence of the new law, which now formally forbids the transfer of embryos after a partner's death, it is our contention that the underlying legal, moral, and social issues are far from being totally understood. They have certainly not been sufficiently explored and discussed, and the position adopted by the new 'bioethics' law probably does not represent closure or deep social consensus on this issue (as suggested by a clause which requires its revision every five years). This is why our chapter has proposed, not answers, but an analysis of this paradigmatic dilemma, in order to bring out the component elements more clearly and sharpen our understanding of their social implications.

If, in virtue of IVF, the embryo is now, from a physical point of view, a visible discrete entity which seems to exist independently of the female body, from a social point of view, its position is unclear in that it is immersed in a far more complex network of relationships. Deprived of its 'natural' setting and traditional references to the woman's body, the embryo seems to be at present immersed in an ambiguous 'no (wo)man's land' with an increasing number of actors who, for different reasons, feel responsible for its destiny. However, even though some feminist groups clamour, and justly so, for 'recontextualization' of the embryo, this should not lead us to conclude that a context is missing. On the contrary, in consonance with their state of suspended animation, frozen embryos (and even fetuses) may be found in a limbo-like space characterized by internal disputes and by incipient normative references regarding the question of how the arguments and criteria of actors who feel concerned with an embryo's future and fate should be ranked. The outcome of this social dispute will have crucial consequences, not only for the future of individual embryos, but also on definitions of their moral and legal status, as well as on institutional policies and practices. Arbitration necessarily involves deciding whose interpretation of the embryo's welfare must prevail. In this sense, the embryo's moral status and concrete destiny reveal, and will always reveal, arbitrary social choices.

7

The Price of Eggs: Who Should Bear the Costs of Fertility Treatments?

JUSTINE C. BURLEY

> Voyez-vous cet œuf? C'est avec cela qu'on renverse toutes les écoles
> de théologie, et tous les temples de la terre.
> (See this egg? It is with this that all the schools of theology and
> all the temples of the earth are to be overturned.)
> (D. Diderot, 1769)

Introduction

Diderot's insight into the radical implications of the science of reproduction is in many ways as acute today as it was in the eighteenth
century. Two hundred years on, technological advances have made it
possible not only to prevent conception, but also to facilitate the creation of human life through a variety of assisted conception techniques
(ACT). Although disagreement exists over how infertility is most accurately characterized, it will suffice for the purposes of this article to define
infertility as the failure to conceive after twelve months of regular unprotected intercourse or the occurrence of more than two consecutive
miscarriages or stillbirths.[1] According to this standard medical definition, as many as 20 per cent of all couples[2] in developed countries will

I am much indebted to G. A. Cohen who provided detailed comments on successive drafts
of this chapter. I should also like to thank Matthew Clayton, John Harris, David Miller,
Nick Owen, and Seana Shiffrin for many helpful discussions and suggestions.

[1] *Black's Medical Dictionary*, 38th edn., ed. G. Macpherson (London: A. & C. Black,
1995), 252.

[2] Note that the standard medical definition applies the term infertility to *heterosexual* couples. This usage may in part be accounted for by the fact that the cause(s) of
infertility cannot always be clearly identified. Even in those cases where the cause(s) of
infertility can be established treatment often involves both partners. S. Holm, 'Infertility,

experience infertility sometime during their reproductive years; 6–10 per cent of that number have no chance of conceiving at all without technological intervention.[3] Of the different fertility treatments available, including *in vitro* fertilization (IVF), gamete intra-Fallopian transfer (GIFT), and zygote intra-Fallopian transfer (ZIFT), virtually all are prohibitively expensive for most individuals.[4] That such treatments are so costly has engendered considerable debate over who rightfully should bear these costs: ought they to be covered by the individual(s) concerned, or by the state?[5]

In this chapter, I explore the issue of the locus of financial responsibility for the treatment of infertility within the context of Ronald Dworkin's conception of liberal equality.[6] Roughly, on this view, any

Childlessness, and the Need for Treatment: Is Childlessness a Social or a Medical Problem?', in *Creating the Child* (Dordrecht: Clair Law International, 1996), 70. I embrace this definition for the sake of argument only. Clearly, single heterosexual men and women, as well as gays and lesbians (single or partnered), might also suffer from infertility.

[3] L. J. Kaplan and R. Tong, *Controlling our Reproductive Destiny* (Cambridge, Mass.: MIT Press, 1994), 187. Figures for the prevalence of permanent infertility are difficult to procure. M. Belsley, 'Infertility: Prevalence, Etiology, and Natural History', in *Perinatal Epidemiology* (New York: Oxford University Press, 1984), 255–82.

[4] For an explanation of these and other ACT, consult Kaplan and Tong, *Controlling our Reproductive Destiny*, 187–95. Most ACT are not curative, e.g. *in vitro* fertilization does not unblock tubes, and success rates are not high, contributing substantially to the overall costs of fertility treatments. The costs of ACT vary across countries but are high in each case. P. J. Neuman *et al.* estimate the average cost of a single cycle of IVF at six different sites in the United States to be $8,000. Ten to fifteen per cent of initiated cycles result in at least one live birth. Accordingly, a successful delivery for couples undergoing their first cycle of treatment is $66,667 and for couples attempting a sixth cycle $114,286. P. J. Neuman *et al.*, 'The Cost of a Successful Delivery with In Vitro Fertilisation', *New England Journal of Medicine*, 331/4 (July 1994), 339–43. The cost/benefit analysis on IVF conducted by M. Granberg *et al.* in Sweden finds the cost of IVF per successful delivery to be £9,410. M. Granberg, 'Couples' Willingness to Pay for IVF/ET', *Acta obstetricia et gynecologica scandinavica*, 74/3 (Mar. 1995), 201. P. Poulain *et al.* in a study of 152 cases of IVF estimate the mean price of one IVF cycle at 11,084 francs. 'Socioeconomic Approaches to the Practice of In Vitro Fertilisation in the Brittany Region in 1993', *Contraception, fertilité, sexualité*, 23/4 (Apr. 1995), 261–6.

[5] The question of who should pay for ACT has been raised repeatedly in a variety of forums in developed countries over the last decade. For example, the British media has highlighted this debate in numerous feature articles, e.g. 'Hospitals Charge NHS Patients for Fertility Treatment', *Daily Telegraph*, 15 Feb. 1996, p. 1. The issue of funding ACT is also being scrutinized by government policy advisers such as the Canadian Royal Commission on New Reproductive Technologies. See *Proceed with Care. Final Report of the Royal Commission on New Reproductive Technologies: Summary and Highlights* (Ottawa: Canada Communication Group, 1993).

[6] For a comprehensive account of this view see 'The Foundations of Liberal Equality', in S. Darwall (ed.), *Equal Freedom* (Ann Arbor: University of Michigan Press, 1995), 190–306.

difference between individuals' mental and physical capacities warrants redistributive compensation, other things being equal, if one individual prefers to have power(s) another possesses, and if the perceived deficit in powers at issue is not traceable to any preference, taste, or choice affirmed by the claimant. The central claim that I shall develop and defend by recourse to Dworkin's liberal political philosophy is that justice demands that individuals be compensated for all or part of the costs of the assisted conception techniques that they undergo.

The present inquiry is informed by Dworkin's egalitarian approach because it provides principled answers to many pressing questions regarding justice in health care in a way that other liberal accounts do not. For example, in stark contrast to Rawls's theory of justice as fairness,[7] Dworkin's theory of equality of resources serves to guide decisions about how much in total should be spent on health care, what kinds of treatments should be offered, and how the burdens of financing them might be fairly distributed.[8] Rawls, for the most part, is silent on these questions. Animating his view are two ideals: a well-ordered society, and free and equal moral personality.[9] Rawls argues that we all have a higher-order interest in exercising and developing our moral powers and therefore are motivated to obtain what he calls 'primary goods' (basic liberties, opportunity, income, wealth, and the social bases of self-respect).[10] One obvious disadvantage of this index of primary goods is that it is restricted to *social* primary goods, and excludes such *natural* primary goods as health, intelligence, etc.[11] Rawls has acknowledged that this constitutes a practicable defect in his approach, conceding that

---

[7] J. Rawls, *A Theory of Justice* (Cambridge, Mass.: Harvard University Press, 1971).

[8] Dworkin's conception of egalitarianism shares with Rawls's theory a commitment to basic rights and freedoms, equality of opportunity, and distributive justice. However, the two thinkers conceive of justice in distribution in markedly different ways. Rawls endorses a *priority* view: the 'difference principle' requires that inequalities in wealth be arranged to the greatest benefit of the worst-off (defined strictly in economic terms) in society. As will be elaborated below, Dworkin's theory of equality of resources permits inequalities resultant on those tastes, preferences, and choices which are linked to an individual's particular conception of the good, but mandates redistribution for inequalities traceable to instances of brute luck, such as the brute luck of being born blind. Derek Parfit identifies and provides incisive discussion of the priority view in his 'Equality or Priority?', The Lindley Lecture, University of Kansas, 21 Nov. 1991.

[9] J. Rawls, *Political Liberalism* (New York: Columbia University Press, 1993), Lecture 1. See esp. pp. 18–20 for a definition of moral personality.

[10] For a fuller exposition of the primary goods index see *A Theory of Justice*, 60–5.

[11] It is assumed by Rawls throughout his discussion of justice 'that while citizens do not have equal capacities, they do have, at least to the essential minimum degree, the moral, intellectual, and physical capacities that enable them to be fully cooperating members of society over a complete life'. *Political Liberalism*, 183.

variations in people's capacities, the need for medical care, and its cost render the application of the same index of primary goods to everyone unfair.[12] In concentrating on achieving fairness in the distribution of social primary goods to the exclusion of natural primary goods, Rawls's theory only indirectly addresses the host of thorny problems that differences in people's mental and physical powers pose for justice.[13]

Dworkin's theory is also of interest because it stands as an attractive alternative to needs-based approaches to health care. Typical of the current debate over state-sponsored ACT is that both opponents and advocates of it appeal to the notion of 'fundamental need', where y is needed fundamentally by x iff x will be harmed and/or would not be x, if he does not have y.[14]

The case against state funding for ACT is premissed on understanding infertility not as a disease but as a disability, relative to a contingent desire; infertile individuals are not so much ill as they are incapable of performing a specific optimal function. Opponents of state-subsidized ACT argue that infertile individuals will not be *physically* harmed if they are not enabled to conceive a genetically related child and therefore there is no fundamental need to have one's own offspring. Burdening

---

[12] *Political Liberalism*, 178–87. Both Arrow and Sen have criticized Rawls's theory for excluding natural primary goods from his primary goods index. Arrow's critique focuses on the issue of preference satisfaction and differential endowments. K. Arrow, 'Some Ordinalist Notes on Rawls' "Theory of Justice" ', *Journal of Philosophy*, 70 (1973), 253 n.; Sen argues that Rawls's focus on primary goods produces unfairness in the distribution of people's basic capabilities. What matter fundamentally from the point of view of justice, according to Sen, are individuals' capabilities to perform certain kinds of actions to attain certain states of well-being. A. Sen, 'Equality of What?', in *Choice Welfare and Measurement* (Cambridge, Mass.: MIT Press, 1982), 364–9; A. Sen, 'Justice: Means versus Freedoms', *Philosophy and Public Affairs*, 19 (Spring 1990), 113–14; A. Sen, *Inequality Reexamined* (Cambridge: Cambridge University Press, 1992).

[13] Features of Rawls's theory have been misappropriated by a number of philosophers interested in defending a variety of health care policies. See, for example, Peter Singer *et al.*, 'Double Jeopardy and the Use of QALYs in Health Care Allocation', *Journal of Medical Ethics*, 21 (1995), 148–9. This criticism does not apply to Norman Daniels's admirable book *Just Health Care* (Cambridge: Cambridge University Press, 1985), esp. 36–48. Daniels draws from Rawls's equality of opportunity principle and develops his own account of equal access to health care. Also see his *Justice and Justification: Reflective Equilibrium in Theory and Practice* (Cambridge: Cambridge University Press, 1996), chs. 9–11. T. Pogge provides a useful albeit relatively brief discussion of medical opportunities and Rawls's theory of justice in *Realising Rawls* (Ithaca, NY: Cornell University Press, 1989), 181–96.

[14] For further elucidation of the concept of fundamental need see D. Wiggins, *Needs, Values, Truth* (Oxford: Basil Blackwell, 1987), 1–58. Wiggins concentrates on distinguishing different kinds of needs statements, defining what he calls 'absolute' need and discussing the relationship between this class of needs and rights. His project does not involve specifying any particular content of the concept of absolute need.

others economically to satisfy what amounts to a *desire* for a child genetically related to oneself, they conclude, cannot be justified.

Certain proponents of state-funded fertility programmes affirm the minor factual premiss of the above argument, namely that infertility is a disability, and still claim that there is a fundamental need to have genetically related offspring. They argue that the desire of infertile individuals for a genetically related child shades into a fundamental need in that these people suffer serious *psychological* harm if this desire is not satisfied.[15] Others argue that there is a medical need for infertility treatment because infertility constitutes a lack in species-normal functions: a normal range of human biological functions includes the capacity to conceive offspring.[16] From both of these alternative perspectives of fundamental need state funding for ACT is deemed to be justified.

There is, I think, little promise of a ready solution to the debate over funding ACT so long as it is framed within the strictures of a needs-based approach. First, any attempt to provide a list of fundamental needs inevitably invites controversy over essentially contested ethical concepts of what makes a life go best. Second, the concept of species-normal functions is too open-ended: which person's functionings are to serve as the standard for normality?[17] Third, the fundamental needs approach begs the question of how to justify the imposition of a ceiling on what is spent meeting these needs. In the absence of additional distributive principles an enormous number of medical needs might be classed as fundamental, entailing a crippling level of health care expenditure. Dworkin's theory avoids the pitfalls commonly besetting needs-based approaches to health care.

Dworkin neither endorses an objective list of fundamental needs in which a determinate view of the good life is implicit nor introduces a benchmark for what counts as normal powers for a person. Instead, his idea of a just distribution of resources recommends that policy decisions concerning the provision of various treatments should be responsive to how much citizens, on average, value them, and how they rank the public provision of health care relative to other goods and services in society. I seek to demonstrate below that Dworkin's approach to distributive

---

[15] It is not claimed that having genetically related children is a fundamental need for everyone.

[16] Norman Daniels, for example, states that infertility could be classified as a disease using his biomedical model of disease and health. *Justice and Justification*, 186.

[17] For discussion of this point see John Harris, 'Should we Attempt to Eradicate Disability?', *Public Understanding of Science*, 4 (1995), 233–42.

equality supplies a set of coherent principles which could support the state provision of so-called non-essential medical treatments such as ACT.

I divide my discussion into three parts. In the first section, to situate my ensuing arguments, I provide a skeletal overview of Dworkin's theory 'equality of resources'. I then go on to explore the manner in which tax-generated state subsidies for fertility treatments can be justified within Dworkin's liberal framework. Here I argue that infertility is plausibly categorized as a 'handicap'[18] and, as such, warrants redistributive compensation. Finally, I shall assess the practical implications of Dworkin's theory for actual health care policy.

Equality of Resources

Dworkin's conception of a just distribution requires that each individual possess a total share of resources which is of equal value to that of each other individual. People control two kinds of resources, personal and impersonal. Personal resources include people's mental and physical capacities, talents, and skills. Impersonal resources, in contrast, are part of the external world and can be distributed and traded; consumer goods, land, and money all being examples. In Dworkin's theory, a fair share of resources (personal and impersonal) is not measured in terms of the amount of *well-being* it secures for an agent.[19] Rather it is measured in terms of the *opportunity costs* to others of their not possessing it. The device employed for identifying opportunity costs is the economists' 'envy test'.[20]

To illustrate an ideal distribution of resources Dworkin invites us to suppose that a number of shipwreck survivors have been washed up on an uninhabited desert island, abundant in resources.[21] The 'immigrants', who, we are to assume, have equal talents and an equal risk of developing various diseases, accept the principle that no one is antecedently

[18] Following Dworkin, I employ this term in a semi-technical sense. See p. 134 below.

[19] 'Foundations of Liberal Equality', 223.

[20] Envy is to be construed as preferring something that someone else has. It does not necessarily involve feelings of hostility or resentment.

[21] Unless indicated otherwise, the following exposition of Dworkin's theory of equality of resources is drawn from his 'What Is Equality? Part II: Equality of Resources', *Philosophy and Public Affairs*, 10 (1981), 283–345.

entitled to any of the resources found on the island, and agree that they shall be divided equally among them. One person is elected to parcel the island's resources into different bundles, for which he sets prices and which he auctions off to the islanders equipped with an identical number of counters to serve as money. Rational agents participating in the auction will bid in accordance with how they wish to lead their respective lives: an individual who values a life devoted to surfing big waves might bid for land with beach access; someone intent on farming would perhaps bid for fertile land in the interior. When the market has cleared, each participant is asked whether she would now prefer someone else's total bundle of resources. The envy test is met if, of all the auctioned-off bundles, no one prefers anyone else's bundle to her own. When there is complete envy freedom with respect to people's personal and impersonal resources perfect equality has been achieved. The division is held to be equal because, *ex hypothesi*, any individual could have purchased another bundle of impersonal resources had they wished to.[22] So long as the envy test is met there is no inequality even if the auctioned-off bundles differ substantively.

Once the simplifying assumptions regarding people's mental and physical capacities are dropped, and the envy test is applied diachronically, it is readily apparent that achieving perfect equality is impossible. Such is the case because a vast number of contingencies might affect both impersonal and personal resource holdings, and give rise to envy. While Dworkin's theory permits inequalities which stem from tastes, preferences, etc., it requires redistribution for those inequalities which are the product of 'brute luck'. Dworkin distinguishes between two types of luck: 'Option luck is a matter of how deliberate calculated gambles turn out—whether someone gains or loses through accepting an isolated risk he or she might have declined. Brute luck is a matter of how risks turn out which were not deliberate gambles.'[23] Accordingly, an individual who places a losing bet at the craps table has bad option luck, and one whose crops are razed by lightning suffers bad brute luck. Differences in wealth which result from either good or bad option luck do not frustrate the envy test whereas differences in wealth which can be traced to brute luck do and, as such, impose redistributive demands.

The option/brute luck distinction has invited much criticism, not least for its apparent indeterminacy. However, some of this criticism proves misplaced once the two ideas motivating the distinction are clarified.[24] On Dworkin's view, it is unfair to make individuals pay the costs of others' bad option luck not because they chose to do *x* but because the choice to do *x* reflects (at least) one idea they have about what leading a good life involves. Risk-taking for mountain climbers and gamblers, for example, is, for them, part of what gives life value. Victims of bad brute luck, on the other hand, have a valid claim to financial assistance from others because, by definition, brute luck is caused by factors unconnected to an individual's life plans, tastes, and choices.

Much of Dworkin's discussion of brute luck focuses on the brute luck of unchosen differences in individuals' mental and physical capacities.[25] This class of deficits in personal resources Dworkin calls handicaps.

Handicaps

Dworkin is unspecific about how handicaps are to be defined in precise terms.[26] As I understand the notion, two conditions must obtain for a difference in personal resources to qualify as a handicap. I label these conditions C1 and C2 respectively.

C1. The individual has a deficit in her personal resources in the sense that she envies:
someone else's personal resources, or
the impersonal resources that someone has been able to acquire because of the personal resources they possess.
C2. The individual cannot fairly be held responsible for the deficit in her own set of personal resources.

Taken together C1 and C2 are sufficient for a difference in personal resources to count as a handicap. It will be useful at this stage to elucidate these two conditions.

C1, the envy condition, which necessarily involves disidentification with the relevant feature of one's personal resources, establishes that

[24] Dworkin's examples of bad option luck make reference to risk-taking and risk-averse individuals but the general principle of denying compensation to shortfalls traceable to preferences which the individual affirms obtains whether the activity in question is risky or not. Dworkin refines the idea motivating his distinction between option and brute luck drawn in 'Equality of Resources' in 'Foundations of Liberal Equality', 293–7.

[25] In this article, I do not consider differences in personal resources *qua* talents and/or skills. I note here only that the difference between talents and handicaps is one of degree, and the scheme Dworkin deploys to mitigate differential talent is similar to that of handicaps. 'Equality of Resources', 313–23.

[26] Ibid. 292–304.

an inequality with respect to mental and/or physical capacities is at issue. As previously explained, in the absence of envy there can be no inequality on Dworkin's construal of the term. Two points of interest about this condition are worth stressing. First, in Dworkin's theory there is no standard for what constitutes normal powers for a person.[27] For example, suppose that technological advances have made a sight-restoring operation possible for a woman who has been blind since birth. If this woman refuses to undergo the operation because she has come to identify with her sightless condition, then she has no handicap, notwithstanding the fact that she is clinically blind. Hence two people could suffer an identical deficiency in personal resources, e.g. blindness, and yet only one of them have a handicap. Dworkin's approach to justice in health care, then, marks a departure from more familiar views which make reference to (often controversial) objective conceptions of normal human functionings or capabilities.[28]

Second, the two objects of envy distinguished in C1 make clear that a handicap, and thus a legitimate claim to compensation, may be present even when there is no difference between people's wealth holdings. It is possible, in other words, for someone to have a handicap even if it does not reduce her earning potential, and also if her impersonal resource holdings are identical to those of the individual whose holdings she envies. Moreover it is the case that if two people's resource bundles differ solely because of the life choices they have made (i.e. it is a just inequality in impersonal resources) and the wealthier of the two envies the other's mental or physical capacities, she would be compensated for this difference in personal resources despite the fact that she is already financially better off.

C2 links Dworkin's distinction between option and brute luck, spelled out above, to the question of handicaps. When differences in personal resources are viewed in light of the distinction between option luck and

[27] Dworkin is not textually consistent on this point in his discussion of handicaps. Compare, for example, the following two quotations drawn from his 'Equality of Resources': '[T]he suggestion that a design of equality of resources should provide for an initial compensation to alleviate differences in physical or mental resources, is troublesome in a variety of ways. It requires, for example, some standard of "normal" powers to serve as a benchmark for compensation. But whose powers should be taken as normal for this purpose?' (p. 300). 'Someone who is born with a serious handicap faces his life with what we concede to be fewer resources just on that account' (p. 302). The bulk of Dworkin's writings suggest that he is not proposing a standard for normal mental and physical powers and I have interpreted them accordingly.

[28] See, for examples, Sen, 'Equality of What?' and Daniels, *Justice and Justification*, ch. 9.

brute luck it becomes clear that not all differences between individuals' mental and physical capacities which give rise to envy will be handicaps in Dworkin's sense of the term: those traceable to individuals' choices, convictions, etc., which they affirm, are not handicaps, whereas those traceable to brute luck are, and so merit financial redress. Take the case of two bungee jumpers: one jumps successfully and so has *good option luck*, the other jumps, detaches her retinas, becomes sight-impaired, and thus suffers *bad option luck*. In this case even though the latter envies the former's eyesight she does not have a handicap as I have defined it. She, unlike someone who suffers the brute luck of blindness caused by a congenital defect,[29] took an avoidable gamble with her health (with which she identified) and it turned out badly.

Having elucidated the notion of a handicap I now turn to discuss the strategy Dworkin deploys to mitigate personal resource shortfalls. In Dworkin's desert island scenario the auction is accompanied by a hypothetical insurance scheme. Each individual placed behind a 'veil of ignorance' is asked how much she would be prepared to insure against various kinds of handicap.[30] All handicaps that the islanders *on average* stipulate they would have insured against in this hypothetical situation will merit compensation. The veil of ignorance is 'thin': general knowledge is permitted, including information concerning the actual incidence of certain diseases; all knowledge particular to individuals is allowed, e.g. their tastes and conceptions of the good life,[31] except for information about individuals' own risk of suffering various handicaps —the risk of developing different handicaps is assumed to be equal for everyone.[32] The information constraints are justified on the grounds

---

[29] It is therefore not the case, as has been suggested to me, that C2 is redundant. As the example illustrates, the bungee jumper who suffers bad option luck does envy her fellow jumper's personal resources but she also identifies with the activity of bungee jumping. Were C2 omitted the blind bungee jumper would have a valid claim to redistributive compensation and this would contravene Dworkin's aim of achieving a choice-sensitive distribution.

[30] G. A. Cohen misinterprets Dworkin's theory when he suggests that individuals would not be compensated for welfare deficits *tout court*. It is actually the case that people can insure against the eventuality of any kind of problem relating to health, including pain. See G. A. Cohen, 'On the Currency of Egalitarian Justice', *Ethics* (July 1989), esp. 916–21. But Cohen is correct that small welfare deficits (which could amount to one large deficit) would not be compensated for the reason specified below.

[31] Contrast this with a Rawlsian veil of ignorance which permits only general facts about the world to be known by a representative individual in the original position.

[32] Dworkin does not mention whether individuals are permitted knowledge of their gender. It is clear that in the absence of such knowledge the insurance scheme would present fewer problems. If such knowledge is allowed individuals, application of the averaging

The Price of Eggs   137

that they are required to achieve convergence in the results of the insurance market.

This approach to mitigating handicaps is defective inasmuch as the averaging assumption, required to make the scheme practicable, entails that not all unchosen differences in personal resources will be compensated.[33] Thus Dworkin concedes that his scheme is only a second-best strategy. Despite this inherent weakness it bears stressing that Dworkin's approach to mitigating handicaps affords a significant degree of choice over which handicaps people could choose to purchase coverage for.

How substantial will compensation be? The amount of redistributive compensation that would be provided individuals is indexed to how much the average islander would have paid in insurance against a given handicap in the hypothetical insurance scenario. In this way Dworkin's theory imposes a limit on the amount of money that the state will be charged with paying out. Health care expenditure is capped by allowing individuals to decide how much they value compensation for certain handicaps in relation to others, and also in relation to the provision of different goods and services in society such as roads and schools.

We may summarize the view just outlined in terms of two core principles: ambition-sensitivity and endowment-insensitivity. A distribution is ambition-sensitive when it reflects differences in people's tastes, ambitions, life plans, etc. It is endowment-insensitive when differences in wealth which stem from brute luck are, so far as possible, corrected for by redistributive compensation.

Infertility, Handicaps, and the Preference for Children

Kids as expensive tastes

The preceding outline of Dworkin's theory makes clear that inequalities in wealth which stem solely from people's convictions, choices, and

---

assumption would result in people being denied compensation for many gender-specific diseases. My ensuing arguments do not turn, however, on the question of whether this type of information can or cannot be known, as the standard medical definition I employ in this chapter applies the term infertility to couples for the reasons outlined in n. 2 above. For detailed discussion of Dworkin's insurance model and gender-related issues see my 'Reproductive Capacities and Bad Brute Luck', in J. C. Burley (ed.), *Ronald Dworkin and his Critics* (Oxford: Basil Blackwell, forthcoming).

[33] The averaging assumption therefore curtails the extent to which a distribution of resources will reflect different individuals' respective conceptions of the good and so impedes the aim of ambition-sensitivity.

Justine C. Burley

preferences are morally permissible. Does this include the preference for children? Given the high costs associated with having children it is clear that the preference for offspring amounts to what Dworkin calls an expensive taste.[34] Dworkin believes that ministering to expensive tastes is counter-intuitive from an egalitarian standpoint, and insists that a relative merit of his theory in relation to welfarist conceptions is that it is not committed to redistribution in order to compensate people for the costs of such tastes.[35]

Liberal equality does not count among the personal resources which affect the equality of someone's circumstances, the preferences, tastes, convictions, predilections, ambitions, attachments and other features of a personality that will in fact play an important role when he decides how content he is with the life he leads. So even though one person aims high—he has costly tastes or great expensive ambitions—and another needs only modest resources to lead the life he wants, liberal equality does not adjust impersonal resources to take account of that difference in their situations.[36]

One line of argument against Dworkin's treatment of the preference for children is suggested by G. A. Cohen's critique of equality of resources. Cohen's own ideal 'equal access to advantage' is aimed at eliminating involuntary disadvantage, i.e. disadvantage for which the individual cannot be held responsible because it does not appropriately reflect choices that she has made or will make.[37] Thus, while Cohen agrees with Dworkin that egalitarians should not cater to deliberately cultivated expensive tastes, he argues that strict egalitarianism would support redistribution for those expensive tastes which people could not help forming or could not now unform. 'There is no moral difference between someone who irresponsibly acquires (or blamelessly chooses to develop) a particular taste and someone who irresponsibly loses (or blamelessly

---

[34] According to one estimate it costs a middle-class family $100,000 to raise a child to the age of 18. J. Rauch, 'Kids as Capital', *Atlantic Monthly* (Aug. 1989), 56–61.

[35] The bulk of Dworkin's discussion of expensive tastes focuses on his rejection of a well-being equalisandum. See 'What is Equality? Part I: Equality of Welfare', *Philosophy and Public Affairs*, 10 (1981), 185–345. For criticisms of Dworkin's treatment of welfarist approaches to equality and expensive tastes see Cohen, 'On the Currency of Egalitarian Justice' and Richard Arneson, 'Equality and Equality of Opportunity for Welfare', *Philosophical Studies*, 56 (1989); id., 'Liberalism, Distributive Subjectivism and Equal Opportunity for Welfare', *Philosophy and Public Affairs*, 19 (1990).

See Rolf George for a thought-provoking treatment of the view that children are public goods. 'Who Should Bear the Cost of Children?', *Public Affairs Quarterly* (1987), 1–42; id., 'On the External Benefits of Children', in *Kindred Matters: Rethinking the Philosophy of the Family* (Ithaca, NY: Cornell University Press, 1992).

[36] 'Foundations of Liberal Equality', 84.

[37] Cohen, 'On the Currency of Egalitarian Justice', 916–17.

chooses to consume) an expensive resource.'[38] Therefore, argues Cohen, Dworkin's cut between preferences and resources is in the wrong place. The right cut is between responsibility and bad luck because if a person is not responsible for her preferences then it is hardly fair to charge or reward her for the choices she makes on the basis of them.

Several different arguments might be advanced to defend the claim that individuals are not responsible for having developed the expensive taste for children, and hence that justice requires we compensate resource shortfalls arising from it. We could argue that the preference for children is instinctual. Indeed, it would be spurious to deny wholly that there is such a thing as a procreative instinct. Alternatively, we could argue that the preference for children is deeply ingrained in individuals during childhood by a series of socialization processes. Or we could highlight the pressures on people in their adulthood from family and society at large to explain why individuals are not responsible for their preference for children. Perhaps the most persuasive vein of argument would be that the preference for children is involuntary due to a combination of nature and nurture. It is not that Dworkin deems the reasoning in this catalogue of arguments inchoate. Rather Dworkin sidesteps the question of responsibility for one's preferences by introducing a different issue, namely, whether people's preferences, however formed, are linked to their views about the good life.

It would be incoherent for me to regard some ethical conviction I have—that the only important thing to do with my life is to create religious monuments, for example,—as a limitation on the goodness of the life I can lead. If it is my view about what a good life would be for me, then I must think that my having this view *essential* to leading a good life; it cannot be a *limitation* because I would be worse, not better off, without it. So the distinction between handicaps and personality is as little arbitrary as ethics itself. People insist on the distinction not because they make the silly mistake of thinking they choose their ethical convictions like their neckties but because the distinction is at the centre of their ethical lives.[39]

Important for Dworkin is not whether individuals chose to develop the preferences they currently hold, but the fact that they can reflect on these

[38] Ibid. 923. For discussion of other approaches to responsibility and justice see John Roemer, 'Equality and Responsibility', *Democracy Project* (Apr.–May 1995), 3–6 and the Replies to Roemer by Scanlon, Scheffler, and Hurley, ibid. 7–9. See also S. Hurley, 'Justice without Constitutive Luck', in A. Phillips Griffiths (ed.), *Ethics, Royal Institute of Philosophy Supplement*, 35 (1993), 179–212.

[39] Dworkin's italics. 'Foundations of Liberal Equality', 293–7.

140   *Justine C. Burley*

preferences and choose how to behave on the basis of these reflections. If, upon reflection, they affirm their preferences, justice does not require that the state compensate individuals for the costs associated with them. Cohen's additional point, namely, that an individual who has an expensive taste might disidentify not with the actual taste but with the fact that it is expensive, also fails as a challenge to Dworkin's position. Because Dworkin does not believe that welfare matters *as such*, he is untroubled by the fact that certain individuals might suffer if the tastes they affirm prove expensive.

If people do not affirm the preference they hold, i.e. if these tastes can be plausibly characterized as cravings which the agent regrets having but cannot control,[40] then Dworkin's theory does supply grounds for compensation following an initial equal distribution of resources. While equality of resources considers preferences in general to be constitutive of people's ethical convictions about the good life, those with which they disidentify or are unable to control are treated as a kind of handicap. Cohen objects here that the disidentification criterion, when applied to the case of cravings, is too demanding, as in many instances it impossible for individuals in the grips of an addiction to repudiate the desire for what is craved.[41] This is doubtless substantiated by empirical evidence. The applicability of Cohen's argument to the preference for children, however, is questionable. Arguably, the case for conceiving of this preference as akin to an uncontrollable craving is much weakened by the increasing number of women choosing not to have any children at all, and also by the widespread practice of family planning.

Thus Dworkin rebuts Cohen's charge that his approach to mitigating brute luck is too austere to yield egalitarian results. I am inclined to side with Dworkin here. It would, I think, be unfair following an equal distribution of resources to compensate individuals for resource shortfalls arising from their preference for children. Granted individuals do not deliberately develop the preference for children, but this is true of many preferences. Indeed, if we are to compensate people for inequalities solely traceable to preferences of this kind we are also, according to Cohen's reading of egalitarianism, committed to compensating, for example, Etonians for their expensive tastes for steak and cigars whenever it can be demonstrated that they did not intentionally initiate the development of these preferences.

---

[40] 'Equality of Resources', 302–3.
[41] Cohen, 'On the Currency of Egalitarian Justice', 922.

We have arrived at the following provisional conclusion: as a matter of principle Dworkin's theory does not endorse redistribution to people whose inferior economic position is traceable to a preference for children when this preference forms part of their view about what leading a good life is.[42]

The price of eggs

It would appear as though Dworkin's theory can provide no justification for government-subsidized ACT; that infertile individuals share the same preference as most fertile individuals for genetically related children scarcely bears stating. This conclusion, however, is too hasty. There is a salient difference between the case of fertile individuals who have a preference for offspring and that of infertile individuals who share this same preference. In the former case, (fertile) parents, other things equal, will have less wealth than people without children. This shortfall in *impersonal resources holdings*, however, stems from their view about what kinds of projects and attachments the good life involves and therefore is not unjust. In the latter case, by contrast, infertile individuals suffer a deficit in their *personal resources holdings*. For this deficit to count as a handicap two conditions must be satisfied: the infertile person must envy the capacity of others to bear genetically related offspring (C1); and the deficit in personal resources at issue must not be traceable to her tastes of choices (C2). C1 and C2 are jointly sufficient for a deficit in personal resources to qualify as a handicap; therefore, in standard cases, infertility is a handicap. While equality of resources deems that individuals should bear the costs of their *decision* to have children, it requires that people be compensated for their *inability* to have them. To illustrate, consider the case of Louis. Suppose that Louis fell ill and permanently lost his sense of taste, and that now he envies this aspect of others' personal resources. Suppose further that Louis only values his taste buds for the pursuit of his expensive taste for claret and plover's eggs. How would his claim to redistributive compensation be regarded? Clearly, Louis has a handicap; he envies others' capacity to taste, and his loss of this sense was the product of bad brute luck. Likewise, infertile individuals seek compensation for a deficit in personal resources in order to pursue an expensive ambition, namely, that of conceiving children. However, because their deficit in personal

---

[42] Benefits could be justified by paternalistic reasons concerning a child's welfare.

resources is the product of bad brute luck they too have a handicap. Louis merits compensation for lacking the capacity to taste and infertile individuals merit compensation for lacking the capacity to conceive children.

A resource egalitarian would deny compensation to Louis for his expensive taste for plover's eggs, and to infertile individuals for their expensive taste for human eggs. It might therefore be thought paradoxical that Dworkin's approach to distributive justice allows individuals to be compensated for deficits in personal resources so that they can pursue such tastes. But the paradox is illusory because, once a handicap has been defined, Dworkin's view is agnostic on what a person then chooses to use compensation for.

We have yet to establish whether infertility, while it clearly is a handicap, would be a candidate for redistribution. Recall that only those handicaps individuals in the aggregate would have insured against will be compensated. In the hypothetical insurance scheme people would have knowledge of the actual incidence of this handicap. They would know that 20 per cent of all couples experience infertility, and that up to 10 per cent of this number will not conceive other than through artificial means. Individuals are denied knowledge of their own personal risk of developing the handicap of infertility by the constraints on information imposed by the veil of ignorance. I contend that in this situation the average individual would deem having genetically related offspring a constitutive element of leading a good life. The social (not to mention economic) importance of children to members of society is uncontestable. It is therefore plausible to insist that individuals in the aggregate would stipulate infertility as one handicap they were particularly concerned to receive compensation for. The amount of compensation that would be forthcoming as a product of this thought experiment is not something that can be precisely pinpointed here. The level would depend on aggregate decisions concerning the value accorded to having a genetically related child relative to the treatment of other medical conditions, and also the provision of other non-health-related public goods and services.

In principle, the form of compensation that Dworkin endorses is that of cash transfers. This is because many handicaps may not, in fact, be treatable and/or individuals may prefer to use the money for other purposes. For example, infertile individuals who had a poor prognosis of conceiving genetically related offspring through artificial means might choose to use the compensation they received to cover the costs of adoption instead of the costs of ACT. Although Dworkin does endorse state-sponsored health care (see below), he does not address the question of compensating individuals through in-kind transfers. His approach does not, however, preclude compensation of this form. Indeed, there may be good practical reasons for in-kind compensation with respect to ACT. Were cash payments awarded, an infertile person could deceptively report that she envied the capacity of others to conceive genetically related offspring and be more advantaged than those who were similarly situated but honest. If payments were in kind, e.g. treatment or a voucher for adoption, then this unfairness would be removed, because no one would benefit from falsely reporting envy. Furthermore, not all infertile individuals want to have children, and in-kind compensation eliminates the possibility of the person who does not want to conceive envying the cash compensation payment transferred to the person who does.[43]

To summarize, I have demonstrated in this section that, in standard cases, equality of resources does supply a coherent set of principles which could support redistributive compensation, generated by taxation revenue, for all or part of the costs of ACT required to enable infertile individuals to conceive. I now turn to consider a number of objections to the argument that I have just developed.

Objections

A plethora of interesting objections might be raised to the case I have just made for the justice of state subsidies for ACT. Here I restrict myself to discussing three which highlight more general difficulties with Dworkin's approach to distributive justice. The first objection I wish to entertain concerns C2, to wit a deficit in personal resources must not be traceable to an individual's choices, convictions, etc. Suppose that an individual decides in her early twenties that she does not want to have children and is voluntarily sterilized. Now in her thirties she regrets the fact that she had infertility induced, envies other couples' capacity to conceive children of their own genetic make-up, and proceeds with her partner to conceive by recourse to technological intervention. According to the argument that I advance above, this woman would not be eligible for redistributive compensation: her infertile condition will not count as a handicap because C2 has been violated.

---

[43] Matthew Clayton suggested these points to me.

This example illustrates in a forceful way, I think, why it might be problematic to deny assistance to individuals who have made lifestyle choices which have permanent effects. It may be that a person's identity undergoes such radical transformation(s) over the course of a lifetime that the notion that it is fair to hold people to account for choices that they once thought fundamental to their conception of the good, but now just think foolish, is wholly lacking in appeal.[44] The philosophical complexities of the personal identity debate are beyond the scope of the present inquiry. It suffices to note that there may be an insurmountable problem for Dworkin along the lines discussed.

The second objection concerns the disidentification requirement imposed by C1, according to which an inequality exists if an individual prefers to have the powers another possesses. Throughout this chapter I have been employing a definition of infertility which applies to heterosexual couples (for the reasons given in note 2). In fact, some lesbians seek fertility treatments and I should now like to discuss one implication of such cases for Dworkin's view. Suppose that a lesbian seeks to be impregnated by AID (artificial insemination by donor), or perhaps by a more costly technique. Assuming that she does not disidentify with her sexual orientation, it is plain that this woman will not be eligible for financial assistance under the terms of Dworkin's theory. If she affirms her preference for same-sex relations then Dworkin would argue that she cannot simultaneously regard her orientation as a limitation on her leading a good life. I argue at length elsewhere[45] that the disidentification requirement in this case is unfair. There is, I venture, a principled difference between this case and Dworkin's own example in the quotation above (p. 139) of the person for whom the good life involves the creation of religious monuments. That is to say, I believe that there are certain aspects of the person which are so fundamentally bound up with an individual's sense of herself that it would be unfair to deny redistributive compensation for shortfalls traceable to them.[46] I am therefore

---

[44] Philippe van Parijs argues that an unconditional basic income is far preferable to a Dworkin-style one-off distribution, in part for this reason. See his *Real Freedom for All* (Oxford: Oxford University Press, 1995).

[45] I develop this point in detail in my 'Reproductive Capacities and Bad Brute Luck'.

[46] Dworkin hints at this objection: 'what counts as voluntary? Should sexual behaviour of a particular kind be treated as voluntary for this purpose? It would seem wrong for insurance companies to charge active male homosexuals higher premiums because they are considered more likely to contract AIDS. Is this because sexual preference is less under people's control than nicotine addiction? Or because the sacrifice of giving up sex is so much greater than giving up smoking?' 'Will Clinton's Plan Be Fair?', *New York Review of Books*, 13 Jan. 1994, p. 22 n. 10.

inclined to think that here, and in a limited number of other cases, Cohen's cut between responsibility and bad luck discussed above does capture our intuitions far better than Dworkin's. While Cohen does not make his own points about expensive tastes in quite the way I have, it is clear that this case stands as a palpable example of why he thinks it objectionable for Dworkin to insist on forfeiture with respect to expensive tastes.

The force of Cohen's position on expensive tastes relies not only on the possibility that individuals can reflect on the preferences, convictions, etc. they have, but also on whether they possess the capacity to revise these tastes and preferences in light of information about their associated costs. If they cannot revise such preferences Cohen argues that it is unfair to deny compensation for resource deficits stemming from them. But, whereas Cohen thinks that welfare matters as such, and that therefore *any* resource shortfall traceable to *any* expensive taste not deliberately cultivated, and which causes an individual to suffer, warrants redistribution, I believe that very few welfare considerations, in and of themselves, have moral import. All that said, I am not persuaded that one or two examples serve to undermine an entire theory. Nevertheless the case we have just considered aptly serves to underline a limitation in Dworkin's theory and a concomitant merit of Cohen's.

The third and final objection that I shall address concerns Dworkin's distinction between preferences and handicaps. Dworkin has been criticized for being unduly sanguine about the possibility of distinguishing sharply between the two. The following variant of the case of infertility gives shape to this objection. Consider that typical of certain fertility treatments is that they predispose individuals who undergo them to multiple pregnancies. The risk of multiple pregnancy therefore nests in with the notion of the handicap of infertility.[47] Why, then, shouldn't an

---

[47] The Mandy Allwood case will help clarify my point here. The estimated cost to taxpayers of treating this British woman, recently carrying eight fetuses, was a staggering £500,000. Some of the more sensationalist press coverage of this case implied that Ms Allwood's multiple pregnancy might have been prevented had she followed medical advice after taking the fertility drug prescribed, and that because she failed to do so it was unfair that taxpayers had to foot the bill. However, given that the infertility treatment that Ms Allwood underwent predisposes all individuals to multiple pregnancy, the risk of this kind of complication itself is most appropriately viewed as an integral part of the handicap of infertility. Thus were it true that Ms Allwood failed to follow her doctors' orders, insisting that she is responsible for the associated costs of her actions conspicuously ignores the possibility that she might have conceived octuplets even had she done all that was medically advised. For press coverage of this case see 'I Got My 8 Babies from Boots' (and other articles), *Sun*, 12 Aug. 1996, pp. 1–6; 'Health Service Ban Hits 8-Baby Mother', *Guardian*, 17 Aug. 1996, p. 1.

individual who successfully brings such a pregnancy to term receive compensation for the costs associated with raising these children? Suppose, for example, that an infertile woman, following treatment, gives birth to sextuplets. Clearly, she would, for that reason, be comparatively financially worse off than a fertile woman who conceived only one child. Arguably, if the former envies the latter's impersonal resource holdings, because her inferior economic position is traceable to a handicap subsidizing the costs of raising her children is justifiable. Even though infertile individuals consent to fertility treatments against a background of information concerning the risk of multiple pregnancy there appears to be no cogent reason why the brute luck of complications arising from the treatment of handicaps, however long-lasting they prove, should not continue to be considered an integral part of the handicap in question over time.

Available to Dworkin are two responses here. First, he might say that the mother expecting sextuplets could undergo a selective termination of one or more of the fetuses. If she did not do so because she was morally opposed to abortion it is fair to deny her financial assistance for the upkeep of the six infants because the deficit in impersonal resources this woman experiences is not, properly speaking, now traceable to the handicap of infertility. Rather, her inferior wealth holdings stem from one of her deep-seated convictions about the sanctity of life. Second, Dworkin might also reply that the mother does have the choice to put up one or more of her newborn babies for adoption, and if she declines to pursue this option, say because she wants to have a large family, then she has no valid claim to additional resources following the birth. It would be precipitate to conclude that these responses are adequate. Both preserve the distinction between the handicaps and preferences. Arguably, however, they do so only at the cost of rendering Dworkin's theory overly demanding.

Justifying ACT in the Real World

One of the main criticisms levelled at Dworkin's theory in the literature is that it is amorphous when we come to ask how it might be applied in practice. Indeed, some maintain that the hypothetical insurance scheme in particular is wholly impracticable.[48] While I agree with

[48] See, for examples, J. Carens, 'Compensatory Justice and Social Institutions', *Economics and Philosophy*, 1 (1985), 39–67; W. Kymlicka, *Contemporary Political Philosophy: An Introduction* (Oxford: Clarendon Press, 1990), 81–4; H. Varian, 'Dworkin

the claim that an exact replication of the scheme in contemporary society is impossible (and possibly undesirable), I contend that it does have some practical import, and can inform the debate over funding for ACT, albeit in limited fashion. Dworkin has suggested that:

> [a]lmost all government-sponsored or supervised health schemes now in existence, and almost all of those that have been proposed as vehicles of reform in the United States, define a basic health-care package of benefits that must be made available, at responsible cost, to everyone, and supplied without charge to those who cannot pay that responsible cost themselves. We might use our speculations about the imaginary society to help us define what should be in that basic package, and what that responsible cost should be.[49]

Dworkin has made two controversial claims about the kinds of treatments people would *not* choose to have made available to them. The first is that people would not favour government expenditure on life-sustaining equipment used to prolong the existence of individuals in a persistent vegetative state, or in the late stages of senile dementia. To do so, argues Dworkin, would be a 'dominant mistake'. That is to say, the sums required to prolong life in either of these conditions could, no matter what, be used to better effect in making people's earlier lives more worthwhile, e.g. education, training, investment. Second, Dworkin believes that people would not favour government expenditure on life-saving treatments in very old age not because most people do not want to live as long as possible but because people would not prefer to live an extra day/week clinging to life at the sacrifice of what they might do earlier on in their lives when the same sum spent would, to a far greater degree, make these lives better ones.

One notable implication of these suggestions is that while individuals might not prefer money to be spent on expensive life-sustaining or life-saving technologies in PVS or the last stages of life, they might well choose to have money spent on either the development or provision of medical treatments or expensive technology which would serve to enhance their lives when they were younger. I hazard that, given how essential children appear to be most people's respective conceptions of what it means for a life to go well, reproductive technologies such

on Equality of Resources', *Economics and Philosophy*, 1 (1985), 115–19. Compare these criticisms with Eric Rakowski's sanguine view of the applicability of Dworkin's theory to actual health care policy. E. Rakowski, *Equal Justice* (Oxford: Clarendon Press, 1991), 313–18.

[49] R. Dworkin, 'Justice in the Distribution of Health Care', *McGill Law Journal*, 38 (1993), 883–98.

as ACT would be stipulated for coverage by rational individuals in the real world.

Conclusion

Throughout the western world the question of which health care services ought to be provided by the state is not a matter in which citizens appear to have much say at all.[50] When funding cutbacks occur, as they increasingly do, the first treatments denied are those such as IVF, cosmetic surgery, eye tests, etc. The justification frequently given for denying funding for these treatments is that they are non-essential from a medical perspective. The nomenclature 'essential' and 'non-essential' invokes a particular interpretation of the concept of fundamental need, an approach to justice in distribution which Dworkin rejects in both theory and practice.

In the preceding pages I sought to convince the reader that Dworkin's conception of justice is of great theoretical interest to the question of who should pay for ACT. I showed that Dworkin's theory mandates redistributive compensation in cases where individuals have suffered the brute luck of handicaps. Handicaps were defined as a deficit in personal resources with which an individual disidentifies and which is not traceable to her views about the good life. I then argued that, on this definition, infertility is plausibly characterized as a handicap, and that this handicap would be compensated according to the terms of the hypothetical insurance market. Finally I gestured at a largely speculative method by which aspects of Dworkin's theory might support the state provision of ACT in contemporary society. I suggested that just policy decisions concerning both aggregate expenditure on health and the provision of different medical treatments require citizens to play a greater role in shaping health policy. I believe that, were individuals to be provided with the relevant information concerning the costs and efficacy of different medical treatments, they would, in fact, favour government expenditure on technologies such as ACT.

Two features salient to Dworkin's theoretical approach to the provision of health care bear stressing. First, Dworkin invokes no essentially contested ethical concepts in his theory about what it means for a life to go well. If, upon reflection, people deem that so-called non-essential

---

[50] One notable exception is the Oregon health care plan.

treatments would enhance their lives, Dworkin believes it appropriate for health policy to reflect this. Second, Dworkin does not insulate the issues of limiting health care expenditure and rationing various treatments from a wider conception of justice. His answers to these questions issue from his theory of equality of resources which links the question of just health care to a comprehensive theory of distributive justice. Dworkin's theory therefore recommends itself because, unlike rival approaches, it is responsive to the main real world factor which adversely affects people's health status, e.g. inegalitarian wealth distribution. It is now widely accepted both that poverty is the greatest cause of ill health world-wide, and that in the West ill health is most prevalent in those countries where disparities in wealth between citizens are extreme.[51] These facts alone should move all policy-makers contemplating the justice of various health care arrangements to take Dworkin's model seriously.

[51] R. Wilkinson, 'Health, Redistribution and Growth', in *Paying for Inequality* (London: Rivers Oram Press, 1994), 24–43.

8

Sperm as Property

BONNIE STEINBOCK

The new reproductive technologies force us to think about embryos and gametes in ways never before necessary or possible. In particular, cryo-preservation enables sperm and fertilized eggs to be maintained for long periods outside the body, giving rise to questions about to whom they belong and what may be done with them. For example, frozen embryos created by married couples intending to undergo *in vitro* fertilization have become the subjects of 'custody' disputes, when the marriages ended in divorce.[1] Men have long sold their sperm for a small fee, but today women who agree to be egg donors receive about $2,000—a practice that has caused consternation among some ethicists. Such scenarios prompt the questions: how should we think about gametes and embryos? Are they property? In an interesting 1993 California case, *Hecht* v. *Superior Court*,[2] the issue was whether frozen sperm was part of a deceased person's estate, to be bequeathed like his other assets.

Hecht *v.* Superior Court

Deborah Hecht and William Kane lived together for five years. Six times in 1991, as Mr Kane simultaneously contemplated fatherhood and suicide, Ms Hecht accompanied him to California Cryobank, Inc.,

Some of the ideas in this chapter will be familiar from a related paper of mine which appeared in the *Stanford Law and Policy Review*'s Spring 1995 issue on Legal, Ethical, and Policy Implications of New Reproductive Technologies.

[1] *Davis* v. *Davis* 842 SW 2d 588 (Tenn. 1992). Although widely reported in the popular press as a 'custody' case, in fact this terminology begs the question of whether extra-corporeal embryos are children or property.

[2] *Hecht* v. *Superior Court* 20 Cal. Rptr. 2d 275 (Ct. App. 1993). Cited in John A. Robertson, 'Posthumous Reproduction' 64 *Indiana Law Journal* 1027, at 1036 (Fall 1994), and reported in David Margolick, '15 Vials of Sperm: The Unusual Bequest of an Even More Unusual Man', *New York Times*, 29 Apr. 1994, B18.

where he made deposits of his sperm so that Ms Hecht could conceive his child by artificial insemination after his death. About a month before he committed suicide on 30 October 1991, he executed a will that left his residual estate to Ms Hecht.

Mr Kane had executed a written 'Authorization to Release Specimens' specifying that the sperm was to be given to Ms Hecht and her physician. However, after Mr Kane died, California Cryobank refused to release the sperm to her because Ms Hecht did not give the authorization to Cryobank while Kane was alive, and Cryobank's original agreement with Mr Kane contained a clause that stated, 'In the event of the death of the client, the client instructs the Cryobank to . . . [r]elease the specimens to the executor of the estate.' The will was then contested by Mr Kane's two children by a previous marriage. They maintain that the will should be declared invalid because permitting Ms Hecht to bear a child by their father would violate the integrity of their family and open his estate to additional claims.

In December 1992, Judge Edward M. Ross of Los Angeles County Superior Court directed that the sperm be destroyed, as Mr Kane's children had requested, but he stayed his order pending an appeal. The Court of Appeal of California vacated the trial court's order, maintaining that the trial court abused its discretion in ordering the sperm destroyed. It ruled that sperm is property that can be bequeathed by will, and ordered the case remanded to the trial court to decide the decedent's actual intention regarding disposition of the sperm, an issue that the Court of Appeal emphasized was not before it.

There appears to be little doubt about the deceased's clear intention, expressed in his sperm banking directive and his will. Mr Kane also expressed his intention in a suicide note to Ms Hecht and in a final letter to his grown children in which he said:

[I]t may be that Deborah will decide—as I hope she will—to have a child by me after my death. I've been assiduously generating frozen sperm samples for that eventuality. If she does, then this letter is for my posthumous offspring, as well, with the thought that I have loved you in my dreams, even though I never got to see you born.[3]

In March 1994, a probate judge in Los Angeles ruled that under a division-of-property agreement signed by the parties after Mr Kane's death, Ms Hecht was entitled to at least three of the fifteen vials of sperm

---

[3] 16 Cal. App. 4th 836, at 844; 20 Cal. Rptr. 2d 275, at 277.

he left behind. The Kane children plan to appeal, and the Cryobank will release nothing until final resolution of the court fight.[4] According to Ms Hecht, to deny her access to the sperm would violate her constitutional right to procreate as well as Mr Kane's right to direct how his sperm shall be used. Individuals clearly have the legal right to dispose of their property after death by means of wills. But is sperm property?

Is Stored Sperm Property?

The ruling of the California appellate court that sperm is property was based, in part, on its finding that Mr Kane 'had an interest, in the nature of ownership, to the extent that he had decision-making authority as to the use of his sperm for reproduction'.[5] John Robertson also interprets property in terms of decision-making authority. He writes:

> Yet a property interest in gametes must exist, regardless of whether an action for conversion will lie. The term 'property' merely designates the locus of dispositional control over the object or matter in question. The scope of that control is a separate matter and will depend upon what bundle of dispositional rights exist with regard to that object.[6]

According to Robertson, someone has the right to decide what is to be done with stored sperm, and therefore someone 'owns' or has a 'property' interest in stored semen. The logical candidate is the one who made the deposit. Robertson says, 'It is "his" semen both in a biological and property sense, and thus he has the right to decide what happens to it.'[7]

Leaving aside the apparent circularity in first deriving ownership from dispositional authority, and then deriving dispositional authority from ownership, the equation of dispositional control and ownership seems dubious. Parents have the right to control virtually every aspect of their children's lives, from the medical care they will receive to where they will live to the kind of education they get. Yet parents do not own their children, and children are not property. Next of kin often make decisions about what should be done with incompetent patients, including whether the patients should be kept on life support, yet next of kin do not own their relatives, and incompetent patients are not property. Dispositional control is part of the concept of property, but not the whole

---

[4] Margolick, '15 Vials of Sperm'.
[5] 16 Cal. App. 4th at 849; 20 Cal. Rptr. 2d at 283.
[6] Robertson, 'Posthumous Reproduction', 1038.   [7] Ibid.

story. It is, to use the law school metaphor, one of the sticks in the bundle, but not the whole bundle. In particular, the reduction of property to dispositional control leaves out a very important element of property, namely, the idea that property is something that can be bought and sold in a market.[8] It is this aspect of property—not the idea of dispositional control—that makes some people extremely reluctant to regard human bodies or their parts as property.

Robertson specifies that ownership does not settle the question of the scope of control—that is, what the owner is permitted to do with the stored sperm. Perhaps one can own something that one is not permitted to sell. For example, the Queen of England owns a great deal of land and many art treasures that she may not sell. Thus, even if sperm is considered as property, it does not follow that it is or should be a marketable product. However, since ordinarily one may sell one's property, the identification of sperm as property creates a (rebuttable) presumption that its owner can do with it as he likes, that is, donate, store, sell, or bequeath it. As Robertson says, 'There is no apparent reason why these usual attributes of ownership should not apply to frozen semen that remains in storage at the time of the source's death.'[9] In other words, because Robertson identifies ownership with dispositional control, he considers stored sperm to be property, but once it is taken to be property, the assumption is that its owner can do with it as he likes. The trouble with this approach is that it ignores the moral question whether sperm is the sort of thing that should be donated, bought, sold, or bequeathed by will.

A more complex analysis of property comes from Stephen Munzer.[10] Munzer's analysis of property conjoins Hohfeld's vocabulary of claim-rights, privileges, powers, immunities, duties, liabilities, and disabilities[11] with an analysis of ownership suggested by Anthony Honore.[12] Honore

---

[8] Elizabeth Anderson expresses a similar view about commodities. 'To say that something is properly regarded as a commodity is to claim that the norms of the market are appropriate for regulating its production, exchange, and enjoyment. To the extent that moral principles or ethical ideals preclude the application of market norms to a good, we may say that the good is not a (proper) commodity.' 'Is Women's Labor a Commodity?', *Philosophy and Public Affairs*, 19/1 (Winter 1990), 71–92, at 72.

[9] Robertson, 'Posthumous Reproduction', 1039.

[10] Stephen R. Munzer, *A Theory of Property* (Cambridge, Mass.: Cambridge University Press, 1990), 50.

[11] Wesley Newcomb Hohfeld, *Fundamental Legal Conceptions as Applied in Judicial Reasoning*, ed. Walter W. Cook, foreword Arthur L. Corbin (Westport, Conn.: Greenwood Press, 1978 [1919]). Discussed in Munzer, *A Theory of Property*, 17–21.

[12] A. M. Honore, 'Ownership', in A. G. Guest (ed.), *Oxford Essays in Jurisprudence (First Series)* (Oxford: Clarendon Press, 1961). Discussed in Munzer, *A Theory of Property*, 22–7.

sought to specify the standard 'incidents' of ownership common to western legal systems. His list of incidents includes the claim-rights to possess, use, manage, and receive income; the powers to transfer, waive, exclude, and abandon; the liberties to consume or destroy; immunity from expropriation; the duty not to use harmfully; and liability for execution to satisfy a court judgment. 'If a person has all of these incidents, or most of them, with respect to a certain thing, then he or she owns it.'[13] Munzer extends Hohfeld and Honore as follows:

> The idea of *property*—or, if you prefer, the sophisticated or legal conception of property—involves a constellation of Hohfeldian elements, correlatives, and opposites; a specification of standard incidents of ownership and other related but less powerful interests; and a catalog of 'things' (tangible and intangible) that are the subjects of these incidents.[14]

Munzer maintains that body rights—rights to use, manage, dispose of, transfer, exclude others from, and so on, a body—should be seen as limited property rights, rather than ownership. 'Too many incidents are lacking to say that persons own their bodies. Restrictions on transfer and the absence of a liberty to consume or destroy, for example, indicate that persons do not own their bodies in the way that they own automobiles and desks.'[15] On the other hand, given all the things that people can do with their bodies (such as donate or sell certain parts), it would be a mistake to say that they have no property rights in them at all. Thus, the correct answer is that persons do not own their bodies, but that they do have limited property rights in them.

Munzer divides body rights into property rights and personal rights. Property rights are body rights that protect the choice to transfer. Personal rights are body rights that protect interests other than the choice to transfer.[16] To note that someone has dispositional authority over a body or body part is thus not necessarily to acknowledge a property right. Dispositional authority may indicate a personal right. The criterion for determining which body rights are property rights is transferability. Munzer further distinguishes between *weak* property rights, which involve only a choice to transfer gratuitously, and *strong* property rights, which involve a choice to transfer for value. Most countries permit the donation of organs, but forbid their sale; in these countries, people can be said to have a weak property right in their organs. In countries where it is permitted to sell blood and semen, individuals have strong property rights

---

[13] Munzer, *A Theory of Property*, 22, referring to Honore, 'Ownership', 108–12.
[14] Munzer, *A Theory of Property*, 23.   [15] Ibid. 43.   [16] Ibid. 48–9.

in these bodily fluids. However, this merely catalogues existing legal rights. As Munzer points out, 'one cannot avoid the underlying moral issue of what body rights persons should have . . . [T]o resolve this issue one must provide moral argument rather than appeal to what a given legal system recognizes.'[17]

Thus, to decide whether sperm is property, we need first to ask, for what purpose? For the moral arguments regarding the selling of sperm may differ from those concerning its donation, and both may differ from the arguments about storing it for posthumous reproduction. The basic argument in favour of recognizing strong property rights in sperm is an argument from autonomy: that individuals should be allowed to use their own bodies and body parts as they please, so long as they do not harm others. The arguments against a strong property right in sperm take several forms. One is an argument against posthumous reproduction, based on the desire to protect the resulting offspring. Other arguments oppose selling sperm, either on the ground that this commodifies the body, or that it commercializes reproduction.

Posthumous Reproduction

For public policy reasons, a state could decide that semen should not be subject to posthumous transfer or use. If so, stored semen would not be an asset of the estate and could not be transferred by will for posthumous reproduction.[18] One reason would be to protect the children from the disadvantage of being born without a father. Children of single parents, especially single mothers, are more likely to be poor, more likely to have difficulty in school, and more likely to get into trouble with authorities.[19] However, Robertson dismisses protection of offspring as an argument against posthumous reproduction because 'that child cannot be born any other way. Protecting the child's welfare by banning the posthumous use of sperm would protect the child by preventing it from being born.'[20] In other words, for the child who would be created by posthumous reproduction, it is life without father or no life at all. Robertson plausibly suggests that few, if any, children who lack fathers find their lives so miserable that they would prefer non-existence. Being

[17] Ibid. 44.   [18] Robertson, 'Posthumous Reproduction', 1039.

[19] Sarah McLanahan and Karen Booth, 'Mother-Only Families: Problems, Prospects, and Politics', *Journal of Marriage and Family*, 51 (1989), 557–80.

[20] Robertson, 'Posthumous Reproduction', 1040.

born to a deceased father 'does not make a child's life so painful or stressful that being born amounts to wrongful life'.[21] It is not possible to protect children by preventing them from having the only existence possible for them.

The mistake in this argument, in my view, is the assimilation of two very different kinds of situation. In one kind of situation, we are faced with the decision whether to continue treating an existing child with a very poor prognosis. The question facing the child's parents and doctors is whether continued treatment benefits the child, or whether non-treatment—and death—would be in the child's best interest. In this situation, it is important to take, if possible, the child's perspective. Perhaps even a very limited existence, with severe mental and physical handicaps, can be a life worth living, a life that has value for the child. If so, death is not in the child's best interest.[22] Causing a child's death is justified only when death is reasonably considered a blessing.

The situation is very different when the issue is whether to bring a child into existence. The prospect of having a child who is likely to have a substandard life should make one consider very carefully whether procreation is justified, even though precisely the same chance of suffering would not justify killing a child. If asked why this asymmetry exists, I can say only that refraining from procreating just is not the moral equivalent of killing. Causing the death of an existing child deprives that child of its life, a life that may be of value to the child, despite its limits, despite its suffering. By contrast, no one is harmed or deprived by not being brought into existence. Nothing is taken away from the child who is never conceived. The decision not to procreate makes no one worse off, and so the decision not to procreate need not be justified.[23] The decision to procreate, however, makes one responsible for the welfare of the children one brings into the world. In deciding whether to have children, people should be concerned not only with their own interests in reproducing, but also with the lives their children are likely

[21] Robertson, 'Posthumous Reproduction', 1040.

[22] For a nuanced discussion of the treatment of handicapped newborns, and the limits of the best-interest standard, see John D. Arras, 'Toward an Ethic of Ambiguity', *Hastings Center Report*, 14/2 (Apr. 1984), 25–33.

[23] That is, no child is worse off for not having been conceived. Of course, potential grandparents may wish their children would reproduce, and may even demand a justification. However, the idea that one has a duty to reproduce to please one's parents, given the enormous responsibility of parenthood, seems implausible. R. M. Hare is one philosopher who thinks that the decision not to reproduce does require justification. See 'Abortion and the Golden Rule', *Philosophy and Public Affairs*, 4/3 (Spring 1975).

to have. If they are condemned to miserable lives, then reproduction should be avoided if possible.[24] The fact that the children, once born, may not long for death or wish they had never been born does not justify bringing them into the world in the first place.[25]

The above argument focuses on the moral obligations of individuals to avoid procreation if they cannot provide their offspring with a decent chance at a reasonably good life. What are the public policy implications, if any? On the one hand, few people would be willing to have the state make for them the decision whether to have a child. This intrusion into one's personal life would constitute the worst sort of fascism. On the other hand, if there is reliable evidence that a particular policy —say, commercial surrogacy—is likely to produce psychologically impaired children, it would be irresponsible of judges and lawmakers simply to ignore that evidence. The difficulty is that often we do not know what the impact will be. While fatherless children are statistically more likely to get into trouble, it is not clear whether the problems arise from not having a father, or from a particular cause of fatherlessness, e.g. divorce. If it is divorce that causes emotional problems in children, public policy does not require rules preventing single women from being artificially inseminated.

An unusual feature of the *Hecht* case is that any offspring created from Mr Kane's frozen sperm will not only be fatherless, but will also have a father who committed suicide before they were born. Children whose parents commit suicide often have psychological problems, and are at greater risk of killing themselves.[26] It would be surprising if Mr Kane's posthumous offspring escaped unscathed. The assurance that their father loved them in his dreams might not be enough to assuage feelings of rejection and abandonment. However, this situation is so unusual as to make any policy decisions difficult. Unless there is conclusive evidence that posthumous reproduction is worse for children

[24] I am not suggesting that it is wrong for poor people to have children, since income level is not the only, or the main, determinant of a good life. Moreover, society can help poor parents provide necessities for their children. Nor am I suggesting that potential parents are obligated to avoid having handicapped children, if it is possible to enable their children to have good lives, despite their disabilities.

[25] The idea that individuals have a moral obligation to avoid parenthood if they cannot provide their children with a decent chance at a good life is more fully developed in Bonnie Steinbock and Ron McClamrock, 'When Is Birth Unfair to the Child?', *Hastings Center Report*, 24/6 (Nov.–Dec. 1994), 15–21.

[26] Bonnie Frank Carter and Allan Brooks, 'Child and Adolescent Survivors of Suicide', in A. A. Leenaars (ed.), *Life Span Perspectives of Suicide: Time-Lines in the Suicide Process* (New York: Plenum Press, 1991), 246.

than many other stresses of childhood, such as divorce, moving to a new neighbourhood, or losing a beloved pet, banning the practice would unduly infringe individual autonomy. We should not use the effect on children as an excuse for prohibiting what may be considered peculiar or bizarre.[27]

Thus, I agree with Robertson that protecting children is not a compelling reason for banning the posthumous use of sperm. However, this is not because the welfare of children is not relevant, or not relevant unless the disadvantage amounts to wrongful life. Judges, lawmakers, and voters should certainly consider the impact of policies and practices on the lives of children. However, the harm must be substantial and the risk well documented before reproductive liberty is infringed.

Should Stored Sperm Be Capable of Transfer?

The commodification of the body

Another objection to treating stored sperm as property is based on opposition to treating bodily parts in general as property, 'especially if a monetary value is to be assigned and market transactions involving them are to occur'.[28] The basic idea is that it is demeaning to human dignity to commodify the body. But why exactly? Perhaps the idea is that selling part of a human body is uncomfortably close to slavery. Slavery demeans slaves by treating them as mere things, completely subject to the will of their masters. Deprived of autonomy, slaves are stripped of their specific human dignity. However, human body parts, as opposed to human persons, do not have autonomy. Why, then, does it undermine human dignity to sell them, especially if the sale is made by the person whose bodily parts they are? In the children's classic *Little Women*,[29] Jo cuts off her long chestnut hair and sells it to raise money to send to her father serving in the Union Army. Jo secretly mourns the loss of her hair, but the sale certainly does not deprive her of dignity or autonomy. If anything, her willingness to sacrifice her hair (her one beauty!) shows her to be—and helps to make her—a better person.

---

[27] I take this view about commercial surrogacy in 'Surrogate Motherhood as Prenatal Adoption', in Larry Gostin (ed.), *Surrogate Motherhood: Politics and Privacy* (Bloomington: Indiana University Press, 1990), 123–35, at 132–4.

[28] Robertson, 'Posthumous Reproduction', 1038.

[29] Louisa May Alcott, *Little Women* (New York: Grosset & Dunlap, 1947), 179–82.

The arguments against commercial traffic are much more compelling when the body part is, or may be in the future, essential to good health, and where the removal involves a risky, invasive procedure, as in the case of kidneys. Few people would be willing to part with their kidneys unless they were desperate. Thus, allowing the sale of kidneys has great potential for exploitation or coercion. Offering large sums of money for kidneys may be seen as exploitation of the poor, or a 'coercive offer'.[30]

What should we conclude from our different reactions to selling hair and selling kidneys? The lesson seems to be that commercialization of body parts is not intrinsically demeaning to human dignity, but only when supported by an independent moral argument, such as that based on exploitation or coercion. According to Munzer, *morally justifiable* property rights in the body do not undercut autonomy:

It is hard to see that, for example, a power to give or sell blood does so—save in circumstances where poverty forces people to sell their blood to survive, and in those circumstances a strong property right in one's blood seems morally unjustifiable.[31]

A different objection to the selling of blood comes from Richard Titmuss.[32] His objection to commercial blood banks is not that they are coercive or exploitative, but rather that they diminish social solidarity. Titmuss favours a completely voluntary donation system. However, neither the coercion/exploitation argument nor the social solidarity argument plausibly applies to the buying and selling of sperm. Too little money is offered for sperm for us to regard the offer as coercive or exploitative, nor is offering money for sperm likely to diminish social solidarity. Sperm, unlike blood, is not lifesaving, nor necessary for health. I doubt that sperm has the same symbolic significance as blood, or that altruism is fostered by its donation.[33]

[30] In 'Noncoercive Exploitation', in Rolf Sartorius (ed.), *Paternalism* (Minneapolis: University of Minnesota Press, 1983), Joel Feinberg characterizes proposals made to people who have 'no choice' but to accept them as 'coercive offers'. Alan Wertheimer, on the other hand, regards such offers as (merely) exploitative. See *Coercion* (Princeton: Princeton University Press, 1987), 68–9. Some people argue that markets in organs are not necessarily coercive or exploitative. See Lori Andrews, 'My Body, my Property', *Hastings Center Report*, 16/5 (1986). See also Charles A. Erin and John Harris, 'A Monopsonistic Market: Or How to Buy and Sell Human Organs, Tissues and Cells Ethically', in I. Robinson (ed.), *The Social Consequences of Life and Death under High Technology* (Manchester: Manchester University Press, forthcoming).

[31] Munzer, *A Theory of Property*, 56.

[32] Richard Titmuss, *The Gift Relation* (New York: Pantheon, 1971).

[33] For an argument that sperm should never be donated, because this abrogates the duties of a father, see Daniel Callahan, 'Bioethics and Fatherhood', *Utah Law Review* (1992), 3: 735–46.

160   *Bonnie Steinbock*

The commercialization of reproduction

Another objection to treating sperm as a commodity focuses specifically on the wrongness of commercializing anything to do with human reproduction. In its Final Report, *Proceed with Care*, Canada's Royal Commission on New Reproductive Technologies said, 'we believe that certain aspects of the human experience must never be commercialized'.[34] 'Human beings, their reproductive capacities or tissues should not be treated as commodities to be traded for money or other goods.'[35] Using this 'guiding principle', the Royal Commission opposed the buying or selling of eggs, sperm, zygotes, embryos, or fetuses, and the use of financial incentives in pre-conception or adoption arrangements.

One fear is that the commercialization of any aspect of reproduction would open the door to commercialization of everything, including surrogacy. The Commission also expressed the fear that allowing the sale of gametes would lead to the creation of a huge industry in assisted insemination, something it believes would be contrary to Canadian values. *Proceed with Care* looks with dismay at the estimated $164-million-a-year industry in the United States, and warns that 'This kind of activity in the United States shows what could happen in Canada without regulation.'[36] Canadians who testified at hearings before the Commission expressed the fear that commercial motives may be driving the development and provision of reproductive technologies inappropriately, and that the private sector's pursuit of profit may promote high-tech approaches to the treatment of infertility to the detriment of other alternatives.[37] While Canadians differ about the appropriate role for commercial involvement in the new reproductive technologies, they agree that the profit motive should not be 'the deciding factor behind the provision of reproductive technologies'.[38]

Fears of a profit-driven assisted-conception industry may justify reluctance to regard gametes as a marketable commodity. However, objections of this sort do not seem to apply when sperm is not sold, but is rather bequeathed to particular individuals for reproductive purposes. If one accepts as a plausible guiding principle that personal choice in procreative matters should be strongly respected,[39] then individuals should have the right to use their gametes to procreate as they please, unless

[34] *Proceed with Care: Final Report of the Royal Commission on New Reproductive Technologies*, vol. ii. (30 Nov. 1993), 718.
[35] *Royal Commission on New Reproductive Technologies: Update* (Dec. 1993), 8.
[36] *Proceed with Care*, 708.   [37] Ibid. 696.   [38] Ibid. 697.
[39] Robertson, 'Posthumous Reproduction', 1028.

doing so would cause substantial harm to others or the community at large. The arguments I have considered against permitting sperm to be bequeathed for reproductive purposes do not seem compelling.

Conclusion

Cases like *Hecht* require judges to ask whether sperm is property because, if it is not, then it cannot be bequeathed by will. This suggests that we should first decide what property is, determine whether sperm is that sort of thing, and then conclude whether sperm can be bequeathed. However, this approach is backward. Whether sperm is property depends on what we think may permissibly be done with it. If there is a strong moral argument against allowing individuals to store sperm for the purpose of posthumous reproduction, then sperm should not be considered property for that purpose. If there is no such argument, sperm is rightly regarded as an asset that can be bequeathed by will.

9

Some Comments on the Ethics of Consent to the Use of Ovarian Tissue from Aborted Fetuses and Dead Women

CHARLES A. ERIN

Why do it?

Technical feasibility

On 7 January 1994 the United Kingdom's Human Fertilisation and Embryology Authority (HFEA) produced a public consultation document, *Donated Ovarian Tissue in Embryo Research and Assisted Conception.*[1] This was a proactive move. It is likely to be some time yet before science will allow us to harness the potential of ovarian tissue.[2] However, assuming that we will one day be able to retrieve ovarian tissue from aborted, human, female fetuses and from dead women, and to grow to maturity human eggs from that tissue, why would we wish to do so? Technical feasibility is not, of itself, a reason for doing something, and one cannot derive 'ought' from 'can' on this ground alone. An obvious point, but many people do feel that all too often we do things simply because we can. If we are concerned to allay people's fear that science produces monsters which it cannot control, public consultation

---

An early version of this piece was presented at the British Medical Association's Conference on Donated Ovarian Tissue, 12 July 1994, BMA House, London.

[1] Human Fertilisation and Embryology Authority, *Donated Ovarian Tissue in Embryo Research and Assisted Conception* (London: HFEA, 1994).

[2] Note that in this case the aims of the consultation exercise were, to some extent, pre-empted by Section 3a of the Human Fertilisation and Embryology Act inserted by Section 156 of the Criminal Justice and Public Order Act 1994, which effectively prohibits the use of cells derived from embryos or fetuses in fertility treatment. See Jean McHale, John Murphy, and Marie Fox, *Health Care Law: Text, Cases and Materials* (London: Sweet & Maxwell, 1997), 659.

exercises of the kind conducted by the HFEA are surely a step in the right direction.[3]

The need for ova

There is, in the case at hand, an obvious concern which may give us a reason for countenancing the use of ovarian tissue from aborted fetuses and dead women, and it is the *need* for oocytes and ova, for use both in research, and in assisted conception techniques, this need coming of the outstripping of supply by demand.

As far as research use is concerned, the purposes listed in the Human Fertilisation and Embryology Act 1990,[4] for example, represent, I think most would agree, important and valid lines of research. They certainly have the potential for enhancing the public good. The use of ovarian tissue in assisted conception techniques seems to be rather more controversial. Nearly twenty years on from the birth of the first 'test-tube baby', debate continues over whether technological assistance with conception is morally justified, and some still maintain that the various treatments currently available ought not to be thought of as 'therapy'. I will not enter into that debate here, but let me just say that I feel that denying people the opportunity of becoming parents on account of their need for technical assistance to achieve that goal is invidious. It must not be forgotten that '[t]he desire to have children and to rear them is powerful and almost universally acknowledged to be one of the chief benefits and points of human existence',[5] it strikes me that to assist those who cannot conceive but for that assistance, and these are often people who would otherwise suffer a heavy psychological burden, is indeed to provide therapy.

---

[3] I should admit to a personal bugbear here. I am perplexed by the reluctance of non-philosophers to countenance future-looking thought experiments, and I know from experience that moral philosophers are often criticized, particularly by scientists, for considering the ethical implications of technologies which do not (yet) exist, even though one of the lessons of recent history must be that much of today's scientific reality was yesterday's science fiction.

[4] Under Schedule 2, 3 (2): '(a) promoting advances in the treatment of infertility, (b) increasing knowledge about the causes of congenital disease, (c) increasing knowledge about the causes of miscarriages, (d) developing more effective techniques of contraception, or (e) developing methods for detecting the presence of gene or chromosome abnormalities in embryos before implantation.'

[5] Charles A. Erin and John Harris, 'Surrogacy', *Baillière's Clinical Obstetrics and Gynaecology*, 5 (1991), 631.

Let us accept, if only for the sake of argument, that we have some fairly powerful reasons for considering the use of ovarian tissue from aborted fetuses and dead women. What I wish to address in this short piece is the issue of consent as it might be raised in relation to the procurement of ovarian tissue from such sources.

'Donation' by Non- and Ex-persons?

It is as absurd to talk of the autonomy of the unborn as it is to talk of the autonomy of the dead, and it is just this, autonomy, that is a prerequisite for making the choice to donate. Neither of the two types of entities we are considering here is autonomous, nor can either even sensibly be termed a 'person'.[6] The fetus, certainly, is unable to choose to donate, is unable to consent to the removal of tissue. We do have, however, established procedures for obtaining a *legally* valid consent for the removal of organs and tissues from cadavers, and I will discuss ovarian tissue donation from cadavers first.

Ova from Cadavers

The Human Tissue Act 1961[7] provides that the person 'lawfully in possession' of a cadaver may authorize removal of parts to be used for therapeutic purposes, if, prior to death, that person has expressed a request that his or her body or specified parts of it be used for such purposes. This request may be made in writing at any time during a donor's life, or orally before two witnesses during the individual's final illness. This 'opting-in' system[8] is something to which we in the UK are habituated.

Nevertheless, some may be left wondering just *why* we should respect the wishes of an individual, albeit wishes declared while that person was alive, when she is dead. On death, this individual loses the capacity for

---

[6] 'Person' in the technical sense which moral philosophers would attach to that term. See, for example, John Harris, *The Value of Life: An Introduction to Medical Ethics* (London: Routledge & Kegan Paul, 1985), 15–18. (There are, of course, alternative views of personhood to be found elsewhere in the literature.)

[7] The 1961 Act may not be the most relevant piece of UK legislation in respect of the procurement of gametes or ovarian tissue, but it is, I think it fair to say, largely responsible for the 'system' we have in the UK, at least as far as that system is perceived in the public consciousness.

[8] This is how the UK system is normally viewed.

autonomy and ceases to be a moral agent. The dead cannot be harmed or benefited. The dead are *ex*-persons.[9] It seems, on the face of it, to be absurd to speak of the protection of the autonomous decisions of those who are now dead. But looking at the situation in this simplistic way misses an important point.

Taking critical interests seriously

Many will be familiar with what Ronald Dworkin calls 'critical interests'.[10] These interests are to be distinguished from 'experiential interests',[11] the interests we have in doing things for the enjoyment of the experience. Our critical interests guide and shape—define even—our lives; they are crucial to an understanding of the integrity of our existence and the sense we make of it.

I cannot hope in this short piece to do justice to this concept,[12] but let me try to pick out some of the key aspects of critical interests which bear on the question at hand. There are many different possible conceptions of the good life, and whilst some of these notions can claim the standing of philosophical theory, for most people they are only 'ramshackle ideas'.[13]

Most of these different ideas about a good life we hold intuitively and in the background; we do not reexamine them except in moments of special crisis or drama. But these background ideas are always there, guiding decisions and choices that may seem to us automatic, and accounting for at least some part of the exhilaration or boredom or shame or sadness we find ourselves feeling, from time to time, about the way our lives are going. It is absolutely crucial to notice, however, that these various opinions and convictions, however inarticulate or submerged, are *critical* in the sense that they concern what makes a life successful rather than unsuccessful—when someone has made something of his life,

---

[9] Cf. John Harris, *Wonderwoman and Superman: The Ethics of Human Biotechnology* (Oxford: Oxford University Press, 1992), 100.

[10] Ronald Dworkin, *Life's Dominion: An Argument about Abortion and Euthanasia* (London: HarperCollins, 1993), 199–213.

[11] Ibid. 201. I cannot help but feel that there may be a useful analogy with this distinction between critical and experiential interests to be found in the distinction which Robert Young draws between the 'occurrent' sense of autonomy—'autonomy of the moment'—and the 'dispositional' sense—'where the focus is on the person's life as a whole'. See Robert Young, *Personal Autonomy: Beyond Negative and Positive Liberty* (London: Croom Helm, 1986), 5.

[12] And, in view of the eloquence and persuasiveness of Dworkin's argument for the importance of this concept, it would be impudent to attempt to do so in the space of a few paragraphs available to me here.

[13] Dworkin, *Life's Dominion*, 200.

not just wasted it. They are not, that is, opinions only about how to make life pleasant or enjoyable minute by minute, day by day.[14]

It would seem, then, that these are interests of which we may never even be conscious, and, furthermore, that people can have powerful interests the *fulfilment* of which may not benefit them in actuality.

Dworkin brings his critical interests argument into play in a discussion of euthanasia, and his focus is thus on death, as a process and an event, on people's interests both in the manner of their death and in when to die:

> [H]ow does it matter to the critical success of our whole life how we die? We should distinguish between two different ways that it might matter: because death is the far boundary of life, and every part of our life, including the very last, is important; and because death is special, a peculiarly significant event in the narrative of our lives, like the final scene of a play, with everything about it intensified, under a special spotlight. In the first sense, when we die is important because of what will happen to us if we die later; in the second, how we die matters because it is how we *die*.[15]

But these critical interests are interests which, it seems to me, may extend not only to the moment of death, but, crucially, beyond death. I may have an interest in the manner of my death, but if I lose consciousness prior to and until my death I will not—I cannot—experience just how I die.[16] And even if I am conscious of this interest during my lifetime,

---

[14] Dworkin, *Life's Domination*, 200–1 (emphasis in original).

[15] Ibid. 209 (emphasis in original). Cf. Jean-Paul Sartre, from *Being and Nothingness* (London: Routledge, 1969), 538–9: 'For Leibniz we are free since our acts derive from our essence. Yet the single fact that our essence has not been chosen by us shows that all this freedom in particulars actually covers over a total slavery. God chose Adam's essence. Conversely if it is the closing of the account which gives our life its meaning and its values, then it is of little importance that all the acts of which the web of our life is made have been free; the very meaning of them escapes us if we do not ourselves choose the moment at which the account will be closed. This has been clearly perceived by the free-thinking author of an anecdote echoed in the work of Diderot. Two brothers appeared at the divine tribunal on the Day of Judgement. The first said to God, "Why did you make me die so young?" And God said, "In order to save you. If you had lived longer, you would have committed a crime as your brother did." Then the brother in turn asked, "Why did you make me die so old?" If death is not the free determination of our being, it can not *complete* our life. If one minute more or less may perhaps change everything and if this minute is added to or removed from my account, then even admitting that I am free to use my life, the meaning of my life escapes me. Now the Christian death comes from God. He chooses our hour, and in a general way I know clearly that even if it is I who by temporalizing myself cause there to be minutes and hours in general, still the minute of my death is not fixed by me; the sequences of the universe determine it.'

[16] Cf. Charles A. Erin and John Harris, 'Living Wills: Anticipatory Decisions and Advance Directives', *Reviews in Clinical Gerontology*, 4 (1994), 274.

in such a set of circumstances I cannot know whether it will ever be satisfied. And the same is true of other non-experiential interests which, though it may never occur to me that I have them, if raised to my consciousness, I would certainly have to admit to having. I have a powerful interest, for example,[17] that my child be not tortured after my death although, because it never occurs to me, during my life, that such a heinous thing might happen, I never become conscious of this interest.

In *Wonderwoman and Superman*, John Harris calls these kinds of interests 'persisting interests'.[18] A crucially important aspect of persisting interests is that they '*survive* the permanent loss of the capacity to know whether or not these interests are being fulfilled'.[19] Harris notes in this connection that 'if I could be said to have such an interest in the manner of my burial or the disposition of my assets, then such an interest would also survive death'.[20]

So, it is not the autonomy of the dead we are protecting, but the interests of those (not dead) (ex-)persons in having their autonomous decisions (made while alive) respected, even when they no longer possess the capacity to make any such decisions, even when they are no longer capable of being aware of whether or not those decisions are being respected. As Harris puts it: '[T]he interests of actual people persist after their deaths. When they are alive you can harm (or benefit of course) both the individual and her interests. Once she is dead only her interests remain to be harmed.'[21] It seems then that, if critical interests are to be taken seriously, we have a reason for respecting the wishes, made while alive, of the (now) dead. And if a woman makes an advance directive giving consent to the use of ovarian tissue for therapy, or research, it is not unethical to make such use of that tissue. Equally, where a woman makes an advance directive withholding consent to the use of ovarian tissue, if her critical interests are to be taken seriously, it would be unethical to make use of that tissue.

The extent of disclosure: specific or general?

Where consent to the use of ovarian tissue from a dead woman is forthcoming, in the form of an advance directive, the question we must address

---

[17] And I have used this example before. Again, see ibid.
[18] Harris, *Wonderwoman and Superman*, 100–1.
[19] John Harris, 'Euthanasia and the Value of Life', in John Keown (ed.), *Euthanasia Examined: Ethical, Clinical and Legal Perspectives* (Cambridge: Cambridge University Press, 1995), 14 (my emphasis).
[20] Ibid.   [21] Harris, *Wonderwoman and Superman*, 101.

is: what level of disclosure is necessary for that consent to be valid?;
that is, does the consent need to be specific, or may it be general? I
return to these questions below.

In the absence of consent . . . ?

It would appear that where there exists a prior declaration, either giving or withholding consent to the use of cadaver tissue, matters are,
ethically, fairly straightforward. More contentious is where there is no
such advance directive in existence. Again, the Human Tissue Act 1961
has something to offer here.[22] If the donor has made no declaration,
whilst alive, as to her wishes concerning the use of her body parts, the
person lawfully in possession may nevertheless authorize removal of
organs for transplantation provided that he has made 'such reasonable
enquiry as may be practicable' as a result of which he has no reason to
believe that the deceased has raised an objection during her lifetime or
that the deceased's relatives object.

Now, I am no lawyer, but despite the fact that, in practice, in the
United Kingdom we have adopted a *de facto* 'opting-in' system, it strikes
me that the 1961 Act *could* be interpreted as establishing a form of
'opting-out' system of organ procurement:[23] inasmuch as, in the absence
of an objection, the default assumption seems to be that the deceased
would have consented to the use of her tissue. Is such a default assumption morally supportable? Is it ethical to remove tissues from a cadaver
in the absence of prior objections from the deceased, or objections from
surviving relatives? And what interests have surviving relatives in this
matter in any case?

There is a line of argument which may provide answers to these
questions *and* shed light on the question of whether, in cases where we
do have an advance directive giving consent, that consent should be
specific or general. It will not have escaped the reader's notice that I
have, until now, proceeded as though there is no qualitative difference
between reproductive tissue and other human tissues.

---

[22] Again, I am using the 1961 Act as an exemplar of legislation which has influenced
social policy, and to this extent I am not particularly worried that this might not be the
most appropriate legal instrument specifically dealing with the procurement of ovarian
tissue.

[23] It does not matter, to the line of thinking I am running with here, whether this is a
fair interpretation of the 1961 Act. But this is *my* interpretation of the language of the
law, and it is a nice way to introduce the questions I wish to ask.

'Reproductive tissue is "different"' : the 'genetic endowment' argument

But can we really say that the nature of the tissue itself does not make a difference? 'Many people, including Dr John Polkinghorne . . . believe that people have a special interest in controlling the destiny of their own genetic material.'[24] This is, supposedly, why many would consider reproductive tissue to be intrinsically distinct from other types of tissue. A plausible-sounding distinction, to be sure, but question begging none the less—just why we are afforded this 'special interest'? And, even assuming that there are good reasons, what are the moral implications of such a distinction?

Nevertheless, let's try to work through the logic of this argument, which we might like to term the 'genetic endowment argument'. The genetic information contained in our gametes can be passed on from generation to future generation. Quite what we are to deduce from this fact is far from clear, but let us adopt a principle which, though perhaps philosophically arbitrary, has a great deal of intuitive appeal about it: let us say that because we have this 'special interest' in the destiny of our genetic material we ought to be afforded control over, and should bear responsibility for, the uses to which our gametes are put. If this holds, it is thus the nature of the tissue which points up the need for informed consent: an implication of this principle is that any use of an individual's gametes must be sanctioned by the individual and her autonomous choice must be safeguarded. Just as significant, this special interest in genetic endowment would seem to be of the critical, or persisting interest, kind, and thus one which extends beyond the individual's death.

Some tentative conclusions

Assuming that all of this makes some kind of sense, what are we to deduce? First, the prospective donor of ova must be made fully aware of the uses to which her ova may be put, particularly if they are to be used in assisted conception and there is a chance that her genetic material may be passed to future generations. This applies equally to those who would donate ova whilst alive and to those who would make a posthumous donation. If full disclosure is not made, then the choice to donate cannot reasonably be termed autonomous.

---

[24] John Harris, 'Rights and Reproductive Choice', Ch. 1 above.

In view of the assumed special interest in genetic endowment, it seems fair to assume that some who hold a conviction that their genetic information should not find expression in a new life and would thus withhold consent for therapeutic uses may, none the less, not object to the use of gametes, and ovarian tissue, for research. On the other hand, some may disagree with research using reproductive tissue, for whatever reasons, but may simultaneously condone the use of their eggs for therapy. This latter view could be explained in terms of a particular woman's interest in engendering a child, an interest which we might say persists even after the curtailment of that woman's life. On practical grounds alone, it could thus be argued that a specific consent would yield a greater supply of ova for research and therapy.

Where there is no advance directive giving consent to the use of gametes after death, it would be unethical to assume that by default the individual would have wished to donate ova. Even though it is absurd to talk of undermining the autonomy of the dead, this would be to ignore the individual's persisting or critical interests. Put simply, and generally, an individual's ova ought not to be retrieved in the absence of that individual's specific consent.

Ovarian Tissue from Aborted Fetuses

So much, for the moment, for ova retrieval from dead bodies. Let us now consider what appears to be a more controversial subject to many people's minds, ova retrieval from aborted fetuses. I am going to take an approach which rests on 'personhood' as the overarching moral criterion by which to judge to what we owe moral respect and concern. I will not have the time to rehearse the argument in detail here, but, thankfully, this will be a familiar argument to many whether they agree with its strict implications or not. So the argument goes: a fetus is not a person and is not due any special concern or respect in our moral reasoning. Now, some deny this implication of the personhood view by recourse to what has become known as the 'potentiality argument': a fetus is a potential person and, due to this potential for personhood, should be shown the same moral concern as an actual person. I reject the potentiality argument as being conceptually flawed and inconsistent. I will not have time to rehearse that argument either, but we do not need to address this debate here, since an *aborted* fetus certainly has *no* potential—at least not in this (very particular) sense of 'potential'.

Our starting point is the aborted fetus. This is not a person, just as a deceased woman is not a person. It cannot make choices, and it makes no sense to talk of the rights, for example, of an aborted fetus. This being so, I see no reason why we should not make use of fetal tissue made available by abortion. Whatever one's views on the morality of abortion, those issues are pre-empted by the fact that the abortion has already been carried out.[25]

The point is that if we consider bringing a child into existence (where her existence will not be considered by her to be worse than no life at all) *as doing good*, then doing some good is, other things being equal, better than doing no good.[26] And making some good use of this tissue is, other things being equal, better than allowing it to go to waste. And using this tissue to help people, whether in terms of research in the public interest, or in terms of therapy for some particular persons, *is* doing good.

Manifestly, an aborted fetus cannot make a valid consent to the use of ovarian tissue. However, consent is an issue here.

The genetic endowment argument II: consent should be specific

Again, the argument concerning our supposed special interest in genetic endowment comes into play. Any ovarian tissue obtained from an aborted fetus will contain genetic information from the two relevant gamete-supplying individuals. If we apply the special interest in genetic endowment principle, we must conclude, surely, that a specific informed consent should be obtained to the retrieval and use of fetal ovarian tissue from those whose gametes went into the creation of that fetus.

---

[25] A concern regularly raised in this context is the worry that women might be induced to have abortions simply to make tissue available for 'particular purposes' (HFEA, *Donated Ovarian Tissue in Embryo Research and Assisted Conception: Public Consultation Document* (London: HFEA, 1994), 5), or even be induced to become pregnant with the aim of having an abortion to make tissue available for transplantation, for example. However, there is a simple way of preventing this, and that is to ensure that the woman's consent to the use of the fetal tissue is sought *only after* she has made a final decision to have an abortion, having met all the legal criteria which entitle her to do so. The consent could then be a specific consent, with the full disclosure which that involves, and yet obviate any worry as to the woman's motivation in seeking an abortion. Such a consent has the merit that the woman's autonomy is not undermined.

[26] I am grateful to John Harris for discussion of this point.

Genetic endowment and conflicts of interest

This raises a further issue which concerns a possible scenario in which the male and female gamete suppliers disagree as to whether ovarian tissue from the fetus should be used either for research or for treatment. On the grounds of the genetic endowment argument alone, can we discern a morally valid criterion on which to judge which partner's view should be respected in such a case? If we allow the individual control over the destiny of the genetic material which they have contributed to the engendrure of the fetus, then both parties would seem to have an *equal* interest. However, the effect of this is not equal. If the consent of both the genitors is considered necessary for the use of reproductive tissue, then, in cases of conflict, the wishes of the person who objects to the use of the tissue will be respected at the expense of the wishes of the other. It is only in cases where there is consensus between the two parties that the tissue should be retrieved that it would be morally permissible for it to be retrieved.

'My "mum" was a dead fetus': a note on psychological impact

Before moving on, I just want to say something briefly about what has been used as the chief reason for denying the use of ova from aborted fetuses for therapy—the supposed 'horrific'[27] psychological impact on a child so engendered of knowing that its genetic 'mother' was an aborted fetus.[28]

As do many others, I believe that some lives are not worth living. But the more relevant question here is whether some lives are so awful that it is worse to live them than to have never lived.[29] Could it be that, for those who are born as a result of the use of ovarian tissue obtained from an aborted fetus, it would have been better never to have been born? I think, if one considers all aspects of the question carefully, one may be led to believe that the causing of a person's existence, even though the psychological impact of knowing the manner by which it was caused

[27] See, for example, Celia Hall, 'Doctors Approve "Egg Donor Cards"', *Independent*, 6 July 1994, p. 6, and Chris Mihill, 'BMA Presses for Ovary Donor Scheme to Help the Childless', *Guardian*, 6 July 1994, p. 4.

[28] One could say much about what criteria we should employ when deciding who is a 'real' mother. Most of what could be said would be of the nature of a red herring. A genetic link with a child is no guarantee of the ability to be an adequate (rearing) parent, for example. See Erin and Harris, 'Surrogacy', 611–35.

[29] A difficult question; perhaps a paradoxical question, even, some might say, an absurd question.

may be burdensome, can, and in all likelihood will, be viewed as a benefit by that person.[30]

Genealogical interests in the control of genetic destiny

This is probably not a very clever thing to do, but I want to end by briefly looking at a question which I feel points up a major flaw in the argument so far. Consider again the case of the dead woman. Her interest in the destiny of her genetic material is an interest which persists beyond death. And it is respect for this special interest which has led me to suggest that we should seek the woman's fully informed and specific consent and that we cannot assume a default 'yes' to ova retrieval. This being so, do we not also need the consent of the dead woman's parents; and her grandparents? *Their* genetic information, too, will be transmitted down the line, though not in as great abundance, and surely their 'special interest' must be considered.

The logic of the genetic endowment argument would seem to dictate that, in the absence of (advance) directives giving consent by *all* previous genetic ancestors, we are acting unethically in retrieving ova from the dead woman's body, and from the aborted fetus. Moreover, without these consents, it would seem that we are prevented from procreating: pushing the argument to extremes, it could be said that we need ancestral consent in deciding with whom we may procreate: this will clearly affect the genetic make-up of consequent offspring, and it may also undermine the special interest in genetic endowment of our forebears.

Now, whilst moral intuition may not have the academic force of rational argument from philosophically justifiable premises along logical lines, this is one case in which I would say that intuition has the upper hand. I cannot believe that the bringing of my daughter into the world was ethically suspect because I did not have the consent of my now long dead grandmother and all the rest.[31]

Is there an answer to this apparent dilemma? It is tempting to limit our genetic endowment argument to the closest generation. That is,

---

[30] Note that some believe that being brought into existence always constitutes a harm. See, for example, David Benatar, 'Why it is Better Never to Come into Existence', *American Philosophical Quarterly*, 34/3 (1997), 345–55.

[31] Having said that, the first time I voiced the ideas that have ultimately gone to make up this chapter was at an Open Lecture arranged as part of the HFEA Consultation (Manchester Royal Infirmary, 26 Apr. 1994), and on that occasion this power of control over the procreative proclivities of their offspring seemed to be one of the few things that appealed to those in the audience.

we could say that the special interest in genetic destiny is a significant consideration for genetic 'parents', and that we should not be concerned with the interests of more distant genetic relations—grandparents, great-grandparents, and so on. Is there a moral argument which will support such a view. Well, yes, there is. Maybe.

One view of morality incorporates what has become known as the 'Social Discount Rate' and has it that we should be morally concerned about the effects of our choices on future persons, but that it is morally justifiable to be less concerned about effects felt in the 'further future'. This argument is more normally associated with discussions of our obligations to future generations, but I am sure that with a little finesse—which I shall not give it here—it could be amended for application to the present debate. On this view, we can discount the more temporally remote effects of our acts at a rate of some certain percentage per year. So that, if we are considering the safe disposal of nuclear waste, depending on what percentage discount rate we adopt, we are justified in being, indeed we ought to be, far more concerned with one death next year than ten deaths in fifty years. And a million deaths in 500 years may be morally trivial.

Derek Parfitt rejects this view, and in doing so makes an interesting general point. He says:

Remoteness in time has, in itself, no more significance than remoteness in space. Suppose that I shoot some arrow into a distant wood, where it wounds some person. If I should have known that there might be someone in this wood, I am guilty of gross negligence. Because this person is far away, I cannot identify the person whom I harm. But this is no excuse. Nor is it any excuse that this person is far away. We should make the same claims about effects on people who are temporally remote.[32]

Another answer would be that, in the absence of a clear directive to the contrary, we ought to take it as a default that all persons would consent to the use of reproductive tissue in assisted conception and research. Whilst such a view ignores people's critical interests, it takes a less cynical view of their altruism than the assumption that they would not wish to contribute to research in the public good or to the alleviation of suffering. It is strongly paternalistic none the less.

But perhaps we *should* limit the effects of critical interests. I have some lingering doubts about critical interest theory which stem from my

---

[32]   Derek Parfitt, *Reasons and Persons* (Oxford: Oxford University Press, 1984), 357.

uncertainty as to whether the dead can be wronged any more than they can be harmed. Even if we admit the existence of critical interests, the question remains: just how seriously should we take them? And what are we to do when the critical interests of the dead conflict with the interests of the living? This is probably most clear where we are talking about organ retrieval where living people may stand to benefit by the saving of their lives, where respect for an advance directive confirming that the deceased does not wish her organs to be used in such a manner could lead to the death of those in need of an organ.[33]

Do We Really Need Consent from Non- and Ex-persons?

The main point which seems to drop out of this consideration is that, if the genetic endowment principle, reliant as it is on an assumed special, persisting interest in the destiny of our genetic material, falls down,[34] the need for seeking consent to the retrieval and use of ovarian tissue and ova from dead women and aborted fetuses, this consent taking the form of advance directives from the former or the consent of the relevant gamete suppliers in the case of the latter, is thrown into doubt.

[33] The view I currently support holds that dead bodies, and I would probably include aborted fetuses here, should automatically enter the public domain. Let me be clear: this is neither an opting-in nor an opting-out system, but a 'no-option system'—see Charles A. Erin and John Harris, 'A Monopsonistic Market: Or How to Buy and Sell Human Organs, Tissues and Cells Ethically', in Ian Robinson (ed.), *Life and Death under High Technology Medicine*, Fulbright Papers 15 (Manchester: Manchester University Press in association with the Fulbright Commission, 1994), 135–6. There are some problems with this notion, of course. For a start, it would seem to go against various religious views as to the 'sanctity of the dead', if I might call it that, and thus it could be said to undermine a right to freedom of religious expression. However, this does not seem to be a consideration which is given a particularly high priority when it comes to autopsy procedure.

[34] And, remember, this was introduced as an arbitrary 'principle', almost as a 'designer' principle, which seemed most suited to do the job of determining the need for consent.

10

Ethical Issues in Pre-implantation Diagnosis

SØREN HOLM

Pre-implantation diagnosis is a new technique which makes it possible to investigate the genetic make-up of an embryo produced by *in vitro* fertilization (IVF) prior to its implantation into a woman's uterus. Embryos with unwanted genetic characteristics can then be destroyed, and only 'healthy embryos' implanted. Pre-implantation diagnosis thereby makes it possible to perform very early diagnosis of hereditary diseases and chromosomal defects, but the technique can also be used to search for genes which are not disease genes, but which the commissioning couple do not like. The technique creates a number of ethical problems. Many of these are, however, similar to the ethical problems raised by the traditional methods of pre-natal diagnosis (amniocentesis, chorionic villus biopsy). In this chapter I will try to identify and discuss those ethical issues which are specific to, or intensified by, pre-implantation diagnosis.

The Scope and Use of Pre-implantation Diagnosis

Pre-implantation diagnosis is based on the biological fact that all the cells in a human zygote at the four-cell or the eight-cell stage are totipotential (i.e. none of the cells is yet committed to a specific developmental path), and that it is possible to remove one or two cells and still get a normal development of the embryo and the fetus.[1] With modern gene-amplifying techniques it is then possible to produce multiple copies of the genetic material in the removed cell, and subsequently to analyse

[1] J. D. Delhanty, 'Preimplantation Diagnosis', *Prenatal Diagnosis*, 14/13 (1994), 1217–27.

the genetic make-up. At present the technique is limited to either an analysis of chromosome abnormalities like trisomy-21 which gives Down's syndrome, or an analysis of one or two specific genes or genetic defects, for instance the genetic defects causing cystic fibrosis, Duchenne muscular dystrophy, Tay-Sachs syndrome, or Lesch-Nyhan syndrome.[2] It is also possible to detect the sex of the zygote, and the technique has therefore been used in families with X-linked recessive diseases to make sure that only female embryos are implanted.[3] It is at present not possible to make a full genetic map of the embryo from just one cell, and it is highly unlikely that it will be possible at any time in the near future. Pre-implantation diagnosis is thus specific in the sense that you have to know exactly what you want to look for before performing the analysis. If the genetic disorder is highly polymorphic (i.e. if it is caused by many different underlying mutations) it may be necessary to develop a new analytic assay for each new family to be diagnosed.

Because the technique is performed at a very early stage in embryonic development it is only possible as a part of an IVF procedure. The main side-effect is that 25–50 per cent of the zygotes perish. There are also problems with the diagnostic accuracy, and the number of false negatives is still fairly high.[4] These technical problems indicate that most of the uses of pre-implantation diagnosis must still be considered as experimental. The biological long-term effects of the technique on the children who have been subjected to pre-implantation diagnosis as zygotes are also unknown at the present time. The technique has been used in cattle for a number of years with no apparent ill effects, and

[2] Ibid.; R. Avner, A. Laufer, A. Safran, B. S. Kerem, A. Friedmann, and S. Mitrani-Rosenbaum, 'Preimplantation Diagnosis of Cystic Fibrosis by Simultaneous Detection of the W1282X and Delta F508 Mutations', *Human Reproduction*, 9/9 (1994), 1676–80; J. Liu, W. Lissens, C. Van Broeckhoven, A. Lofgren, M. Camus, I. Liebaers, and A. Van Steirteghem, 'Normal Pregnancy after DNA Diagnosis of a Dystrophin Gene Deletion', *Prenatal Diagnosis*, 15/4 (1995), 351–8.

[3] Y. Verlinsky and A. Kuliev, 'Human Preimplantation Diagnosis: Needs, Efficiency and Efficacy of Genetic and Chromosomal Analysis', *Baillière's Clinical Obstetrics and Gynaecology*, 8/1 (1994), 177–96; J. C. Harper, E. Coonen, F. C. Ramaekers, J. D. Delhanty, A. H. Handyside, R. M. Winston, and A. H. Hopman, 'Identification of the Sex of Human Preimplantation Embryos in Two Hours Using an Improved Spreading Method and Fluorescent In-Situ Hybridization (FISH) Using Directly Labelled Probes', *Human Reproduction*, 9/4 (1994), 721–4; A. Veiga, J. Santalo, F. Vidál, G. Caldéron, C. Gimenéz, M. Boada, J. Egozcué, and P. N. Barri, 'Twin Pregnancy after Preimplantation Diagnosis for Sex Selection', *Human Reproduction*, 9/11 (1994), 2156–9.

[4] W. E. Gibbons, S. A. Gitlin, and S. E. Lanzendorf, 'Strategies to Respond to Polymerase Chain Reaction Deoxibribonucleic Acid Amplification Failure in a Preimplantation Genetic Diagnosis Program', *American Journal of Obstetrics and Gynecology*, 172/4 pt. 1 (1995), 1088–96.

there are similar data from studies on mice,[5] but we do not yet know whether this is true for the use of the technique in humans. This further supports labelling the technique as experimental for the time being.

Pre-implantation diagnosis is still a very new technique, and it is impossible to assess the limits of its future use at the present time. What we do know is, however, that there is a demand for the technique, both in families with known genetic disease, and for other purposes such as sex selection.

With the present limitations of the technique three groups of users are likely to demand access to pre-implantation diagnosis:

1. infertile couples in IVF treatment wanting to screen their embryos for chromosomal abnormalities prior to the transfer of the embryo to the woman's womb;
2. couples with a known risk of genetic disease wanting to avoid pre-natal diagnosis and possibly abortion by having IVF and pre-implantation diagnosis;
3. couples wanting to choose a child of a specific kind, for instance a child of a specific sex.

The couples in groups 2 and 3 are not infertile (i.e. they can produce children in the 'natural way') and therefore fall outside the present indications for IVF, but they will now want IVF only because it is a necessary prerequisite for having pre-implantation diagnosis. The development of pre-implantation diagnosis will thus create a redefinition of the purpose of IVF from a treatment for infertility, to a more general element of the possible procreational choices facing a couple wanting to have children.

The number of pre-implantation diagnoses likely to be performed is difficult to predict; it depends partly on technical developments and on the progress in identifying and sequencing specific genes as part of the human genome project, partly on the number of couples in group 3 choosing IVF and pre-implantation diagnosis as a means of exercising choice in reproduction. In this context it is relevant to note that pre-implantation diagnosis will not totally replace traditional pre-natal diagnosis even if the technical problem of false negatives is solved. First of all there are serious developmental conditions (like spina bifida and other neural tube defects) which cannot be detected by pre-implantation

---

[5] K. H. Cui, R. Barua, and C. D. Matthews, 'Histopathological Analysis of Mice Born Following Single Cell Embryo Biopsy', *Human Reproduction*, 9/6 (1994), 1146–52.

diagnosis. Secondly it is highly unlikely that the traditional method of reproduction, i.e. sexual intercourse, will go out of fashion in the near future; and when fertilization takes place inside a woman's body pre-implantation diagnosis is not an option.

The reasons for couples in group 2 to want pre-implantation diagnosis are easy to understand. At present the only way in which they can be certain not to get a child with the genetic defect is by using pre-natal diagnosis followed by abortion in cases where the fetus has the genetic defect. Any pregnancy is thus tentative until the result of pre-natal diagnosis is known, and the woman may have to have a number of abortions if the genetic lottery goes against her. With pre-implantation diagnosis the couple can know from the beginning of the pregnancy that this is a pregnancy which is intended to be carried to term, because they can know that the embryo does not carry the disease. The psychological advantages in this approach are evident (as long as the couple have no ethical worries about the moral status of the embryo). This has led some commentators to the conclusion that: 'In spite of the high cost of the preimplantation diagnostic technique at present, its development is highly justified for high risk families as it provides a wider range of options for avoiding the risk of having an affected child.'[6]

For the infertile couples in group 1 the situation is more complex. By having pre-implantation diagnosis for chromosomal abnormalities they can avoid a possible later pre-natal diagnostic procedure, but they gain this benefit by accepting a reduction in the number of fertilized eggs available for implantation; some eggs will be destroyed directly by the procedure, and some will possibly be found to have a chromosomal abnormality. If the couple has a lot of fertilized eggs this may not be a problem, but if they only have a few this will put them in a dilemma, especially in cases where they themselves are paying for the procedures.

There is one empirical study looking at women's attitudes and preferences when given a choice between pre-implantation diagnosis and chorionic villus biopsy (CVS).[7] The study was conducted as a postal questionnaire in Scotland and included five groups of women. One group had had genetic counselling because of a family history of single gene disorder, one group had had CVS for single gene disorder, one group

[6] Verlinsky and Kuliev, 'Human Preimplantation Diagnosis', 177.
[7] Z. Miedzybrodzka, A. Templeton, J. Dean, N. Haites, J. Mollison, and N. Smith, 'Preimplantation Diagnosis or Chorionic Villus Biopsy? Women's Attitudes and Preferences', *Human Reproduction*, 8/12 (1993), 2192–6.

had had CVS for other reasons, one group had recently completed a normal pregnancy, and the last group had experience of IVF. The authors found that in the total sample 38 per cent preferred pre-implantation diagnosis, and 42 per cent favoured CVS and termination of pregnancy. However, in the group of women having had genetic counselling and the group of women having experience with IVF the preference for pre-implantation diagnosis was higher. The authors therefore conclude that: 'a substantial number of women find embryo diagnosis more acceptable than CVS when the pregnancy is at high risk. This is especially true amongst those with experience of IVF or who are at risk themselves. A demand for embryo diagnosis has been demonstrated.'[8]

Pre-implantation and Pre-natal Diagnosis: Similarities and Differences

The similarities in the ethical analysis of pre-implantation and pre-natal diagnosis are obvious. The main aim of the techniques is similar (both are primarily aimed at finding and removing embryos and fetuses with undesired characteristics), and the medical setting where the techniques are performed is also similar.

If the ethical analysis is primarily based on a conception of the moral status of the embryo and fetus which does not entail any major changes in this status in the time span from conception to birth, then pre-implantation and pre-natal diagnosis are morally on a par. If the embryo attains full moral status at conception then it is wrong to destroy it at any point thereafter, and if it does not attain full moral status before it is born (or even later) then it is not wrong to destroy it at any time during pregnancy.

In the following sections of the chapter, discussing specific problems created if pre-implantation diagnosis is not found to be wrong in principle, I will assume that part of this acceptance is based on the view that human zygotes do not have moral status at the four- or eight-cell stage, and that it is therefore not intrinsically wrong to destroy them. Given that many countries allow embryo experimentation and the destruction of surplus embryos, this is not an unreasonable assumption. I will therefore allow myself to leave out all the provisos which would

---

[8] Miedzybrodzka *et al.*, 'Preimplantation Diagnosis or Chorionic Villus Biopsy?', 2192.

be necessary in the following arguments if human zygotes were believed to have significant moral status at this stage. In my own prior work on these issues I have presented arguments aiming to show that human zygotes do have significant moral status,[9] but these are outside the main scope of the present chapter.

There are differences between pre-natal and pre-implantation diagnosis, even if neither fetuses nor zygotes have moral status. It may be psychologically easier to ask for an eight-cell zygote to be destroyed than to ask for an abortion (and it does not affect the mother's health in the same way), and this could lead to pre-implantation diagnosis being used for conditions, or by people in situations, where pre-natal diagnosis and abortion would never be contemplated. Another difference lies in the position of the zygote relative to the position of the fetus. When pre-implantation diagnosis is performed the zygote is in the laboratory in a Petri dish, whereas pre-natal diagnosis is performed on a fetus inside a woman's body. Arguments relying on a woman's right to control her body therefore support a right to have the embryo/fetus destroyed only in one of those situations and not in the other. This has implications for a range of consent issues surrounding pre-implantation diagnosis (see the section 'Pre-implantation Diagnosis and Parental Rights' below).

Pre-implantation diagnosis is not cheap in itself, and in cases where it is sought by fertile couples who would not normally have IVF treatment the quite substantial price of IVF should be added on top. If the use of the technique becomes widespread it will therefore represent a serious drain on health care resources. There will undoubtedly be savings in not having to care for the handicapped persons who were destroyed while they were still embryos, but these savings will mainly fall outside the health care sector and cannot be directly converted to health care funding. Pre-implantation diagnosis will therefore have to compete in the normal priority setting process. If we compare the technique with other similar techniques this would mean that pre-implantation diagnosis and IVF would first be offered to couples with known risk of genetic disease; the next group to get it (if funds are available) would be couples already being offered publicly funded IVF procedures; and it is probably unlikely that couples wanting pre-implantation diagnosis

---

[9] S. Holm, 'The Moral Status of the Pre-personal Human Being: The Argument from Potential Reconsidered', in D. Evans (ed.), *Conceiving the Embryo* (The Hague: Kluwer Law International, 1996), 193–220.

just in order to choose a child of a specific kind would ever be funded by the public health care system.

Pre-implantation Diagnosis and Parental Rights

If we accept pre-implantation diagnosis and offer it to couples as an option in IVF procedures we immediately create a complicated consent problem. Who should consent to the performance of pre-implantation diagnosis and who should consent to the actions taken as a result of pre-implantation diagnosis? In pre-natal diagnosis we usually operate with a firm assumption that the woman is the final decision-maker, but part of the argument for this assumption is that pre-natal diagnosis involves procedures which affect the woman's body. This is not necessarily the case in pre-implantation diagnosis.

Arguments relying on a woman's right to control her own body will give her a veto over which embryos are implanted, and thereby the final right to choose between the embryos after pre-implantation diagnosis has been performed. Such arguments, however, have no direct bearing on a situation where the male partner wants pre-implantation diagnosis performed, and the female partner does not want it performed. In not wanting pre-implantation diagnosis performed she implicitly accepts the implantation of any of the embryos produced which are not screened out by the normal control of the morphology of the zygotes. Since the embryos chosen for implantation after pre-implantation diagnosis belong to this group of embryos she should, in principle at least, have no objection to their implantation. The scenario becomes even more complicated if we consider IVF procedures involving egg donation, sperm donation, surrogacy, or any combination of these.

Gamete donors may have legitimate worries about certain uses of pre-implantation diagnosis, for instance sex selection. It is not immediately self-evident that the usual rule that donation is non-directed and 'no strings attached' should also apply here. A moderately feminist egg donor might have very sensible arguments for not donating to a couple who would use sex selection. Such a couple would be quite likely to hold values concerning the importance of gender and about gender roles exactly opposite to her own. Prospective surrogates would also have an obvious interest in the pre-implantation diagnosis and the decisions following from the knowledge gained.

There is in all likelihood no way of reaching a compelling ethical solution to these consent issues, and the most useful pragmatic solution is probably that pre-implantation diagnosis and its possible outcomes must be discussed very thoroughly with couples presenting themselves for IVF. During this discussion a consensus should be sought, which can then be the basis for the resolution of any later disagreements.

Restriction of Pre-implantation Diagnosis to Serious or Severe Conditions?

In the public debate and in legislative proposals it is often suggested that pre-natal and pre-implantation diagnosis should be restricted to looking for serious or severe conditions. Some have operationalized this idea and suggested the creation of a positive list of conditions for which pre-implantation diagnosis will be available and a negative list of conditions for which it will be prohibited. The underlying idea is probably an extension of the requirement in many European abortion laws that late abortions on eugenic grounds are only allowable if the fetus suffers from a serious or severe condition. The English Abortion Act of 1967, for instance, allows late abortions if there is: 'a substantial risk that, if the child were born, it would suffer from such physical or mental abnormalities as to be severely handicapped'.[10] There are at least two problems with this suggestion for a restriction on pre-implantation diagnosis.

First of all it is questionable whether the state has any right to impose restrictions on pre-implantation diagnosis if such a restriction is not based on an argument giving the zygote moral status. This problem will be dealt with more extensively in the next sections of the chapter.

Secondly, it is very difficult to produce a non-arbitrary dividing line between severe conditions and non-severe conditions. It is reasonable to assume that the notion of severity which is at play here is a global notion of severity which is closely linked to the notion of disability, and which should perhaps ultimately be cashed in terms of an ability to have a good life. The exact understanding of severity is, however, not important for the present argument as long as it is agreed that severity cannot be reduced to mere medical/physical severity in this context.

---

[10] J. K. Mason, and R. A. McCall Smith, *Law and Medical Ethics*, 3rd edn. (Edinburgh: Butterworths, 1991), 104.

Despite the political correctness lobby and its attempts to force the view upon us that there are no disabled people but only differently abled people, there can be little doubt that some conditions are actually disabling in any realistically conceivable human society. It is disabling to be blind and deaf at the same time, and no amount of re-description can change that. Conditions which are universally disabling in this sense (i.e. disabling in any realistically conceivable human society) are clearly paradigmatic exemplars of severe conditions. The same could be said of a condition like Lesch-Nyhan syndrome which leads to mental retardation and compulsive self-mutilation (children with this condition may bite off their fingers or toes, or gouge out their own eyes). An individual with Lesch-Nyhan syndrome has a degree of suffering which clearly places this condition in the category of severe conditions.

There are, however, many conditions where the situation is not nearly as clear. Many conditions are not universally disabling but only disabling in specific circumstances. Severe myopia (near-sightedness) is only marginally disabling in our society, whereas it was a severe disability before the invention of glasses. If changes in the disabling effects of a given condition were only of this historical kind, it would not pose any serious problem to an attempt to find a dividing line between the severe and the non-severe conditions. It would mean that specific conditions would move relative to the dividing line, but at any one point in time a condition would either be severe or non-severe.

A more serious problem is that severity varies not only historically but according to the precise social context of each affected person. Even if we assume that the physical and psychological manifestations of a given condition are constant, there will be many conditions where the impact on the person with the condition will vary quite markedly. The degree to which for instance a severe case of club foot will affect a person will depend on both the kind of family he or she is born into— whether physical or more sedate pursuits are the centre of family life— and the kind of other abilities which the person has. The severity in the global sense of a severe case of club foot is thus not determined by the medical severity of the condition. Two persons with the same medical severity might end up being widely separated on the global severity scale. This indicates that a dividing line operating on the level of specific conditions is at risk of misclassifying individuals. The conceptual basis of the categorization therefore seems to force us towards a case-by-case classification, and away from a classification of a number of cases falling under the same condition label.

It is furthermore unclear whose assessment of severity should count. There will undoubtedly be differences between the general population, politicians, physicians, persons with the condition, and prospective parents in this assessment, both for specific conditions and for the cut-off point. This uncertainty opens the field for pressure groups wanting to have a specific condition classified in a specific way. It is probably most likely that the pressure will be in the direction of labelling more and more conditions as severe, because that would be the only way to get access to pre-implantation diagnosis for these conditions. Because of the conceptual ambiguity underlying the original classification of conditions and the original placing of a dividing line it will be difficult to offer principled arguments against a re-classification. It is therefore foreseeable that 'severity creep' will take place over time, and that more and more conditions will be labelled as severe.

Pre-implantation Diagnosis and 'Frivolous Choices'

A recurrent feature of the ethical debates about pre-natal diagnosis and about gene therapy is the suspicion that these techniques may be used to promote the selection or creation of children with certain characteristics which the parents just happen to want. The same suspicion can obviously be raised about the use of pre-implantation diagnosis. Such choices could be about the sex of the child or about other characteristics such as height, colour of the hair or eyes, or intelligence (not all of these choices are technically possible at the moment, and it may never become possible to test for intelligence). Sometimes such choices are described in the public debate as 'frivolous choices'. Would it be appropriate for the state to try to restrain such choices, either through direct prohibition, or by leaving them out of the range of services funded by the public health care system?

The focus here will mainly be on arguments supporting a general or partial prohibition of pre-implantation diagnosis. The issues concerning restriction of public funding are extremely interesting, but would require an in-depth analysis of justice in health care resource allocation. I have therefore decided to leave the funding issues out of this chapter.

There can be no doubt that examples can be created, and real life situations do occur, where a prohibition against selection according to a certain criterion goes against some persons' deeply felt desires, and causes them harm. This is clearly so in the case of sex selection where for instance British hereditary peers may have a strong desire to select for male offspring (with the ethical blessing of Mary Warnock), or perhaps more importantly women in certain ethnic groups may need male children to maintain their marriages and social status. Are such cases sufficient to vitiate any attempt of state intervention?

If we look at the question of direct prohibition it seems that the state would have to show that allowing people to exercise these kinds of choices would harm other people or other societal interests. Whether such harm could plausibly be argued to exist depends to a very great extent on (1) what kinds of states of affairs we allow to count as harms, and (2) what kind of connection we require between the action of making a specific reproductive choice and the harmful state of affairs.

Harm in the Family

Very direct harm can be imagined within family units if parents want to select against characteristics which already existing children have. Statements like 'it is not because we don't like black hair and brown eyes, it is just that we would also like to have a blond, blue-eyed child' are unlikely to do much toward alleviating any feeling of psychological rejection the already existing child with black hair and brown eyes might feel. But if people only select characteristics for their first child this problem could be alleviated.

We can also envisage scenarios where parents will want to select embryos with a specific condition which is normally seen as a handicap or disability. There is anecdotal evidence that some American deaf couples have used pre-natal diagnosis to detect and abort non-deaf fetuses, so that they could be certain to have a deaf child which could be fully integrated in the deaf culture. Pre-implantation diagnosis could be used for the same purpose. Intuitively most would probably feel that this is a perverse use of the technique and that the child who is born deaf has been harmed in some way. There are, however, arguments purporting to show that this is not the case.[11] These arguments proceed from the observations that (1) if a woman conceives a child this month, the child will be different from the child she could have conceived next

---

[11] Parts of the following section draw on my article 'Embryology and Ethics' in the forthcoming *Encyclopedia of Applied Ethics* published by Academic Press, Inc. The original ideas behind replacement arguments can be found in D. Parfitt, *Reasons and Persons* (Oxford: Oxford University Press, 1984).

month, because they will come from the union of different gametes and be genetically different, and more generally (2) any change in reproduction which entails a change in the timing or manner of conception leads to the production of different children (children with different identities). In the case of the deaf child we may believe that we are comparing the welfare of the child growing up deaf with the welfare of the same child growing up hearing and deciding which would be the better life for the child, but this is not true. What we are doing is comparing two different children, the child growing up deaf and another child growing up hearing. The life of the deaf child is the only life this child can have, and what we have to decide is not whether there are better lives, but whether the life of this child is so bad that it would be better not to have it. This is an unlikely proposition in most cases, so the argument that it would be better for the child not to be born than to be born disadvantaged is in most circumstances false. What we have to decide is whether parents are allowed to choose to bring into the world a child with an impairment, when they could have produced another and 'better' child, or whether they are only allowed to bring 'the best possible' child into the world. If we decide that they are only allowed to bring 'the best possible child' into the world, this will clearly have implications which reach far beyond questions about pre-implantation diagnosis.

Societal Harm

Harm outside the family context is also possible but it will probably be of a much more indirect nature, not mediated through the direct effects of the choice made, but through its symbolic meaning. To choose a specific characteristic must necessarily imply a preference for that specific characteristic when compared to other members of the same set of mutually exclusive options (e.g. the members of the set of eye colours). To deliberately choose brown eyes must imply a preference for brown eyes over other possible colours. It is arguable that to prefer something is to value it more highly than the other possible options, and this assumption actually plays a major role in rational choice theory when the implicit value structure of an individual is determined from his explicit choices and preferences. This entails that by choosing a specific characteristic I signal that it is more valuable to me than the other possible options.

Let us imagine that a person with the less favoured characteristic (characteristic A) claims that he or she feels devalued by the choice made, and that he or she is thereby harmed. What defence could the person choosing have against such a claim? One possibility would be to say something like 'my choice and my values are specific to my situation and it is not intended to entail a general evaluation of all persons with characteristic A'. That defence would, however, be implausible if an analysis of the aggregate of all the choices made in similar situations showed that there was a general tendency to choose against characteristic A. Such a general bias would indicate that the values of the chooser were less situation specific than he or she would have us believe, and would furthermore indicate the existence of an underlying social value structure biased against characteristic A.

Persons with A could in that case plausibly claim that allowing people to choose against A legitimizes and reinforces the underlying social bias against A. What is wrong is thus not the individual acts of choice but their combined effect. In this way the problem resembles the well-known 'problem of the commons' in social co-operation where individual actions which are rational and acceptable lead to an unacceptable combined result. It may not be wrong for any individual couple to select for characteristic A, but it becomes wrong when taken together with all the other choices made by other couples.

If this line of argument is accepted it can support a prohibition of specific forms of pre-implantation diagnosis, but not a general prohibition of the whole technique.

Communitarian and Semi-communitarian Arguments

There is a line of argument which attempts to support a general prohibition of pre-implantation diagnosis. This line of argument has, for instance, been used by some members of the Danish Council of Ethics in their general rejection of pre-implantation diagnosis. The argument relies on a broader notion of harm, and seeks to establish that an introduction of pre-implantation diagnosis is harmful because it further medicalizes and technologizes human reproduction. According to this way of looking at reproductive techniques they are harmful because they transform something which has (appropriately) been seen as natural and not subject to human intervention into something where technology, medical knowledge, and human choice become essential. This is often connected to a general sceptical view on the 'blessings of technology'. It seems relevant to ask 'but what is wrong with technologizing reproduction?'. Here two different kinds of answers have been proposed. One kind of answer focuses on the social effects of the various reproductive techniques, and argues that the changes in values which accompany the new possibilities are detrimental to society as a whole. This assertion may then be backed by arguments of a general communitarian kind, or by more specific arguments attempting to show that our currently held ideas about parenting and motherhood are valuable to society (or maybe more accurately the ideas about parenting we held twenty years ago). From this last evaluation of some specific ideas about parenting it could then be argued that the value of upholding these ideas overrides the possible benefits to specific individuals by allowing new reproductive techniques.

Another kind of answer criticizes the assumption that having these reproductive choices, including the choice of pre-implantation diagnosis, is necessarily a good thing. We normally assume uncritically that it is better to have many choices than to have few, but this is an assumption which can be questioned. If I am a truly believing Jehovah's Witness it is, for instance, not a benefit to me to be offered the choice of whether or not to have a blood transfusion, but a distinct disadvantage to be forced to choose. Having to choose between killing one, or letting twenty be killed, is also a choice which is of no benefit to the chooser, but only causes him or her harm.

The claim is then that the choices offered by the new reproductive techniques are choices of this kind, choices which are forced upon us, and which do not make us any more free. Can this claim be made good?

It will not help just to refer to the mental anguish caused by having to choose, because many choice situations where choice is usually appreciated can be accompanied by mental anguish (such as choosing university or choosing a school for your children). It must be shown that having the choice in itself is harmful in some way. The claim is highly unlikely to be true if it is stated in the form 'being given the choice whether or not to use pre-implantation diagnosis is harmful to all persons who are given this choice'. We know that there are people who want to have the choice, and unless they are all suffering from self-deception about what is good for them, there must be at least some cases where it is good to be offered the choice. The question is then whether the lesser claim 'being given the choice whether or not to use pre-implantation diagnosis is harmful to a majority of persons who are given this choice' is true. This seems to be a claim which is, at least in principle, amenable to empirical investigation. The question in itself can, for obvious reasons, not be answered prior to the introduction of pre-implantation diagnosis, but evidence from studies of pre-natal diagnosis could shed some light on the problem. If being given the choice whether or not to have pre-natal diagnosis and possibly abortion is not harmful, then it is unlikely that being given the similar choice about pre-implantation diagnosis will be harmful. There is anecdotal evidence of harm in the pre-natal diagnosis situation, especially in cases where couples are being 'persuaded' to have pre-natal diagnosis against their will, but there is, as far as I know, no evidence of widespread harm. Some of this harm can, furthermore, be removed if health care professionals become more sensitive to the fact that it is morally problematic to force choices on persons who clearly are not interested in having them. In the end the argument that creating an opportunity for choice regarding pre-implantation diagnosis is harmful therefore fails.

Conclusion

The arguments in this chapter all point toward the conclusion that the possible ethical problems created by pre-implantation diagnosis are not of a sufficient severity to render the technique as such ethically questionable. There may be reasons to restrict certain uses of the technique but there are no arguments supporting a total prohibition. Before the technique is introduced it is important to solve the complicated consent problems created by pre-implantation diagnosis.

This conclusion does, however, only follow on the assumption that human zygotes at the four- or eight-cell stage have no moral status, and that it is not intrinsically wrong to kill them. For those who do not accept this assumption pre-implantation diagnosis raises serious ethical problems because the technique is aimed at detecting and destroying certain kinds of human zygotes.

11

Reproductive Choice:
A Muslim Perspective

GAMAL I. SEROUR

Reproductive health is defined as a condition in which the reproductive process is accomplished in a state of complete physical, mental, and social well-being. Reproductive health is not merely the absence of disease or disorders of the reproductive process.[1] This implies that people have the ability to reproduce, to regulate their fertility, and to practise and enjoy sexual relationships. It also implies that women can go safely through pregnancy and childbirth, that fertility regulation can be achieved without health hazards, and that people are safe in having sex.

Reproductive Choice

Reproductive choice is the right of the person to choose freely his or her reproductive performance including his or her reproductive potentials. Though reproductive choice is basically a personal decision yet it is not merely so. This is because reproduction itself is a process which does not involve the person who makes the choice alone. It also involves the other partner, the family in all its forms, the society, and the world at large. It is therefore not surprising that reproductive choice is affected by the diverse contexts, mores, cultures, and religions as well as the official stance of different societies.

The reproductive choice of the person not uncommonly may even conflict with the interest of his or her own society. This is likely to occur when his or her choice does not enjoy the approval and support of the society. In reproduction, one cannot always have what one chooses

---

[1] M. Fathalla, 'Reproductive Health: A Global Overview', *Annals of the New York Academy of Sciences*, 28 June 1991, p. 1.

even within one's own society or country. Every day many people cross borders to fulfil a reproductive choice which may not be permitted in their own societies or countries. Such an act is by no means restricted to one country or followers of one religion. It is a well-known fact for physicians working in the field of medically assisted conception that a few Muslims fly over to Europe or the United States to fulfil a reproductive choice which they cannot have in their own country. The same pattern also exists in Europe among residents of different European countries with different regulatory mechanisms for the process of reproduction. The recent birth of a baby by a post-menopausal British woman who had had medically assisted conception in Italy has made headline news all over the world.

Reproductive choice includes two main aspects, reproductive choice practice and reproductive choice research. Reproductive choice practice deals with the choice of the pattern of reproduction: its prevention, promotion, or the use of its potentials. Its objective is the control of one's own present or near future reproductive pattern. It includes: prevention of conception, termination of conception, sex selection (SS) whether pre-conceptional or post-conceptional, medically assisted conception (MAC), and post-menopausal conception.

Reproductive choice research involves the choice and approval of conducting research procedures and techniques on one's reproductive products, namely pre-embryo and fetus, in the early phase of their development. The objective of such choice is mostly beneficence to generations to come, humanity at large, and possible beneficial effects to one's offspring. Reproductive choice research includes: embryo research, gene therapy, and fetal tissue transfer and research.

Islamic Background

Islam is a faith which had over 1.225 billion adherents worldwide in the year 1990, and with the present rate of population growth this figure is expected to increase to 2.5 billion by the year 2020.[2]

Islam is a comprehensive system that regulates the spiritual as well as civil aspects of individual and communal life. It aims at producing a unique personality of the individual, and a distinct culture for the

---

[2] A. Omran, 'UN Data on Demography of the Islamic World', paper presented at the International Conference on Islam and Population Policy, Jakarta and Lhokesumawe, Indonesia, 19–24 Feb. 1990.

community, based on Islamic ideals and values. The teaching of Islam covers all the fields of human activity—spiritual and material, individual and social, educational and cultural, economic and political, national and international.[3]

The instructions which regulate everyday activity, to be adhered to by good Muslims, are called shariah. There are two sources of shariah in Islam: the primary sources and the secondary sources.

Primary sources of shariah

The primary sources of shariah in chronological order are:

1. the holy Quran: the very word of God;
2. the Sunna and Hadith, which are the authentic traditions and sayings of the Prophet Muhammad (peace be upon him) as collected by specialists in Hadith;
3. *igmaah*, which is the unanimous opinion of Islamic scholars or *aimma*.
4. analogy (*kias*), which is intelligent reasoning through which to rule on events the Quran and Sunna did not mention, by matching them against similar or equivalent events which have been ruled on.

A good Muslim resorts to secondary sources of shariah in matters not dealt with in the primary sources.

Secondary sources of shariah

The secondary sources of shariah are:

1. *istihsan*, which is the choice of one of several lawful options;
2. views of the Prophet's Companions;
3. current local customs if lawful;
4. public welfare;
5. rulings of previous divine religions if these do not contradict the primary sources of shariah.

The five categories of human actions

The shariah classifies all human actions without exception into one of five categories:

[3] G. I. Serour, 'Research Findings on the Role of Religion in Family Planning', paper presented at the IPPF Regional Conference, Cairo, 23–4 Oct. 1991.

1. obligatory, such as praying and fasting;
2. recommended, such as marriage and family formation;
3. permitted, such as breaking off fasting during illness and travelling;
4. disapproved but not forbidden, such as divorce;
5. absolutely forbidden, such as killing and adultery.

Even if the action is forbidden, it may be undertaken if the alternative would cause harm.

The shariah is not rigid or fixed except in a few areas such as worship rituals and codes of morality. Islamic shariah is adaptable to emerging situations in different eras and places. It can accommodate different honest opinions as long as they do not conflict with the spirit of its primary sources and are directed to the benefit of humanity.

The development of the science of *fiqh* (jurisprudence) resulted in the establishment of certain guiding principles to help to form rulings. There are several principles on which the science of *fiqh* is based, such as: harm should be removed, one should choose the lesser of two harms, and public interest takes priority over enjoying benefits.

The goals of shariah can be summarized in the preservation and protection of self (life, health, procreation, etc.), mind (prohibition of alcohol, freedom of thought, etc.), religion (freedom of faith, non-compulsion in religion, rituals of worship, etc.), ownership (sanctity of private ownership, legitimate commercial relationships, prohibition of stealing, fraud, and usury, etc.), and honour (purity, marriage and laws of family formation, chastity and prohibition of adultery, etc.).[4]

Muslim ethics is a systematic reflection from a theological perspective, on both moral actions and practices of those in the Muslim community. It also reflects the character, traits, virtues, dispositions, and intentions out of which those actions and practices come.[5] The rules that govern behaviour in the different societies are the instructions of religions, followed by those of ethics, then by those of law. It is well known that religious teachings are of influence in correcting the behaviour of the faithful and have tangible effects in pious societies, but the absence

---

[4] H. Hathout, 'Islamic Origination of Medical Ethics', in G. I. Serour and A. Omran (eds.), *Proceedings of the First International Conference on Bioethics in Human Reproduction Research in the Muslim World* (Cairo: IICPSR, 10–13 Dec. 1991).

[5] G. I. Serour, 'Religious, Secular and Medical Ethics: Are there any Common Themes? A Muslim Perspective', paper presented at the Fifth International Congress on 'Ethics in Medicine', Imperial College, London, 31 Aug.–3 Sept. 1993.

of a material punishment to be enforced for violation makes these teachings effective only when they are approved as laws, at least in societies that are not governed by shariah.[6]

Reproductive Choice Practices

Prevention of conception

No Quranic text explicitly forbids prevention of conception. Islam is inherently a religion of planning and regulation and there is no contradiction between its lofty precepts and family planning. Coitus interruptus was practised at the time of the Prophet Muhammad (peace be upon him) and he did not forbid or discourage it. By analogy, methods of contraception available today which were not available at the time of the Prophet Muhammad would be permitted provided they cause no harm and prevent conception temporarily.[7]

Temporary methods of contraception are acceptable for fertility regulation with the free informed consent of both the husband and the wife. Permanent methods of contraception may only be conducted for therapeutic purposes, when pregnancy would endanger the woman's life or health or is associated with the birth of a seriously handicapped child.[8]

This includes genetic screening for the identification of carriers of harmful genes before they get pregnant or have a family. Appropriate counselling of these carriers may help them tremendously in making an enlightened decision about their reproductive choice. Programmes to detect Tay-Sachs disease, sickle-cell anaemia, and cystic fibrosis are some examples of this situation. Disclosure of such information to the couple on their request is certainly ethical and may help them in taking an enlightened decision and prevent later unhappiness and disappointment at the reproductive choice outcome.

[6] G. Abdel-Salam, 'Legal Aspects of Family Plannning', in Serour and Omran (eds.), *Proceedings of the First International Conference on Bioethics in Human Reproduction Research in the Muslim World*, 118–33.

[7] A. G. H. Gad El-Hak, HE, 'Islam and Birth Planing', *Population sciences* (IICPSR), 2 (1984), 40–5; id., 'Family Planning Islamic Sharia', *Gynecological Problems in the Legacy of Islam* (IICPSR) (1992), 135–41; M. S. Tantawi, HE, *Birth Planning and Islamic Sharia* (Cairo: Dar El-Eftaa, 1988); M. El-Ghazali, Ibn. H. Al-Azhar, In Ihia Ulum El-Din (1269 AH), xi. 45. Cairo.

[8] See n. 7.

Termination of pregnancy

Abortion is unacceptable in most of the Muslim world as a method of family planning. However, it is carried out to protect the mother's health or life or to prevent the birth of a seriously handicapped child.[9] Many high-rank theological authorities would even restrict its use to protection of the mother's health or life only.[10]

Sex selection

Sex selection was practised by the Arabs before Islam, when female babies used to be buried after their birth; Islam forbids such selection.[11]

Pre-conceptional sex selection merely to choose the sex of the baby is forbidden as this constitutes a challenge to the will of God. However, pre-conceptional sex selection for health reasons is acceptable.[12] Post-conceptional sex selection is only acceptable for health indications.

Sex selection, whether pre-conceptional or post-conceptional, is acceptable for health indications to prevent the birth of a seriously handicapped child, but not for the mere choice of the sex of the child.

Artificial reproduction (AR)

Medically assisted procreation was not mentioned in the primary sources of shariah; namely the Quran and the Sunna and Hadith. However, these same sources have affirmed the importance of marriage, family formation, and procreation.[13] Treatment of the infertile couple is therefore encouraged and becomes a necessity as it involves preservation of procreation in the married couple.[14]

[9] G. I. Serour and A. R. Omran, *Ethical Guidelines for Human Reproduction Research in the Muslim World* (Cairo: IICPSR, 1992).
[10] *Al-Azhar Views on the Draft Programme of Action of the International Conference for Population and Development Held in Cairo, 5–13 Sept. 1994* (Cairo: IICPSR, 1994).
[11] Serour and Omran, *Ethical Guidelines*; Ali Gad El-Hak, Gad El-Hak, 'Islam: A Religion of Ethics', in Serour and Omran (eds.), *Proceedings of the First International Conference on Bioethics in Human Reproduction Research in the Muslim World*, 37–9; A. F. El-Sheikh, 'Al-Azhar: A Mosque and a University of Ethics', in Serour and Omran (eds.), *Proceedings of the First International Conference on Bioethics in Human Reproduction Research in the Muslim World*, 34–6; Qur'ān, Ṣūra el-Takweer 81: 8–9.
[12] Serour and Omran, *Ethical Guidelines*.
[13] Qur'ān, Ṣūra al-Shura 42: 49–50; Ṣūra al-Nahl 16: 72; Ṣūra al-Ra'd 13: 38; Hadith Shareef, reported by Abou Daoud; Hadith Shareef, reported by Bukhary and Muslaam.
[14] A. G. H. Gad El-Hak, HE, Dar El-Iftaa, Cairo, (1225) 1/115 (1980), 3213–28.

Islam entitles a woman who does not bear children to seek medical assistance, including advanced technology, to fulfil her most cherished wish: motherhood. The basic concept of Islam is to avoid mixing genes, as Islam enjoins the purity of genes and heredity. It deems that each child should relate to a known father and mother. Since marriage is a contract between the wife and the husband during the span of their marriage, no third party intrudes into the marital functions of sex and procreation.[15] A third party is not acceptable, whether providing an egg, a sperm, or a uterus. Therefore, sperm donation, egg donation, and surrogacy are not allowed in Islam.[16]

Any excess number of pre-embryos can be preserved. The frozen pre-embryos are the property of the couple alone and may be transferred to the same wife during the validity of the marriage contract.[17] If the marriage contract has come to an end because of divorce or the death of the husband, AR cannot be performed on the female partner even using sperm cells from the former husband.[18]

Multifetal pregnancy reduction is only allowed if the prospect of carrying the pregnancy to viability is very small. It is also allowed if the life or health of the mother is in jeopardy.[19] Surrogate motherhood was at one time allowed;[20] but the present situation is that surrogacy is forbidden.[21]

[15] G. I. Serour, 'Bioethics in Artifical Reproduction in the Muslim World', *Bioethics Special Issue: Inaugural Congress of the International Association of Bioethics*, 7/2–3 (Apr. 1993), 207–17; I. S. Kattan, 'Islam and Contemporary Medical Problems', in Abdel Rahman A. El-Awadi (ed.) (Kuwait: Organization of Islamic Medicine, 1991), 365–74; G. I. Serour, M. A. Aboulghar, and R. T. Mansour, 'In Vitro Fertilization and Embryo Transfer: Ethical Aspects in Techniques in the Muslim World', *Population Sciences* (IICPSR), 9 (1990), 45–53; G. I. Serour, M. A. Aboulghar and R. T. Mansour, 'In Vitro Fertilization and Embryo Transfer in Egypt', *International Journal of Gynecology and Obstetrics*, 36 (1991), 49–53; M. A. Aboulghar, G. I. Serour and R. T. Mansour, 'Some Ethical and Legal Aspects of Medically Assisted Reproduction in Egypt', *International Journal of Bioethics*, 1/4 (1990), 265–8.

[16] Serour, 'Bioethics in Artificial Reproduction'.

[17] Serour and Omran, *Ethical Guidelines*.

[18] Ibid.; Gad El-Hak, Kattan, 'Islam and Contemporary Medical Problems'; Serour *et al.*, 'In Vitro Fertilization and Embryo Transfer'; Serour *et al.*, 'In Vitro Fertilization and Embryo Transfer in Egypt'; Aboulghar *et al.*, 'Some Ethical and Legal Aspects'; G. I. Serour, 'Medically Assisted Conception: Dilemma of Practice and Research. Islamic Views', in Serour and Omran (eds.), *Proceedings of the First International Conference on Bioethics in Human Reproduction Research in the Muslim World*, 234–42. 'Proceedings of 7th Meeting of the Islamic Fikh Council in I.V.F. & E.T. and A.I.H., Mecca (184)', *Kuwait Siasa* (Mar. 1984).

[19] Serour and Omran, *Ethical Guidelines*; S. Tantawi, 'Islamic Sharia and Selective Fetal Reduction', *Al-Ahram* (Cairo) (1991).

[20] 'Proceedings of 7th Meeting of the Islamic Fikh Council'.

[21] Serour and Omran, *Ethical Guidelines*.

Pregnancy in the post-menopause

Artificial reproduction allows post-menopausal women to become pregnant and have children of their own. Pregnancy in the post-menopause appeals to the egalitarians, as it is just for older women to have children since older men have always been able to father children. However, the issue is not that simple. Men are not directly involved in the process of pregnancy, childbirth, and to a great extent in the process of caring for the newly born child at least in the first few months of life. Such physiological processes no doubt tax and exhaust the health reserves of women. Also, pregnancy in the post-menopause may be unjust to the child as it violates the rights of the newly born child to get his or her share of adequate love, care, and tenderness. For all these reasons many regard this as raising ethical issues as to the suitability of older women as mothers.

Pregnancy in the post-menopause at least at present involves:

1. egg donation;
2. increased maternal risks;
3. problems with the rearing of the child.

Pregnancy in the post-menopause using donated eggs is ethically unacceptable in the Muslim world. Apart from mixing genes it exposes mothers to increased maternal risks and complications and is rather unjust to the newly born child. Pregnancy in the post-menopause using a couple's own frozen embryos is associated with increased maternal risks and needs further evaluation.

Reproductive Choice Research

Embryo research

The main ethical concern has been the alleged immorality of using embryos for research purposes. Embryo research has non-procreative interests which include:

1. improvement of knowledge in treatment of infertility;
2. improvement of contraception;
3. treatment and prevention of cancer;
4. treatment and prevention of birth defects.

Embryo research denigrates the importance of human life by treating embryos as means rather than ends. Embryo research could harm children, if the embryos used in research were then placed in the uterus of a woman.[22]

The ethical concerns which surround embryo research include:

1. creation of embryos solely for research purposes;
2. limits on the purposes of embryo research;
3. transfer to the uterus after research;
4. keeping embryos alive *in vitro* for more than fourteen days.

Research would occur only on spare embryos created as a by-product of IVF treatment of infertility. However, the wide use of cryopreservation of extra embryos has limited the number of embryos donated for research. The other source of embryos for research would be creation of embryos solely for research purposes. This would pose an important question: is creating embryos solely for research purposes a reproductive liberty?

Creating embryos solely for research purposes is not a reproductive liberty. It is an act of liberty in the use of one's reproductive capacity.[23] One should certainly ask: is there a significant moral difference between research on embryos created solely for research purposes and research on spare, discarded embryos?

Though most commissions now accept a wide degree of embryo research, ethical controversy continues to surround the production of embryos solely for research purposes. Do the symbolic benefits of protecting embryos from being created solely for research purposes justify this loss? Creation of embryos solely for research purposes is a non-reproductive use of reproductive capacity. Legally only a few European nations and Victoria, Australia, prohibit the creation of embryos solely for research purposes.[24]

Research of a commercial nature or unrelated to the health of mother or child is not allowed. Cryopreserved pre-embryos may be used for research purposes with the free informed consent of the couple. Research conducted on pre-embryos should be limited to therapeutic research.

The treated pre-embryos may be transferred only to the uterus of the wife who is the owner of the ova and only during the validity of the

[22] J. Robertson, 'Freedom and the New Reproductive Technologies', in *Children of Choice* (Princeton: Princeton University Press, 1994), 198–202.
[23] Ibid.   [24] Ibid.

marriage contract.[25] Research aimed at changing the inherited characteristics of pre-embryos including sex selection is forbidden.

Non-therapeutic research may be conducted on excess pre-embryos
with the free informed consent of the couple, to improve the treatment
of infertility, contraception, reproductive medicine, genetics, cancer, and
embryology. These treated pre-embryos are not to be transferred to the
uterus of the wife or that of any other woman.

Gene therapy

Genetic research on human subjects is part of medical research in general and the ethical requirements and rules of medical research should
apply to it.[26] It should be governed by previous international guidelines
relevant to this problem such as the Nuremberg and Helsinki Declara-
tions (1963 and 1975), the CIOMs (1982), the Inuyama Declaration (1990),
and the Cairo Declaration (1991) for the Muslim Countries.[27]

There are four well-known categories of human gene therapy which
it is helpful to delineate, in order to focus the ethical gene therapy discussion.[28] These include:

1. somatic cell gene therapy;
2. germ line gene therapy;
3. enhancement genetic engineering: (*a*) somatic cell enhancement,
   (*b*) germ line enhancement;
4. eugenic genetic engineering.

Genetic manipulation is desirable to remedy genetic defects. Serious
ethical questions begin to arise at the borderline cases when the aim of
genetic manipulation shifts from therapy to the creation of new human
types.[29] Though there is fairly general approval of somatic cell gene therapy, ethics has not been able to solve the dilemmas of germ line gene
therapy.[30]

[25] Serour and Omran, *Ethical Guidelines*.

[26] G. I. Serour, 'Ethical Issues in Population Based Genetic Research', paper presented
at the International Seminar on Bioethics, Dunedin, 22–7 Nov. 1993.

[27] Serour and Omran, *Ethical Guidelines*.

[28] W. F. Anderson, 'Genetics and Human Malleability', *Hastings Center Report*, 20
(1990), 21–4; R. V. Lebo and M. S. Golbus, 'Scientific and Ethical Considerations in
Human Gene Therapy', *Baillière's Clinical Obstetrics and Gynaecology*, 5/3 (1991),
697–713; LeRoy Walter, 'Editor's Introduction', *Journal of Medicine and Philosophy*, 10
(1985), 209–12.

[29] Benedict M. Ashley, 'Constructing/Reconstructing the Human Body', *Thomist*, 51/3
(1987), 501–20.

[30] Serour, 'Ethical Issues in Population Based Genetic Research'.

From a Muslim perspective human gene therapy should be restricted only to therapeutic indications. Somatic cell gene therapy is encouraged as it involves the remedying and alleviation of human sufferings. However, enhancement genetic engineering or eugenic genetic engineering would involve change in the creation of God which may lead to imbalance in the whole universe and should be prohibited.[31] Gene therapy to manipulate hereditary traits such as intelligence, stupidity, stature, beauty, or ugliness is a serious act as it may unbalance the life of man.[32]

Research on fetal tissue abortuses

Is research performed on fetuses or fetal tissue obtained from abortion permissible? Examples of this are researches connected with the transplantation of fetal tissues into patients suffering from Parkinson's disease.[33] From a Muslim perspective such research and practice are permitted provided the free informed consent of the couple who are the owners of the fetal tissue is obtained.[34]

Fetal ovarian tissue transfer would enable the provision of eggs for use and research in artificial reproduction. Certainly it provides the possibility of creating children who will have a fetus as their genetic mother. The genetic grandparents of these children will be the contemporaries of their birth parents. Though research on fetal ovarian tissue for the improvement of the results of artificial reproduction and other therapeutic purposes is ethically acceptable in the Muslim world, yet its use for the creation of children is unacceptable as these children will not be related to their genetic parents.[35]

Conclusion

Islam is a flexible religion, adaptable to the necessities of life, and what is unethical in one situation may become ethical in another situation or at another time.[36] Islam is a religion which has given great importance

---

[31] Ibid.   [32] Gad El-Hak, 'Islam: A Religion of Ethics'.

[33] *Frame Work for Debate on Ethical Aspects of Scientific Research* (Zoetermeer: The Netherlands Ministry for Education and Science, Sept. 1991); J. Glover, *Ethics of New Reproductive Technologies: The Glover Report to the European Commission* (DeKalb: Northern Illinois University Press, Studies in Biomedical Policy, 1989).

[34] Serour and Omran, *Ethical Guidelines*.   [35] Ibid.

[36] G. I. Serour, 'Islam and the Four Principles', in R. Gillon (ed.), *Principles of Health Care Ethics* (London: J. Wiley & Sons Ltd., forthcoming).

to what are known today as the ethical principles of autonomy, beneficence, non-maleficence, and justice.

No doubt when a person makes his or her reproductive choice, he or
she would like to see that the different ethical principles are observed.
However, because the reproductive choice directly affects human life
and procreation and involves a potential child, a partner, and the society at large, it is not uncommon that different interests conflict with each
other. Also, there is no universal agreement on the meaning of the beginning of human life. Though diversity between physical and religious
definitions may not be vast, yet the cultural definition differs markedly
in different societies with different cultural backgrounds.[37] In Muslim
countries when one makes one's reproductive choice, one has to observe
the ethical guidelines of society, which should not contradict the basic
instructions of Islamic shariah, which is adaptable and accommodative
to new technological development.

[37] G. I. Serour, 'Life: Its Meaning and Sanctity. A Muslim Perspective', in S. Privitera
(ed.), *Bioetica e cultura* (Palermo: Instituto Siciliano di Bioetica, Armando Editore,
1994), ii. 67–81.

12

To Everything there is a Season? Are there Medical Grounds for Refusing Fertility Treatment to Older Women?

FLEUR FISHER AND ANN SOMMERVILLE

Medical Treatment and Social Issues

In October 1994 the High Court upheld the decision of a District Health Authority not to provide publicly funded fertility treatment for a woman aged 36, on the grounds of her age.[1] Although the court case centred primarily on the debate about what constitutes a reasonable use of public resources, it also raised much wider issues about the criteria for women's access to or exclusion from fertility treatment. It is notable that despite featuring prominently in consideration of women's eligibility for fertility treatment, the age criterion has barely received any mention in relation to men's desires for parenthood. Some of the medical justification usually advanced to support this discrepancy is considered in this chapter.

Ironically, concern about the 'appropriate' age for women to become parents arose not only when science provided new opportunities for late motherhood by the use of eggs donated by young women, but also at a time when social trends over several decades had encouraged women to postpone starting a family. Joshi examined links between changes in the birth rate in Britain and the changing economic status of women.[2] She charted the dramatic increase in women's wages *vis-à-vis* male earnings since the 1970s to explain plausibly some causes of delayed childbearing in the UK. As cohorts of women born in Britain after 1945 have progressively delayed motherhood, childbearing rates have fallen

---

[1] *R. v. Sheffield Health Authority, ex parte Seale*, reported in *The Times*, 18 Oct. 1994.

[2] H. Joshi, *The Changing Population of Britain* (Oxford: Blackwell, 1989).

in younger women and risen for the older age brackets.[3] The birth rate for British women in their late thirties and forties has risen steadily over the past decade. The rate for women over 40 years rose by 9 per cent, for example, between 1991 and 1992.

The trend of delayed childbearing has also resulted in a substantial rise in childlessness at each age group among women born since 1945. For many, childlessness or the decision to postpone childbearing is voluntary. In Britain, it partly reflects the accessibility of contraception and abortion. Birth rates are also based on intensely personal choices in response to a host of other social, cultural, and economic forces. Statistics from the Office of Population, Censuses and Surveys[4] show that over a third of women born in 1960 reached the age of 30 without having had a child and this represents the equivalent of twice the proportion for women born in 1945. One of the effects of delayed childbearing in western society is that women discover relatively late that they have problems in conceiving and that they need medical treatment to do so.

Regardless of social trends, female fertility begins naturally to decline from about the age of 25. In many cultures where deliberate birth control can be assumed absent,[5] clear patterns of maternal age and fertility can be traced. Twenty years ago, Bongaarts indicated how natural average fertility rates for women over the age of 40 could be estimated at less than half of fertility rates for women aged 30–40, which in turn were considerably lower than for women in their twenties.[6] Medical science can now circumvent the natural decline in female fertility and facilitate pregnancy after the menopause using donated eggs.

Clinical decisions about the provision of any form of medical treatment depend upon a number of factors, chief among which usually figure considerations of patient need and the likely efficacy of the treatment proposed. When the treatment is aimed at circumventing the consequences of infertility, however, the patient's need and the potential efficacy of the treatment are weighed, explicitly or not, with a range of non-clinical judgements. In Britain, treatment providers are required to

---

[3] 'On the State of the Public Health 1993' (London: HMSO, Sept. 1994).

[4] Ibid.

[5] One of the first analyses of age patterns and natural fertility was made by Louis Henry, who collected data from thirteen societies with varying cultural characteristics. L. Henry, 'Some Data on Natural Fertility', *Eugenics Quarterly*, 8 (1961), 81–96.

[6] J. Bongaarts, 'Why High Birth Rates are so Low', *Population and Development Review*, 1/2 (June 1975), 289–96.

consider such non-medical matters by a statute obliging them to take account of 'the welfare of any child who may be born as a result of the treatment and of any other child who may be affected by the birth'.[7] In fact doctors are often called upon to make judgements about the welfare or 'best interests' of both their patients and people who may exist in the future as a result of fertility treatment. The aptitude of the medical profession to make such social judgements, however, is open to question. Denmark, Austria, France, and Sweden have similar requirements and include the patient's social circumstances amongst the factors doctors are obliged to consider before providing fertility treatment.

In the 1994 High Court case (*Ex parte Seale*), the woman's age was not apparently *one* of the factors relevant to the decision against treating her. It was the *only* factor considered. Six months prior to the hearing, the Health Authority had decided to finance *in vitro* fertilization (IVF) only for women between the ages of 25 and 35 years on the grounds that the treatment was generally less effective in women over 35. (This decision did not address the fact that also excluded are women for whom IVF is likely to be most effective; namely those under 25.)

While medical evidence suggests that IVF may be generally less effective in women over 35,[8] the treatment can be highly effective for particular women beyond that age. General limits necessarily reflect the convenience of statistical computation rather than a sudden Cinderella-like transformation as midnight strikes. Clinical assessment is the means of discovering whether an individual woman could benefit or not from fertility treatment. Reluctance even to consider providing clinical assessment highlights the fact that the major issues under consideration are unrelated to the woman's medical suitability for treatment. The aim of this chapter, however, is not to focus on the moral, social, or legal arguments connected with the provision of fertility treatment for older women but rather to review what few medical data have been published. Separating the strands of hard medical information from the individual moral and social views published by clinicians and others, however, is difficult. Therefore it may be relevant to raise some questions about society's views and prejudices about older women and put these in context with medical data regarding health and fitness in the older post-menopausal population (over 50).

---

[7] s. 13 (5) of the Human Fertilisation and Embryology Act 1990.
[8] Human Fertilisation and Embryology Authority, *Third Annual Report* (1994), 41.

Defining 'Post-menopausal'

A preliminary task must be that of defining 'post-menopausal' since the term is loosely used to cover a wide age range from 45 onwards. For the average woman, menopause occurs around the age of 51 or 52 although some women experience premature menopause when much younger. The age at which the uterus can no longer provide a receptive environment for embryo-implantation is unknown. There is a slowly accelerating decline in natural fertility from the mid-twenties and natural conceptions over the age of 45 are relatively few. UK figures show, for example, that 553 live births were registered for women aged 45 and over in 1992.[9] Here, however, one encounters the primary difficulty in establishing a clear perspective. Mortality, morbidity, conception, and live birth rates are not analysable in an age-specific manner in the post-menopausal population from most of the British statistical tables. Often figures for different generational cohorts of women are analysed in a five-year span up to the age of 30 or 35 but more erratically after the thirty-something watershed. Many of the data collected in Britain about perinatal, neonatal, and maternal deaths, for example, give a detailed breakdown by maternal age up to that of 35 but only aggregated figures for all mothers over the age of 35. Comparing the potential risks for women of 36, 46, and 56 clearly requires more precise data. Attempting to compare data internationally raises even more difficulties and accounts for some of the problems in clarifying the parameters of the debate.

Even so, it is clear that a small minority of women become pregnant naturally in their mid- or even late fifties. Table 1 shows the figures for natural pregnancies resulting in births for women aged over 50 in France between 1980 and 1990 out of an annual overall birth rate of three-quarters of a million. There were between 35 and 39 children born each year to women over 50 and in 1986 the number rose to 51 natural pregnancies. This does not include pregnancies which were terminated or which miscarried and, even though the numbers are minuscule, they serve to show that there is nothing intrinsically 'unnatural' or necessarily dangerous about pregnancy in older women.

Carlo Flamigni, of the Italian Bioethics Committee, talks about women over 40 as 'older women' but draws a distinction between the over-

---

[9] Figures for 1981 to 1992 are published by the Office of Population Censuses and Surveys, General Register Office (Northern Ireland) and General Register Office (Scotland).

TABLE 1. *Natural birth rate for women over 50*

Age	1980	1982	1984	1986	1988	1990
50	22	16	21	23	12	20
51	4	8	8	11	9	6
52	4	8	1	3	7	3
53	4	0	5	8	4	3
54	1	4	4	6	5	5
50–4	35	36	39	51	37	37

Source: J. Belaisch-Allart, 'Le Gynécologue face aux grossesses tardives', *Contraception, fertilité, sexualité*, 22/5 (1994), 307–9.

forties and the over-fifties.[10] Egg donation to the over-fifties should be suspended, he argues, pending analysis of case reports (although this raises the question of how significant numbers of case reports can be obtained unless women undergo the procedure). Another view is that careful case monitoring is needed, together with audit of women of varying ages and with varying medical backgrounds, in order for clinicians to assess effectively the potential risks and benefits.

Much of the clinical debate in Britain has focused on women between 50 and 55, even though this group is not straying beyond the bounds of what is naturally possible (as Table 1 shows). Real controversy arises when fertility treatment for women over 55 or 60 is proposed. The oldest known British woman to have a child as a result of fertility treatment was 59 and in 1994 an Italian, Rosanna Della Corte, reportedly became the oldest mother by giving birth to a son at age 62. For the purposes of this discussion, we concentrate on women between the ages of 50 and 60.

Life Expectancy

Definitions of what constitutes 'old' are relative and depend on how long one expects to live. Life expectancy has changed significantly in developed countries during the twentieth century although the mean age of menopause has remained fairly constant worldwide at 52. Women's life expectancy has not only increased but has increased more than

[10] Carlo Flamigni, 'Egg Donation to Women over 40 Years of Age', *Human Reproduction*, 8/9 (1993), 1343–5.

men's, highlighting what has been called the 'feminization'[11] of later life. In 1906, an average 65-year-old man in Britain expected to live for eleven years,[12] and by 1991 this had crept up to an average of thirteen years. A 65-year-old woman at the beginning of the century could expect to live only one year longer than her male counterpart (i.e. twelve years), but by 1991 her life expectancy at 65 was in the order of seventeen years. This means that a woman undergoing pregnancy at the age of 60 or 62 could reasonably expect to see her child grow into adulthood, all other factors being equal. This may mean that older women have a *better* claim than that of older men to consider parenthood, since in the natural order of things the women will live longer than their male contemporaries.

A lifespan of sufficient length to raise children to adulthood is not the only consideration, however. Although a healthy 60-year-old woman in the UK can expect to survive for an average of twenty-three years, the presumption of continuing health may be more tenuous. Cardiovascular disease and strokes, relatively rare before the age of 50, are prevalent thereafter, forming the third most common cause of all deaths in Britain. Post-menopausally, the risks for women increase and approach those for men; prediction of risk, however, is partly related to lifestyle and genetic factors so that better understanding of these will increasingly help people to gauge the risks more accurately.

Hospital admission statistics show that, overall, many more men than women in the 65–74 age group require hospital treatment.[13] In terms of admission for mental disorder, however, after the age of 45 the statistics for women are significantly higher than for men, and in the 65–74 age range over 30 per cent more women than men are hospitalized for mental disorder. For some women, mental disorder is due to Alzheimer's disease. The recent French development of a 90 per cent accurate genetic test of an individual's potential to succumb to Alzheimer's disease by 65 will clarify the risks. In Britain, between 2 and 3 per cent of the population (about 1 million people) are thought to carry this gene. As science provides new methods for detecting or diminishing the likelihood of certain conditions, individuals who want to embark on projects such as parenthood can do so from a more secure knowledge base.

---

[11] This term is used by P. Coleman, J. Bond, and S. Peace in 'Ageing in the Twentieth Century', in their book *Ageing in Society* (London: Sage, 1993).

[12] S. Arber and J. Ginn, *Gender and Later Life* (London: Sage, 1991).

[13] Hospital Episode Statistics 1989–90 taken from *Health and Personal Social Services Statistics for England* (London: HMSO, 1993).

Although generalizations about health or life expectancy do not necessarily help predict individual circumstances, some health analysts see the problems of disease and dependency being increasingly confined to those aged over 80. Fries, for example, has predicted 'that the average period of diminished physical vigour will decrease, that chronic disease will occupy a smaller proportion of the typical lifespan, and that the need for medical care in later life will decrease'.[14] Some subsequent studies support this view that chronic illness and dependency is concentrated in the population over 85 years old. As they age, however, people suffer not only from specific or chronic age-related disease but also from combinations of relatively minor conditions. The older mother, therefore, must bear in mind that she may become physically dependent at a time when her child is still an adolescent or young adult. The significance of this for the child depends partly upon the financial and other support provisions in place. Where extended families or stable systems of paid carers bear part of the parenting role, they may compensate for the potential physical limitations of older parents.

Attitudes to Infertility

Although British society's attitude to the infertile has changed significantly in recent years, permitting much more openness and debate about the subject, residual stigma attached to infertility has perpetuated some of the traditional secrecy. In 1990, for example, legislation passed in the UK enforced secrecy by forbidding doctors who were providing fertility treatments from disclosing to other doctors any information about their patients.[15] The prohibition applied even if the patient consented. To disclose information direct to the patient's own general practitioner was a criminal offence until the law was amended in 1992. Hostility towards the notion of providing fertility treatment for post-menopausal women may partly be an expression of the societal reservations often felt in regard to new developments. Or, some of the past negativity and secrecy associated with the infertile state may still be implicit in society's attitude to women who are sterile because of their age.

Women's infertility has never been protected from scrutiny in the same way as men's. Dewar, for example, considers the silence surrounding

[14] J. F. Fries, 'Aging, Natural Death and the Compression of Morbidity', *New England Journal of Medicine*, 303 (1980), 130–5.
[15] Human Fertilisation and Embryology Act 1990.

donor insemination as reflective of 'men's reluctance to face the consequences of their own infertility, possibly because our culture attaches
much significance to the association between fertility and power'.[16]
He goes on to say that donor insemination 'both preserves the shame-
ful secret of the male while simultaneously enhancing women's ability
to do without men in the reproductive process in all but the most basic
biological sense'. Giving reproductive power and choice to women without necessarily involving male partners has always been associated with
controversy, especially so when the choices are exercised in a manner
which is seen as 'contrary to nature' because the woman is a lesbian or
is post-menopausal.

Given the power and importance associated with reproductive ability,
sterility inevitably bears complementary associations of powerlessness
and marginalization, even though public attitudes are gradually changing. When a particular aspect of life, such as reproductive ability, is valued by a large segment of society, it takes considerable courage for
an individual to repudiate it openly. Maclean, for example, has drawn
attention to the way in which childless women feel pressurized by social
attitudes to undergo possibly painful and dangerous medical treatments
in order to conform to a perceived reproductive norm.[17] Greer too has
written at length about historical attitudes to post-menopausal women,
whom she sees stereotyped as shadowy grey or invisible figures traditionally allocated a marginal role outside the creative and productive mainstream of society.[18] In fact, women over the age of 50 form 17
per cent of the British population and are therefore one of the largest
population groups, but art, literature, product advertising, and medical
research frequently ignore them. This is a phenomenon which might
be seen as perpetuating the apparently unexceptional viewpoint of an
eighteenth-century male writer who questioned the right of women
over 40 even to exist in the world.[19]

The notion of a woman embarking on pregnancy at the age of 50
or older is criticized for diverse reasons. Traditionalists see it as an
unacceptable tampering with the natural order and fear that it represents disruption to the values which bind society. Yet the whole point
of medicine and research is to improve, so to speak, on nature and the

[16] John Dewar, 'Fathers in Law? The Case of AID', in R. Lee and D. Morgan (eds.),
Birthrights (London: Routledge, 1989).
[17] Unpublished paper by Professor Sheila Maclean given at London Science Museum,
spring 1995.
[18] Germaine Greer, *The Change* (Harmondsworth: Penguin, 1992), 24.
[19] Quoted by Greer, ibid.

natural order. The clinicians who treat older women claim they are simply evening the unfair divergence between the sexes in giving older women the same opportunity to be parents as older men already have. Historically, the purpose of medicine has been perceived as prolonging life and alleviating suffering. Its potential for enhancing the lives of individuals is relatively recent and may not be entirely accepted by society which, for example, refuses to finance most treatment of non-life-threatening conditions. The use of medicine to satisfy individual desires and aspirations is seen by many as inappropriate, particularly so when such procedures benefit only a small élite. Post-menopausal pregnancy has been portrayed by some of the media as the epitome of female egoism and the 'consumerization' of children: feminism and the cult of the individual having encouraged women to elevate excessively the status of their desires. Like men, women lay claim to have interesting lives and careers first and still not miss out on having children later. Some liberal feminists also see late pregnancy as outrageous. 'Pregnancy is barbaric',[20] declared Shulamith Firestone, looking forward to the time when science would liberate women of all ages from the oppressive task of reproducing the species. The use of reproductive technology in this context is seen by some as a euphemism for experimentation on women by the predominantly male scientific community.[21]

Post-menopausal pregnancy seems to have few supporters. Yet when premature menopause occurs in women in their twenties or thirties, broad public and medical consensus supports the provision of fertility treatment to these women. They can be seen as representing an agreed norm of those who should be assessed for treatment. When there is a reluctance to provide clinical assessment of older women, the question must be asked; 'to what degree is the outcome of fertility treatment in older women significantly different from that in these younger post-menopausal subjects?' The very small population of older women seeking fertility treatment, however, makes comparison difficult.

Assessment for Treatment

Women seeking fertility treatment undergo screening and assessment to ascertain the efficacy and potential harm of the procedures. To some

---

[20] Shulamith Firestone, *The Dialectic of Sex* (London: Bantam Books, 1970).
[21] See, for example, Patricia Spallone, *Beyond Conception: The New Politics of Reproduction* (Granby, Mass.: Bergin & Garvey, 1989).

extent, it can be argued that older women are such unusual candidates for fertility treatment that the screening and assessment they currently receive vastly exceeds that provided for younger women and probably means that their pregnancies are more carefully monitored than others where the risks are less identifiable. The British Medical Association's view is that older, post-menopausal women should not be excluded from assessment and that their own health risks and those of any potential children should be discussed with them. The BMA rejects the notion of establishing hard and fast rules on eligibility for fertility treatment as part of a general refusal to classify individuals into groups. The Association's view is that a woman should not automatically be denied access to fertility treatment simply on the grounds of status, such as her marital status or her age. Judgements about whether or not a woman should be offered fertility treatment should, the Association believes, be based on a full assessment of the woman's particular clinical situation and all other relevant factors which might include age. As with any patients, treatment decisions should be made on a case-by-case basis and the fact of providing assessment is no guarantee of treatment.

The medical assessment for egg donation to older women might arguably include all of the following:

- assessment of age-related disease in the woman;
- screening for genetic predisposition to any major disorder;
- consideration of general maternal mortality risks;
- assessment of implantation procedure on the older women;
- assessment of the impact of singleton pregnancy on the mother's health;
- assessment of the impact of multiple pregnancy on her health;
- assessment of the physical or psychological impact of miscarriage;
- effect of labour or Caesarean section on the mother;
- medical prognosis for the child;
- psychological prognosis for the child;
- assessment of demands of child rearing on the mother's health.

As yet the clinical evidence concerning assessment of most of these factors is scanty or speculative. The limited data which exist can only be derived from a small number of centres willing to offer assessment and treatment to older women. An obvious disadvantage, therefore, is that the clinicians providing and analysing the data are those who already support the procedure.

The only assessment required by statute concerns the welfare of the child. In 1990, parliamentary discussion of this requirement drew attention to the fact that:

'Welfare' is an all-encompassing word. It includes material welfare, both in the sense of adequacy of resources to provide a pleasant home and a comfortable standard of living and in the sense of an adequacy of care to ensure that good health and due personal pride are maintained. However, while material considerations have their place, they are secondary matters. More important are the stability and the security, the loving and understanding care, the warm and compassionate relationships, that are the essential for the full development of the child's own character, personality and talents.[22]

Referring to this definition, Lord Mackay drew attention to the need of parents of any age to think about appointing a guardian for the child in the event of their death. In general, however, matters such as the psychological welfare of the child can only be the subject of speculation. The published conclusions of child psychologists seem to be that such psychological effects cannot be predicted but the quality of the parent–child relationship may outweigh other factors.[23] The opinions and cultural images perpetuated by the society around it may, however, affect the child and wider acceptance by society of older parents might arguably reduce the problem. It seems clear that the uteruses of older women after a natural menopause can be maintained in a receptive state for embryo implantation way beyond the ovaries' ability to provide gametes or the hormonal sustenance to support a pregnancy, by using steroid hormone replacement therapy. The main medical barriers to pregnancy using egg donation are the physical and psychological health of potential recipients and much of the information necessary to determine these matters is currently merely speculative. The demands of child rearing on parental health are also individual and unquantifiable. Many women over 60 are caring, with little support, for even older parents with multiple problems, such as incontinence and dementia. Such demands take a toll on carers which is arguably as great as or greater than caring for a child. More predictable is consideration of general maternal mortality risks.

---

[22] House of Lords, Official Report, 6 Mar. 1990, col. 1097. This and other aspects of the concept of welfarism are discussed in *Blackstone's Guide to the Human Fertilisation and Embryology Act 1990*, ed. D. Morgan and R. G. Lee (London: 1991), 141–8.

[23] See, for example, F. Molenat, 'Réflexions du pédo-psychiatre à propos des grossesses chez les couples âgés', *Contraception, fertilité, sexualité*, 22/5 (1994), 312–13.

TABLE 2. *Maternal mortality by age in France*

Age	Deaths per 100,000 births	
	1980–1985	1986–1990
15–9	13.4	6.9
20–4	8.9	5.4
25–9	10.3	6.1
30–4	17.9	13.6
35–9	35.6	20.9
40 and over	74.0	37.9

Source: Belaisch-Allart, 'Le Gynécologue face aux grossesses tardives'.

Table 2 shows maternal mortality figures in France for the same period as the birth statistics shown in Table 1. Separate figures for maternal mortality in women over 50 are not available. A 1991 report estimated that annually there are about 40 births, 45 terminations, and 25 cases of spontaneous miscarriage in women over 50 in France.[24] The table does not distinguish between natural and IVF pregnancies. Risks associated with the vascular system (mainly risks of pregnancy-induced hypertension) increase after 50. This can result in cardiovascular problems or poor fetal nutrition and failure to thrive.

There are limited data about the impact of the implantation procedure. Since donated eggs are used, women do not require the superovulatory drugs which younger women undergoing fertility treatments need. Egg or embryo replacement is a simple and routine procedure, accompanied by the administration of oestradiol valerate and progesterone to encourage implantation. Edwards has drawn attention to the fact that the menopause may confer an advantage in achieving implantation.[25] He reports a pregnancy rate of 25 per cent in acyclic women over 40 years of age compared with 10 per cent or less for cyclic women. Other commentators too have drawn attention to the conclusions of Abdalla's 1993 study showing that, in women over the age of 40 undergoing IVF, embryo transfer, or gamete intra-Fallopian transfer, the pregnancy rate and live birth rate are significantly higher and the miscarriage rate lower

[24] Toulemon, *Rapports sur la situation démographique de la France*, quoted by Belaisch-Allart, 'Le Gynécologue'.

[25] Edwards *et al.*, 'High Fecundity of Amenorrhoeic Women in Embryo-Transfer Programmes', *Lancet*, 338 (1991), 292–4.

than for younger women.[26] In some cases, this may be a misunderstanding of Abdalla's conclusion, which is that the over forties using donated oocytes do better in comparison with other women who are using their own oocytes. Abdalla's study appears to confirm that the age-related decline in fecundity is due to the age of the oocytes rather than the age of the uterus. The higher implantation rate in women using donor eggs means that there is an increased risk of multiple pregnancy with its attendant problems. Comparisons of such studies as Abdalla's and Edwards's also return us to the problem mentioned earlier of how 'post-menopausal' is defined. In Edwards's study—and others he quoted later to support fertility treatment of post-menopausal women—we are only told that the women are 'over 40', and outcomes may be quite different for women of 60.

For women over 40, the main health risks in pregnancy are hypertension, pre-eclampsia, gestational diabetes, placenta previa, uterine fetal distress, and use of Caesarean section. Bellaisch-Allart, like other commentators, presumes it highly likely that pregnancies in the over fifties cause greater obstetric complications and higher maternal mortality rates but notes the lack of supporting data for that conclusion.[27]

Edwards has collected data on almost 200 post-menopausal pregnancies arranged in four clinics in three European countries—thought to be Italy, Belgium, and the UK. His study is as yet unpublished. In March 1994, *Le Monde* carried an article on the findings and, although incomplete, this has provided some material for discussion. According to the information reported, the average maternal age was 49 with a range of 45 to 63. Their partners' mean age was 46, with an age variation ranging from 33 to 80 years of age. (The fact that fathers may have comparatively little life expectancy was not apparently a prohibitive factor). The oocyte donors were all under 35. Two clinics out of four reported increased maternal morbidity in the post-menopausal group but the numbers were insufficient to be significant. Most women received three embryos and a total of 439 embryos were implanted. Pregnancy was achieved in 191 women, producing 174 births.

In California, Sauer concluded that there were no serious complications.[28] In 1993, his study involved women aged 50–9 and included eight

[26] H. I. Abdalla *et al.*, 'Age, Pregnancy and Miscarriage: Uterine versus Ovarian Factors', *Human Reproduction*, 8/9 (1993), 1512–17.

[27] Belaisch-Allart, 'Le Gynécologue'.

[28] M. V. Sauer *et al.*, 'Pregnancy after Age 50: Application of Oocyte Donation to Women after Natural Menopause', *Lancet*, 341/8841 (Feb. 1993), 321–3.

TABLE 3. *IVF multiple clinical pregnancy and embryo transfer* (for all centres, including frozen embryo transfers)

Embryos transferred	No. of transfers	Singleton	Twin	Triplet
One	1,869	154	3	1
Two	4,279	687	193	1
Three	8,067	1,268	513	116
Totals	14,215	2,109	709	118

Source: Human Fertilisation and Embryology Authority, *Third Annual Report* (1994), 53.

TABLE 4. *IVF clinical pregnancy and multiple clinical pregnancy rates* (for all centres, including frozen embryo transfers)

Embryos transferred	Clinical pregnancy rates (%)	Multiple clinical pregnancy rates (%)
One	8.5	2.5
Two	20.6	22.0
Three	23.5	33.2

Source: Human Fertilisation and Embryology Authority, *Third Annual Report* (1994).

pregnancies which were ongoing at time of publication, two Caesareans due to pre-eclampsia, and three births. Antinori reporting the treatment of eleven women aged between 50 and 60, listed four pregnancies, one placenta previa in which the fetus was delivered and died at 29 weeks, and three births at term.[29] In a further thirty-two women aged 45–9, there were twelve pregnancies, two miscarriages, a case of toxemia leading to death of the fetus, and nine births at term.

A multiple pregnancy increases the health risks for women of any age and their newborn children. In Britain, there has been an increase in the rate of multiple births by just over a quarter in the last decade.[30] The increase is believed to be due to the use of superovulatory drugs in fertility treatment. The number of embryos transferred in IVF treatment also affects the multiple birth rate. Tables 3 and 4 show the numbers for the UK in 1992 and the rates of multiple pregnancy for the same year.

[29] S. Antinori *et al.*, 'Oocyte Donation in Menopausal Women', *Human Reproduction*, 8/9 (1993), 1487–90.

[30] From 0.98% in 1980 to 1.25% in 1992 (OPCS).

TABLE 5. *IVF success rates by women's age using own eggs* (all centres)

Age	Treatment cycles	Clinical pregnancy rates per treatment cycle (%)	Live birth rates per treatment cycle (%)
Under 25	178	16.9	9.6
25–9	2,416	22.1	16.5
30–4	6,806	19.0	14.6
35–9	6,039	15.2	11.4
40–4	2,065	8.2	4.5
45 and over	174	3.4	1.7

Source: Human Fertilisation and Embryology Authority, *Third Annual Report* (1994), 41.

In Britain, doctors are prohibited from transferring more than three embryos. For older women, in particular, there can be severe health risks associated with multiple births. In some of the European clinics studied by Edwards, up to five embryos have been implanted in some post-menopausal women. This carries additional risks of selective reduction of fetuses.

Age is an important factor in the outcome of treatment when women use their own contemporaneous eggs. Statistics published by the Human Fertilisation and Embryology Authority (HFEA) indicate that, using their own eggs, women's chances of pregnancy resulting in a live birth decrease with age, except for women under 25.

Age is less significant for pregnancy in women receiving donor eggs (or those who when young stored fertilized eggs for later use). At present, it is not possible to fertilize successfully eggs which have previously been frozen but embryos may be preserved in this way. In the UK, however, such frozen material is subject to statutory storage periods and so women would be unable to store them indefinitely. Gametes can legally be stored for up to ten years and embryos for five although these limits could be extended by regulations. Once the statutory storage period has elapsed, including any additional period agreed by new regulations, the stored material must be allowed to perish.

Between 1991 and 1994, the HFEA recorded twenty-five cases of women aged 50 and over receiving a total of forty-two treatment cycles.[31] Eight pregnancies resulted in five births in this group. The HFEA's Code

[31] Unpublished data from the Human Fertilisation and Embryology Authority.

TABLE 6. *IVF success rates by women's age using donor eggs* (all centres)

Age	Treatment cycles	Clinical pregnancy rates per treatment cycle (%)	Live birth rates per treatment cycle (%)
Under 25	8	37.5	37.5
25–9	55	16.4	7.3
30–4	134	27.6	20.9
35–9	128	25.8	24.2
40–4	142	16.9	12.7
45 and over	79	25.3	17.7

Source: Human Fertilisation and Embryology Authority, *Third Annual Report* (1994).

of Practice obliges centres to pay attention to the age and medical history of the prospective parents and their ability to meet the child's needs. No upper age limit for access to treatment is set for either men or women but the HFEA has stated that it would be 'concerned if any centre were repeatedly treating older women and would require such a centre to justify this practice in terms of the welfare of the child'.[32]

Studies such as that of Abdalla indicate that the age of the oocyte donor is directly related to the miscarriage rate but the age of the recipient is not.[33] The miscarriage rate, therefore, seems to be approximately the same for women pre- and post-menopause if donated oocytes from young women are used.

Conclusion

In Britain, no statutory age limit is imposed on fertility treatment for men or women. France has banned post-menopausal pregnancies by the bioethics law of 29 July 1994, which restricts fertility treatment to cohabiting, heterosexual couples of reproductive age. Belgium and Holland have no regulations. The British woman who gave birth to twins at the age of 60 had received treatment in Italy, following refusal of her case by a British ethics committee. Given the patchwork of different regulations and requirements, it is foreseeable that there will be a transborder flow of older women seeking fertility treatment as part of

[32] Human Fertilisation and Embryology Authority, *Third Annual Report* (1994), 12.
[33] Abdalla *et al.*, 'Age, Pregnancy and Miscarriage'.

so-called 'procreative tourism'. In December 1993 the Health Minister, Virginia Bottomley, called for an international code of ethics governing fertility treatment to 'establish ethical controls over some of the dramatic achievements in modern medicine'.[34] Ethical debate, however, should be accompanied by factual information about the potential risks and benefits of the procedures.

At present, effective use of the data is hampered not only by insufficient case reports but also by the fact of the non-comparability of the terms and figures available. When post-menopausal pregnancies are reported, the ages of the women vary between 40 and 60 and almost all the case reports and analysis come from facilities which demonstrate enthusiasm for the procedure. In order to obtain clinically useful information, there needs to be objective assessment of centrally collected data based on clearly defined criteria. No such information is currently available.

Although the data are scanty, there are likely to be additional health risks for some older women who wish to procreate. Some of the health risks will be increasingly predictable through genetic and other screening measures, but for patients of any age there will always be the possibility of unforeseen and unforeseeable risks and tragedies. Part of medicine's role is to inform the individual and society about the known and potential hazards and to ensure the existence of a framework to monitor the interests of the children created by medical intervention. When, however, medical decisions include considerations about eligibility for treatment or fitness for parenthood, there should be greater public debate about society's expectations. If it is widely accepted that the age criterion is valid for excluding women but not men from parenthood because, for example, the roles of the sexes in child rearing are significantly different, this too should be subject to public scrutiny and debate. It is interesting that Edwards's research shows that somewhere in Europe an 80-year-old man is still intent on becoming a father, and this does not seem to be a controversial issue—whereas a 55- or 60-year-old mother is.

Finally, it may be of note that such debate as has occurred about extending the scope of reproductive choice has taken place against the backdrop of the very different United Nations' discussion about population and reproductive health. The 1994 UN Cairo conference focused international concern all too briefly on the unacceptable global levels

---

[34] *Guardian*, 28 Dec. 1993. p. 2.

of female morbidity and mortality arising from poor access to acceptable methods of contraception. Maternal mortality through unsafe or excessive childbearing is one of the major problems to confront modern medicine and often has deleterious effects for the wider society as well as the children left orphaned. It provides a reminder that the primary need for the majority of the world's women is to limit not extend their reproductive ability.

13

The Post-menopause: Playground for Reproductive Technology? Some Ethical Reflections

GUIDO DE WERT

Introduction

Until recently, most, if not all, clinics for *in vitro* fertilization used some sort of age limit with regard to their female patients. Women over 40 years of age were only seldom treated. This policy was accepted not because all gynaecologists agreed with Plato—who stated that women are allowed to produce children for society up until they are 40—but because of the poor success rate of IVF in older women. Every stage in the IVF process has been shown to be less effective when the source of the egg is an older woman. A study in the Netherlands, for example, showed that the effectiveness of IVF dropped by one-third for women aged 35 to 40 and by two-thirds for women over the age of 40.[1] This gloomy picture, however, no longer applies: using eggs donated by young women, several clinics report fairly good 'take baby home' rates in treating older, even post-menopausal, women. It appears that egg donation makes pregnancy possible in virtually any woman with a uterus.

Egg donation in (post-)menopausal women is a hot topic in the popular media and in medical ethics. It is clear that there is no consensus among the European nations. According to the French Health Minister (Philippe Douste-Blazy) 'it is absolutely shocking to think that when a baby is 18 years old, his mother will be 80'. Apparently, most French politicians agree, or are even more critical: France recently adopted a law forbidding post-menopausal pregnancies.[2]

---

[1] G. Haan, 'Effects and Costs of In-Vitro Fertilization: Again, Let's be Honest', *International Journal of Technology Assessment in Health Care*, 7 (1991), 587.

[2] J.-Y. Nau, 'Bioethics Laws in France', *Lancet*, 344 (1994), 48.

The British Human Fertilisation and Embryology Authority is more liberal. The Authority stated that it is neither necessary nor advisable to fix an upper age limit for the treatment of infertility. Each case should be considered individually. The Authority would, however, be concerned if a centre were repeatedly treating older women, and would require such a centre to justify this practice in terms of the welfare of the child.[3]

In the Netherlands there is an ongoing debate. The Dutch Health Council has recently been asked for advice on, amongst others, post-menopausal pregnancies. It is expected that the Ethics Committee of the Royal Dutch Medical Association will publish guidelines soon. (In the meantime, Dutch practice concerning the access to oocyte donation is quite restrictive. Most clinics still do not treat women aged 41 and above.) Some Italian centres were, as we all know, among the first clinics offering egg donation to older women.

In Germany and Norway the post-menopausal pregnancy is a non-issue. These countries have, indeed, completely prohibited egg donation. This ban will, however, no longer apply to post-menopausal pregnancies when, in the future, there will be alternative ways to assist older women in reproducing, ways which would make the use of *donor* eggs redundant. One option would be the cryopreservation of embryos or oocytes for use at a later date. It might even be possible to develop drugs which enable ovulation (i.e. delay menopause) well into the seventies.

The nations at the other side of the Atlantic ocean show a similar dissensus. Many American clinics offer egg donation to older women, rejecting any upper age limit.[4] The Canadians, however, seem willing to adopt more restrictive regulations: indeed, the Royal Commission on New Reproductive Technologies recommended that 'women who have experienced menopause at the usual age should not be candidates to receive donated eggs'.[5]

Proponents of the 'pregnancy after the menopause' state that the desire to have children is an innate human characteristic and that its fulfilment brings the parents great joy, irrespective of their age—'a child is a joy at any age'. The critics object to this 'reproductive revolution' for very diverse reasons. What, then, are the major moral objections—and are they convincing?

---

[3] Human Fertilisation and Embryology Authority, *Third Annual Report* (1994), 12.

[4] M. V. Sauer and R. J. Paulson, 'Understanding the Current Status of Oocyte Donation in the United States: What's Really Going On Out There?', *Fertility and Sterility*, 58 (1992), 16–18.

[5] Royal Commission on New Reproductive Technologies, *Proceed with Care* (Ottawa: Minister of Government Services Canada, 1993), i. 590.

It is useful to make a distinction between on the one hand 'direct' or non-consequentialist objections—which focus upon the act of creating a post-menopausal pregnancy—and on the other hand consequentialist objections, which involve predictions about the medical, social, and psychological consequences of the post-menopausal pregnancy.

Weighing the Arguments

Direct objections

'It is unnatural'

Some people consider reproductive technologies to be morally wrong because they are 'unnatural'. The argument that 'x is wrong because it is unnatural' can, as Warren eloquently stated, only succeed if there is an interpretation of the term 'unnatural' which enables us both to distinguish clearly between natural and unnatural actions, and to understand what there is about the latter which is morally objectionable.[6] It is doubtful whether there are any such interpretations which are convincing or even plausible. Of course, many ways of assisted reproduction are unnatural in the sense that they would not occur spontaneously, prior to the development of sophisticated technologies. We cannot object to reproductive technologies on this basis unless we wish to advocate a return to a simple gathering-and-hunting lifestyle. Furthermore, it is apparent that proponents of 'the argument from nature' are highly selective in their moral reasoning. It is, for example, well established that many fetuses with chromosome abnormalities are aborted spontaneously—a form of natural selection. There is also evidence that multiple pregnancies are often spontaneously reduced—think of the 'vanishing twin'. These natural phenomena as such, however, do not morally justify interventions such as a selective abortion or a 'multifetal pregnancy reduction'—and I have never heard proponents of 'the argument from nature' defending the opposite.

With regard to the post-menopausal pregnancy many critics state that it is natural for older women to become infertile and that it is, therefore, unacceptable to manipulate this biological age limit. But let us take the example of baldness. It is natural for older men to become bald, but I doubt as to whether one can plausibly argue that a hair transplant is an unjustifiable invasion of older men's biological nature. Of course,

---

[6] M. A. Warren, *Gendercide: The Implications of Sex Selection* (Totowa, NJ, Rowman & Allanheld, 1985), 78–9.

one may point to a morally relevant difference between these two inter-ventions: opting for a hair transplant is a 'self-regarding' act, while a post-menopausal pregnancy is not—it is 'other-regarding' in the sense that it may have harmful consequences for the prospective child. Seen in this way, however, it is not biological nature *per se* which imposes moral restraints on our actions, but the interests of those persons who are (or may be) implicated in our interventions in biological nature.

I suspect that the argument from nature, if used to condemn post-menopausal pregnancies, is often symptomatic of an uneasiness about the risks of these pregnancies, especially the risks for the prospective child. In that case, however, this apparent direct objection is a disguised consequentialist objection.

'There is no medical indication. IVF should only be used for the treatment of pathological infertility'

Women with *premature* ovarian failure are generally accepted as can-didates to receive donated eggs. These women are infertile at a time of life when the ability to become pregnant is normal—their infertility is pathological. The Canadian Royal Commission on New Reproductive Technologies criticizes, however, the use of egg donation to expand the human reproductive lifespan, because it is normal for older women to be infertile—'there is no medical indication for the practice'.[7] In other words: physicians like Sauer and Antinori, who have been directly involved in treating older, post-menopausal women, are not correcting a disease or a malfunctioning organ system, but are reversing part of the *normal* ageing process.

This criticism raises complex questions, such as: what are the goals of medicine? And what is the task of physicians? The objection, how-ever, mistakenly suggests that the domains of medicine and health care have always been surrounded by clear, fixed borders. In fact, there are already widely accepted medical solutions for non-medical problems. Think of sterilizations for the purpose of family planning. And many infertility clinics offer artificial insemination with donor sperm to single women and lesbian couples, even though these women do not suffer from pathological infertility, and, strictly speaking, there is no medical indica-tion. The objections that some people have to these artificial insemina-tions mainly concern the risks for the well-being of the future child—again: a consequentialist objection.

---

[7] Royal Commission on New Reproductive Technologies, *Proceed with Care.*

Although moving the borders of health care raises difficult questions, I doubt whether the absence of a strict medical indication as such is a strong moral objection to offering egg donation to post-menopausal women.

Consequentialist objections

'It is an unjust use of scarce medical resources'

This objection has several versions. Some people criticize any public funding of IVF, because IVF is expensive and they consider infertility to be a somewhat trivial concern. As a consequence, they criticize any public funding of egg donation to post-menopausal women. The second version holds that public funding for traditional IVF treatment, including egg donation to women who suffer from premature ovarian failure, is acceptable, while public funding for creating pregnancies after the 'normal' menopause is not.

In fact, both versions of this objection do not concern this infertility treatment as such: after all, both versions become much weaker when women seeking to have a child by IVF after normal menopause will themselves pay for the treatment.

I will not tackle the problem as to whether traditional IVF, including egg donation, should be (entirely or at least partially) publicly funded from a moral point of view, whether IVF (and similar techniques of assisted reproduction) should be included within the notion of 'an adequate level of health care' that should be provided to every citizen. Let me, for the sake of argument, assume that it should—can we, then, plausibly hold that such public funding should not apply to older, post-menopausal, women? Those who answer this question in the affirmative support the second version of the current objection. This version can only be considered convincing if at least one of the following conditions is being met:

1. it is possible to show that creating a post-menopausal pregnancy is morally wrong (after all, public funding for medical interventions which are morally wrong is highly problematic);
2. it is possible to show that creating a post-menopausal pregnancy, although not necessarily morally wrong, differs in a morally relevant way from traditional IVF.

Some critics might argue that the suffering of older women from their infertility is 'self-inflicted', because they have deliberately postponed their first pregnancy, and that public funding should therefore be withheld. This argument is problematic for several reasons. First, many postmenopausal women opting for donor oocytes have always been infertile. Other post-menopausal women were fertile when younger, but have only recently met a (suitable) partner. In these cases, a prior 'equal opportunity' simply did not exist. Even if some post-menopausal women have deliberately decided to postpone their first attempts to become pregnant, and now discover that they have become infertile, their 'self-inflicted harm' is not a morally valid reason for withholding funding. Such policy would be difficult to reconcile with the public funding of all kinds of treatments for patients with other sorts of 'self-inflicted' harms (skiers with broken legs, etc.).

As I have just said, both versions of the current objection become much weaker when the older woman is herself paying for the infertility treatment. This is not to say that this objection loses its force entirely: after all, there does remain the problem of the higher costs involved in pregnancies at risk, pregnancies which invariably entail a greater number of tests, hospital admissions, perinatal interventions, and admissions to neonatal intensive care units. These 'secondary' costs (which would probably not be paid by the post-menopausal women herself) do not, of course, prove that creating post-menopausal pregnancies implies an unjust use of scarce financial resources. These secondary costs do, however, remain a point of concern. Such financial concerns constitute a good reason—not the only reason! (see below)—to strive for minimizing the risk of medical complications in post-menopausal pregnancies.

'It would increase the shortage of donor eggs'

This objection too has two versions. Both are based on questionable empirical and moral assumptions. The first version reads as follows: 'The large number of potential recipients in the older age group will be difficult to supply with donated eggs because of the difficulty of recruiting sufficient donors. The growing demand for donor eggs, combined with a stable-but-insufficient supply, will reduce the chances of younger infertile patients to receive donated eggs—which is unfair.' The empirical underpinnings of this objection may soon be outdated, given the research aimed at developing new ways to get donated eggs. The so-called *in vitro maturation* of unfertilized eggs will probably deliver huge amounts of donated eggs for infertility treatment and research.[8] Furthermore, this objection would

---

[8] 'Debate: In-Vitro Growth of Oocytes', *Human Reproduction*, 9 (1994), 969–76.

no longer apply if post-menopausal women provided their own egg donors selected among fertile friends and relatives. This strategy is already being promoted by many infertility clinics offering IVF with donated eggs.[9] The moral assumptions behind this objection are questionable too: why should a younger woman of 38 get a higher place on the waiting list for donated eggs than an older, post-menopausal women of 47? Is it because the older woman has had opportunities to become pregnant earlier in her life, and has deliberately decided not to use her 'equal opportunities'? Such reasoning is problematic, amongst other things, because in many cases such 'equal opportunities' simply did not exist.

A second version of the objection concerning the increasing scarcity of donated eggs is defended by Joffe:

The egg donor will probably expect the recipient to be of normal childbearing age. If this assumption were challenged, an oocyte donor might feel anxious about the care of the child she will help to create, and also about the increased chance that her genetic child will want to trace her, if that child's legal mother died or became disabled through old age when the child was still of dependent age. If older post-menopausal women qualify for ART (assisted reproductive technology), the result of these concerns might be that oocyte donors would be even less forthcoming, and this would indirectly damage the chances of young infertile women to have children.[10]

I doubt whether this is a plausible objection to creating post-menopausal pregnancies. After all, the fear that the pool of potential egg donors might decrease can be eliminated by recognizing the right of egg donors to give a specific consent indicating whether or not they agree to using their eggs for treating post-menopausal women.

Post-menopausal women applying for reproductive medical assistance could circumvent both versions of the current objection by 'adopting' excess (cryopreserved) embryos. This might be a real alternative for a subset of older infertile couples, given the increasing number of banked frozen embryos, many of which will be unwanted by infertile couples concluding their treatment. It remains to be seen whether 'pro-life' critics of the post-menopausal pregnancy could accept such 'life-saving' prenatal adoptions.

---

[9] R. Frydman, 'A Protocol for Satisfying the Ethical Issues Raised by Oocyte Donation: The Free, Anonymous, and Fertile Donors', *Fertility and Sterility*, 53 (1990), 666–72.

[10] T. Joffe, 'Life Begins at Sixty: Babies for the Older Woman', *Bulletin of Medical Ethics* (May 1994), 19–24.

228   *Guido de Wert*

'It is too dangerous for the mother'

An important concern is the potential risk to the older pregnant woman. Pregnancy is a major stress on women's organ systems. Obstetric complications and maternal morbidity and mortality increase with maternal age. Some critics condemn post-menopausal pregnancies because of these increasing risks. A Dutch politician even recommended a ban.

I have the impression that some proponents of post-menopausal pregnancies consider the maternal risks to be morally irrelevant: 'It is for the individual woman to decide what risks she is willing to take. The gynaecologist has the duty to inform the post-menopausal woman about the risks of pregnancy. When she considers them to be acceptable, the physician should respect her autonomy and give access to treatment.' This type of anti-paternalism is, in my view, not acceptable. The gynaecologist has his own professional responsibility to avoid excessive maternal risks. I assume that most people would refute the anti-paternalistic argument if confronted with cases involving extreme risks for the patient. A good example is the so-called '(artificial) induction of abdominal pregnancy'.[11] Such treatment has, as far as we know, not yet been attempted, but, theoretically, it should now be feasible as a result of knowledge obtained from IVF technology. For women without a uterus, but with normally functioning ovaries, eggs could be collected from the ovaries and fertilized *in vitro*. One of the embryos could then be implanted into the peritoneal cavity. The same technique could be used in women without a uterus who also lack ovaries, but in these cases donor eggs would be required. Theoretically, if the embryo is implanted in the omentum, it can be expected to develop as an abdominal pregnancy. An induction of abdominal pregnancy might also be successful in biological males. Those who have expressed intense desire to bear a child include male transsexuals reassigned as females, homosexuals in a monogamous relationship, single heterosexual men with a strong maternal instinct, and married men whose wives are infertile. Because it is likely that these pregnancies would create very serious health hazards for the person carrying the fetus, medical assistance in the induction of such pregnancies would, I think, not be acceptable from a moral point of view, even though some patients are willing to undertake the serious risks of an abdominal pregnancy.

---

[11] W. A. W. Walters, 'The Artificial Induction of Abdominal Pregnancy', in W. A. W. Walters (ed.), *Human Reproduction: Current and Future Ethical Issues* (London: Baillière Tindall, 1991), 731–42.

'Medico-moral risk assessment' is, however, a complex issue. After all, pregnancy is never risk free. One thus cannot require that gynaecologists offering infertility treatments avoid *any* maternal risk. The question, then, becomes: is there a point at which the stress imposed by a pregnancy in an 'older' woman represents an unacceptable risk—and, if so, at what point? How old is too old? This question cannot be answered at the present time.

This is not to say that the gynaecologist should refrain from treating post-menopausal women, nor that he can go on, and just treat all women who are prepared to take the unknown risk. Physicians like Antinori and Sauer have developed some sort of 'middle of the road' approach, a policy aimed at 'risk-reduction'.[12] This approach has three components. First, they try to prevent the inclusion of patients with known diseases and risk factors, especially those with cardiovascular and diabetic complications. Second, intense monitoring during pregnancy may lessen the risk that a complication will go unrecognized. And third, to reduce the chance of late adverse events, such as pre-eclampsia, they recommend timely delivery after the fetus reaches maturity (about thirty-seven to thirty-eight weeks' gestation). Such screening and monitoring is necessary—but I doubt as to whether this policy of risk reduction is sufficient. I think it needs to be complemented by *gradually* raising the maternal age limit for IVF. Up until now, there is only very limited experience with pregnancies in women over the age of 45. We know that the maternal risks increase with age, but we do not know exactly how serious the risks will be. Given this uncertainty, I think it is questionable to drop any age limit right now, and to treat women who are in their late fifties and even over the age of 60. Following a step-by-step approach, a second, possibly more risky step could only justifiably be taken after a careful evaluation of the first step has indicated that the risks are acceptable—'Proceed with caution'. Of course, there is no objective method to answer the question as to what precise maternal upper age limit should be adopted during the first stage(s) of the clinical trials. I personally think it would be wise to suspend egg donations to women over approximately 50, with a view to evaluating the risks of pregnancies in older women aged 45–50.

---

[12] S. Antinori, C. Versaci, and G. Hossein Gholami, 'Oocyte Donation in Menopausal Women', *Human Reproduction*, 8 (1993), 1487–90; M. V. Sauer, R. J. Paulson, and R. A. Lobo, 'Pregnancy after Age 50: Applications of Oocyte Donation to Women after Natural Menopause', *Lancet*, 341 (1993), 321–3.

'It will result in more reductions of multifetal pregnancy'

The British gynaecologist Craft has reported a possible causal link between receiving donated eggs and certain maternal complications during pregnancy. Multiple pregnancy is likely to worsen these complications. Therefore, according to Craft, a reduction of multifetal pregnancy 'may need serious consideration for women having a multiple pregnancy after oocyte donation, especially in older women'.[13] A reduction of any multiple pregnancies—even triplet- and twin-pregnancies—might thus become a routine procedure in the context of assisted post-menopausal procreation.

For several years, there has been a growing uneasiness with regard to multifetal pregnancy reductions after infertility treatment, and a call for the prevention of dangerous multiple pregnancies which provoke the demand for multifetal pregnancy reductions. A multifetal pregnancy reduction should be seen as a last resort (*ultima ratio*) in cases of failed prevention. It is worth mentioning one of the conclusions of an international working group on multifetal pregnancy reduction: 'we are distressed that a few physicians have become aggressive with assisted reproduction technologies and view a multifetal pregnancy reduction as merely an adjunct to such therapies with no major medical or ethical consequences.'[14] Given the moral imperative to prevent dangerous multiple pregnancies, and assuming that Craft is right in stating that any multiple pregnancy in older women is dangerous, some critics might condemn assisted post-menopausal reproduction altogether. This conclusion would be too bold. It is necessary and sufficient to insist that IVF clinics modify their transfer policy in order to avoid multiple pregnancies. The routine transfer of four embryos, as practised by the American gynaecologist Sauer and his team, might result in a banalization of multifetal pregnancy reduction.

'Risks for the future child'

Let me make some general remarks first. Suitability for parenthood has been widely established as a valid consideration in determining who may

[13] I. Craft, M. Fedah, and M. Tsirigotis, 'Pregnancy in Post-menopausal Women', *Lancet*, 341 (1993), 697.

[14] M. Evans, 'Efficacy of Transabdominal Multifetal Pregnancy Reduction: Collaborative Experience among the World's Largest Centers', *Obstetrics and Gynecology*, 82 (1993), 61–6.

receive infertility treatment. In Britain, IVF clinics are required by law to consider the welfare of the prospective child. The Ethics Committee of the Royal Dutch Medical Association states that the physician should check whether there are serious risks for the well-being of the prospective child.[15] The Ethics Committee of the American Fertility Society has taken a similar stance with regard to the professional responsibility of physicians offering infertility treatments.[16]

Judging the suitability of infertile patients for parenthood is, however, not without its critics. The main criticism runs as follows: 'Prospective parents who are fertile are not being tested for their suitability for parenthood, so judging infertile patients involves a double standard, which is unjust.' I doubt whether this objection is valid, because it ignores an important difference between the two situations. In the context of 'natural' (non-artificial, non-assisted) procreation there are only two persons involved: the prospective parents. The responsibility for reproducing and the decision-making authority is theirs. Interfering with this authority by others (society, medical doctors) is not acceptable—it would involve an invasion of their (liberty) right to reproduce. In the context of assisted procreation, however, a third person is involved, namely the doctor. He has his own responsibility for the consequences of his acts. A doctor assisting in reproduction shares the responsibility for creating a new human being. Assisting in reproduction is as little morally neutral as is reproducing. From a moral point of view the physician is in some sort of triangle: he should consider the wishes and interests of his patients as well as the interests of prospective children—*salus aegroti et infantis suprema lex*. For this reason, judging the suitability for parenthood of infertile prospective parents is part of the professional responsibility of the physician. He is not an amoral technical agent, an amoral puppet of the prospective parents.

Although this basic principle is, I think, justified, it raises difficult problems, both procedural and material. Let me concentrate on the latter. What criteria should be used to define 'suitability for parenthood'? I assume that most people agree that couples who have a (recent) history of child abuse, or HIV-seropositive junkies, would be difficult to accept. In real life, however, most cases are not that clear. And sometimes the

---

[15] KNMG-commissie Medische Ethiek, 'Verantwoordelijkheid arts bij kunstmatige voortplanting', *Medisch Contact* (1989), 1711–14.

[16] Ethics Committee of the American Fertility Society, 'Ethical Considerations of the New Reproductive Technologies', *Fertility and Sterility*, 46 (1986), Supplement 1.

criteria used to measure suitability for parenthood are unjustifiably discriminatory. For example, I find it difficult to accept that patients who are unemployed are rejected, as is quite common in the UK.[17]

One can discern at least three different standards for judging suitability for parenthood. According to the first standard (the 'minimal risk' standard), medical doctors should refuse access to artificial reproduction if there is any risk for the well-being of the prospective child. This standard—*in dubiis abstine*—is much too high. In fact, it would urge medical doctors to stop assisting in reproduction altogether. The second standard is the 'wrongful life' standard. This standard holds that assisted reproduction should be refused if there is a serious risk that the life of the child would be so harmful to him that no one would want to live such a life. In these cases to be born is itself said to constitute a harm to the child and a violation of his right to be born with at least a chance for a minimally decent life.[18] According to this account, a child suffers the harm of wrongful life if it would be rational for a representative of the child's interests to prefer non-existence to the child's ever having been born. It is obvious that this standard leaves very little room for a psychosocial contra-indication for assisted procreation, based on judgements concerning the suitability for parenthood. The third standard, which I think is the most reasonable, is what Arras calls the 'high risk of serious harm' standard.[19] This standard differs from the second one in that it contains a less minimalistic concept of reproductive responsibility. In the words of Arras: 'The fact that unconceived or unborn children could end up having lives that were on balance worthwhile cannot function as an all-purpose excuse for imposing grievous pain, suffering, and deprivation on them.' Although particular children may not, strictly speaking, be 'victims' because they have no alternatives to either non-existence or their specific 'minimally decent' life, it is still irresponsible and wrong of parents and physicians involved in assisted procreation to expose them to a high risk of great suffering. This third standard is very similar to the criteria proposed by the Royal Dutch Medical Association for judging the suitability of infertile patients for parenthood.[20]

[17] R. M. L. Winston, 'Resources for Infertility Treatment', in Walters (ed.), *Human Reproduction*, 551–73.

[18] J. Feinberg, *Harm to Others* (New York: Oxford University Press, 1984).

[19] J. D. Arras, 'AIDS and Reproductive Decisions: Having Children in Fear and Trembling', *Milbank Quarterly*, 68 (1990), 353–82.

[20] KNMG-commissie Medische Ethiek, 'Verantwoordelijkheid arts bij kunstmatige voortplanting'.

Let me return now to older women (couples) opting for assisted reproduction. In discussing the risks for the prospective child, one can differentiate between medical risks and psychosocial risks.

Medical risks. It is well established that perinatal morbidity and mortality increase with maternal age. This is caused by the higher frequency of premature deliveries, and by the increase of multiple pregnancies and congenital defects. Is this a good (or even a compelling) reason to condemn post-menopausal pregnancies altogether? The problem is that perinatal risks increase gradually. It is, therefore, difficult to define a point at which these risks become 'suddenly' unacceptable. Furthermore: as the egg donors are significantly younger, the increase in chromosomally abnormal embryos seen in older women should not be a concern here. And last but not least: the prevention of multiple pregnancies in post-menopausal women might contribute to the prevention of premature delivery and its associated risks.

At the moment, all we know is that the medical risks for the child will probably be higher in older mothers. It is not known what exactly the perinatal risks are, and whether they can be minimized by preventive measures. Given these uncertainties, a gradual raising of the upper age limit for older women seems appropriate.

Last but not least the *psychosocial risks.* Critics mention all sorts of psychosocial risks. I want to focus on two of these, both of which concern the future inability of the older couple to fulfil the parental roles and responsibilities. First, being a parent is emotionally stressful and physically arduous. People of 55 may be perfectly able to cope with a baby, but at 70 could well be too old to provide the supervision and emotional support needed by the teenager. The second risk is that the growing child will become an orphan at an early age. The question, of course, is: how real are these risks, and what is their moral significance? Let me start with the latter, moral, question.

Implicit in the debate are, I think, particular conceptions of 'reproductive responsibility' or 'responsible parenthood'. The term 'responsible parenthood' is used in at least two different ways. In one meaning, responsible parenthood refers to parents who care for their existing children in a careful manner, meeting all their parental responsibilities. The other meaning refers to wise decisions that people make in becoming a parent. Obviously, the two meanings of responsible parenthood are interrelated, since ideas about what parents are and how they should respond to their children will affect attitudes towards becoming a parent.

I will not try to give a detailed account of the precise content of parental responsibilities and obligations, of what is to be expected of parents. Basically, parents have the task of nurturing and cherishing their children, satisfying their needs, and guiding them until they reach adulthood. A basic element of 'reproductive responsibility', then, is the willingness and ability of parents to assume this responsibility.[21] Decisions to reproduce should not be misinterpreted as just decisions to have a baby. These decisions are in fact decisions to undertake the far longer and more demanding task of bringing up a child to at least the level which will fit the child for independent adult life. Arras rightfully stated that it is a good thing not to have children if a person can predict well in advance that he or she will be incapable of discharging these parental duties in the near future, and that this is especially true in cases where the partner is (or, I would add, will probably be) likewise unavailable for parenting.[22]

Can the post-menopausal pregnancy be morally justified, given this 'minimal' conception of responsible parenthood? A differentiated view seems to be appropriate. 'Geriatric' IVF (that is, IVF for couples aged, say, 60 and older) would be highly problematic, if not completely irresponsible, in the light of the 'high risk of serious harm' standard. Even though life expectancy is approaching 80 years, the risk that the prospective child would become an young orphan seems just too high. Furthermore, Benagiano rightly insists that 'prolongation of life expectancy cannot *per se* be considered an answer to the question of the right of any child to a minimum standard of family life'.[23] Even though people are surviving longer with heart disease, cancer, and strokes, this may well result in their suffering longer a variety of highly disabling illnesses, which make it hardly possible for them to fulfil their parental responsibilities. Apart from the threat of disabling diseases of 'old age', it is highly questionable whether couples aged 75 or even older will be capable of managing the task of supervising teenagers. Offering geriatric IVF would be assisting in frivolous parenthood.

Many critics of the post-menopausal pregnancy tend to stretch these arguments, in that they lump geriatric IVF together with egg donation

[21] Cf. O. O'Neill, 'Begetting, Bearing, and Rearing', in O. O'Neill and W. Ruddick (eds.), *Having Children: Philosophical and Legal Reflections on Parenthood* (Oxford: Oxford University Press, 1979), 25–38.

[22] Arras, 'AIDS and Reproductive Decisions'.

[23] G. Benagiano, 'Pregnancy after the Menopause: A Challenge to Nature?', *Human Reproduction*, 8 (1993), 1344–5.

to post-menopausal patients of, say, 45–60. I doubt whether one can plausibly argue that a couple of 47 asking for IVF irresponsibly risk creating an orphan. The other psychosocial risk, namely the risk that the parents' abilities to fulfil their stressful and arduous parental tasks will diminish prematurely, is far more relevant for this age group. Nevertheless, one must acknowledge that this risk is generally greater for couples aged 55–60 than for couples aged 45–50.

How old, then, is too old? When do the psychosocial risks become excessive? At what age should couples be denied access to IVF, in the best interests of the child? Any age limit is, of course, somewhat arbitrary. Looking at the long-term interests of prospective children, I would say that there are compelling reasons not to treat couples aged 60 and older, and that there are good reasons not to treat couples of, say, 50–5 and older.

I will finish my evaluation by briefly commenting on some of the possible moral justifications of the post-menopausal pregnancy.

A first justification makes use of the 'replacement argument': 'Why worry about the risk that the child will be an orphan soon? After all, if parents are unable to discharge their responsibilities, *adoption* is an reasonable alternative.'[24] The question, however, should be whether parents ought to put themselves and their children into such a dreadful position in the first place.[25] I think the presence of such a risk—if serious —constitutes a compelling reason not to have children. Proponents of the replacement argument ignore that adoption (of older children) is often a very traumatic experience for these children, and that adoption can only be justified as a last resort.

A second justification, which is fairly popular among supporters of the post-menopausal pregnancy, can be called the 'abandonment argument': 'Does it make sense', Flamigni asks, 'to talk about the problems of communication or dialogue a woman of 60 [or 70? or 80?] might have with a child or adolescent? What is the percentage of children who, born because of a mistake or carelessness, are abandoned and brought up by no one?'[26] This kind of 'moral reasoning' is shocking: the fact that

---

[24] M. Huengsberg, 'Routine Testing for HIV at Infertility Clinics', *British Medical Journal*, 303 (1991), 645.
[25] KNMG-commissie Medische Ethiek, 'Verantwoordelijkheid arts bij kunstmatige voortplanting'.
[26] C. Flamigni, 'Egg Donation to Women over 40 Years of Age', *Human Reproduction*, 8 (1993), 1343–4.

families break down, that children are abandoned, can never justify that we deliberately use medical technology to risk such harmful events.

A third—more important—justification is the anti-sexist argument, or 'the argument from justice'. Some people wonder about a double standard. 'After all', they argue, 'men in their seventies often father children and get a slap on the back for it from admiring friends. Why shouldn't older women bear children if older men can father them?' According to Caplan, this sexism debate ignores the biological reality that older men can produce sperm naturally, while older women need expensive medical help: 'No one is talking about devoting a lot of technology to getting impotent old men to have babies.'[27] I, too, doubt whether the sexism debate (the argument from justice) is appropriate—though for other reasons than Caplan. Most important: it ignores the fact that, up until now, old men who father children always have younger women as partners. This is a morally relevant difference, for at least two reasons. First, the medical risks for these younger women are smaller than the maternal risks of post-menopausal pregnancies. And second: the fact that at least one of the parents, namely the mother, is (relatively) young significantly reduces the psychosocial risks for the (prospective) child.

The latter remark might, however, indicate the need for a more differentiated moral evaluation of post-menopausal pregnancies. Partners of women of advanced age also tend to be older. Some post-menopausal women asking for IVF do, however, have husbands significantly younger than they themselves are. Assisted reproduction in these situations might be judged differently, assuming that the 'harm probability' ratio with regard to the prospective child becomes less unfavourable, and assuming that the maternal risks for the older women are acceptable.

A special case would also arise if a post-menopausal woman wished to be a surrogate for her daughter (who was infertile because of the loss of her uterus) and would assume the role of grandmother after the birth of the child.

Conclusions and Recommendations

I come to the following tentative conclusions and recommendations:

1. The ethical evaluation of post-menopausal pregnancies should not ignore the cultural context of these pregnancies. The current trend

---

[27] Cited in M. Beck, 'How Far Should We Push Mother Nature?', *Newsweek*, 17 Jan. 1994.

toward later childbearing, toward postponing attempts at becoming pregnant until a time when the ability to become pregnant is limited, is, at least in the Netherlands, partly caused by our society, which makes it difficult for women to combine a job with motherhood at a younger age. Society should promote facilities which make such a combination easier.

2. The direct objections and most of the consequentialist objections to post-menopausal pregnancies are questionable or just untenable.

3. As with any experimental medical intervention, assisting in the creation of pregnancies in women older than 45 should be applied only in the context of a research project, in well-designed clinical trials.

4. The inclusion criteria for these trials and the minimal requirements for careful medical practice need further debate. It is generally accepted that older women are only accepted after a thorough medical screening, and that a careful monitoring of their pregnancies is required. It seems to be wise to add two further conditions: the prevention of multiple pregnancies, and a provisional upper age limit during the first trials (the 'step-by-step' approach). Because little is known about the medical risks for women over the age of 45 as well as for their children, a provisional maternal upper age limit of 50 seems reasonable.

5. Doctors offering reproductive technologies should consider the welfare of the prospective child. Looking at the long-term interests of prospective children, I would conclude that there are compelling reasons not to treat couples over the age of 60, and that there are good reasons not to treat couples over the age of, say, 50–5. Treating older women with a significantly younger partner (male or female) may be less of a problem, while treating single older women would be more difficult to reconcile with an acceptable 'harm probability' ratio.

6. The right of candidate egg donors to give a specific consent regarding the age group of the recipients should be acknowledged, for two reasons: first, out of respect for their autonomy, and second, to prevent a decreasing willingness to donate eggs for infertility treatment, resulting in an even more acute shortage of donor eggs.

14

Letter from a Post-menopausal Mother

INEZ DE BEAUFORT

My dearest daughter,

For your eighteenth birthday, this milestone of adulthood, I'm writing
you this letter. A plea for the accused? An explanation for more understanding, if need be posthumously? A justification? A testament for later,
for when you are in more reflective mood?

I think that mothers always look back at the birth on the occasion of
the birthdays of their children; it is such an overwhelming event that
you want, maybe have to relive it. Or chew it over, as you would call
it: 'Come on mummy, that's ancient history. Please, not the video of
my baby days.' After the last straining months we were so proud and
happy that you were born. And relieved as well. Quite bitter the contrast with your sixteenth birthday when you so angrily walked out of
the house for the first time. The concrete reason was that I did not give
you permission to stay out all night with your friends. When I told you
that I considered it just too dangerous your reply was, 'You never allow
me anything. Why did you have me if you knew you would be 70 when
I was 16? Now I'm stuck with these ancient parents who do not understand me at all.' I, of course, realize that this is not the first sixteenth
birthday that, because of some parental ban, was not what the birthday
girl expected. Rumour has it that there are other teenagers who have
the distinct impression that their parents do not understand them, but
still your words were like stabs in my heart. I've always been afraid,
of course, that this reproach would come, I counted on it, but still I was
unprepared. It's not that I don't have an answer for you, but I know
that you don't accept my answer, at least not yet. It is awful if your
child is ashamed of you. I see that happen to many parents (thank God
for the consolation of sharing). Often the parents don't even realize
how much their children are feeling ashamed, which makes the children feel even more embarrassed. In a way it is almost touching if you

see it happen to someone else, but I've never known what to do with your shame. When you were 12 and started secondary school you told your friends that your parents and your two small brothers died in a car accident and that you were brought up by your grandparents. You had even cut a picture of a father, a mother, and three children out of a magazine and put it in a frame next to your bed. Your friends thought it very interesting, romantic, and sad and I didn't know whether or not to undeceive them when they came to play with you and you would address me as 'grandma' with this begging look in your eyes.

I've always resisted the idea that as a parent one would have to account to one's child for having it. I think it is a private decision of the parents, so intimate that it is nobody's business, not even the child's. I also wonder if it is possible to give a satisfactory answer. Each answer will probably look either sentimental or trivial in the eyes of the children. 'We wanted you so much.' 'Why, you didn't know that I would be myself anyway. If I had been somebody else would you have wanted me as much?' 'We loved each other so much.' Wrong: too many associations with the embarrassing phenomenon of parental sex. 'You just came.' 'Why, wasn't I planned?' 'We thought we would enjoy it.' Probably one of the best answers, but definitely belonging in the category trivial. Rationalizations of a primordial feeling? A deeply felt need to produce a link in the genetic chain of humankind? The promise of immortality by living through your children?

There is a lot you can reproach me with, but not that I've acted on an impulse. Parents who are trying to have children for thirty years don't do that out of frivolity; they have thought too much about it rather than too little. You can blame me for being optimistic, but not for being frivolous. You also have to understand my resistance to giving an account in the context of the fact that your father and I were constantly asked to account for ourselves. When I was pregnant everybody thought they had a right to know why I did it, how much it had cost, if we still had a sexual relationship and, if so, how it was influenced by the pregnancy, if I intended to breastfeed you, etcetera, etcetera. Young as I then was— sorry for the cynicism—I still thought that I could influence the prejudices. But we were execrated by our wholesome fellow men. We gave interviews, appeared in numerous talk shows on television. The modern but scarcely more humane alternative to the freak show. From the fattest lady of the country to one of the oldest mothers of the country. Let's gaze and judge . . . We even refused a lot of money, offered by a magazine in exchange for the exclusive rights to your story.

I wanted to show that I could go through pregnancy and be a good mother to you even if I was 54. I wanted to explain how empty my life was before, how indispensable you were even before you existed. It's not that I had nothing to do or was constantly lamenting over an imaginary crib. It was because a child is different from anything else; it means a unique alliance, and gives you a wonderful feeling. Tell them how I had to fight for what for so many others simply falls into their laps, their reaction sometimes an almost indifferent casualness. Your father always accompanied me to what he called the 'justification circus'. He didn't want the publicity, but accepted that I had a message for the bigoted public. With my happiness and my honesty I would convert them. But they weren't interested in my story, they only wanted to pass judgement on geriatric mothers. Later your father told me that he was often ridiculed at work; there were constant smirks and jokes about his virility. 'Look here's our Abraham. We have this crabby spinster in our family, couldn't you pay her a visit?' He never told me then. It is curious, considering the fact that many men of his generation had ventured on second relationships with younger women and fathered 'love babies'. But that apparently was different because those children were conceived in a bed and not in a laboratory. I hated the hypocrisy and the cavilling. I still do. Now I sometimes think that we should never have accepted the publicity, but at the time I would have had to consider that as cowardice. They even called my hairdresser to ask if I dyed my hair and if I had started dyeing it when I became pregnant. Poor man. (Do hairdressers have an obligation to professional secrecy?) Anyway, he told them that the pregnancy was not good for my hair, but very good for me.

In those days I thought my example would find some following, that it would help others cross the threshold so that they would consider it not to be too unusual, although it might not be normal. This didn't happen and it's one of the reasons that have caused you misery. People felt very uncomfortable about it and I think that by the end of the century it was forbidden in most European countries. Few dared to venture on the undertaking of post-menopausal motherhood. That was considered as an argument in favour: 'why bother, it's not going to spread anyway.' For you, of course, the consequences made a difference: it meant that you were one of the very (unhappy?) few. When finally a 58-year-old woman died in childbirth the 'enthusiasm' vanished altogether. One did see more women having their eggs cryopreserved at a young age and then fertilized and implanted in a surrogate mother later on. A legal rigmarole, but at least one didn't die from it. In the end that also was forbidden. The world is populated by busybodies feeling this moral obligation to interfere. Policies were based on gut feelings ('Isn't it disgusting?') and not on arguments. Does the freedom to procreate only hold for those who are between 20 and 40 and who can offer their children harmonious and warm (don't make me laugh!) nests? Mint-coloured baby rooms with dinosaurs or whatever other cute animal is forced upon us by the admen? Isn't the fact that one is not supposed to differ from the common morality, the principles of Mr Average, a sign of ideological poverty?

My dearest daughter, I still feel that way but I have underestimated what it would mean for you, how you would be discriminated against; underestimated how much you wanted 'normal' parents. I really try to have understanding for your inclination to consider the average as an iron standard, whether it's your clothes, your holidays, or the home situation. The grief of children of divorced parents in your eyes is less terrible because so many children have divorced parents and then it is 'normal'. And if it is 'normal' it is okay. I don't blame you for your conformism; I just state a fact. That is the way the world looks to you. I also know that probably you will learn to relativize, but I'm not sure if I'll still be around to witness it. The funny thing is that I don't remember if at your age I was like that. I probably was, although I prefer to think of myself as a person who was not afraid of moral rebellion. Maybe I had less to complain about. Did I, or were we more contented? No, not likely, although old people like to think they were.

I remember a television programme with an ethicist (himself the father of five children, naturally conceived, just like that) who with a confidence bordering on fanaticism said that what I did was absolutely morally reprehensible. It was 'an excrescence of modern technology', 'an expensive madness' (by the way: we paid for everything ourselves), 'no human being had the right to defy nature by violating her laws'. 'Where was our respect for the natural course of human life?' He depicted me, (mind you, I was there) as a poor wretch, as a technology junkie who could not accept her fate, as an egoistic person who was prepared to sacrifice her child's happiness to fulfil her own consumerist desires. 'Pre-implantation diagnosis, sex-selection: our civilization was gliding down the slippery slope.' (I personally thought that sex-selection was indeed consumerist. I guess it is strange for you to hear there were fierce debates on the subject. Think how easy it now is with the Super Sperm Selector you can buy over the counter.) He was one of the worst preachers of penitence I've ever met, and I met quite a lot of specimens of the species. (Quite comforting that my memory is still so good that I can remember what he said word for word.)

Without wanting to justify myself (well, maybe I do want just that), aren't all persons who bring children into the world in a certain sense egoistic? They do it for themselves. For who else? Don't ever believe someone who tells you he begot a child for altruistic reasons. He is as mad as a hatter, either incredibly vain or just plain naïve. Not really healthy for the child if you ask me.

I asked this ethicist how he thought that he could measure the suitability of parents. Was age a criterion? No! Old fathers could be suitable, because *qua* nature they had it in them to beget children. (Also a sexist, this man.) (It helped to be a famous painter or movie star, Anthony Quinn, Picasso, Yves Montand.) Intelligence? Income? No, no, he didn't know how that could be judged, although certainly he thought of himself as eminently qualified, being a superior parent, personally to inspect all potential parents on behalf of the Ministry of Responsible Parenting. He argued that the fact that other 'non-perfect parents' could not be prevented from reproducing was not a good reason to give *carte blanche* to the post-menopausal mothers. We ought to consider our diminishing strength (quite a surprisingly polite way of putting it, he meant our decay), as well as the risk that you could become an orphan at an early age. For example: your father wouldn't be able to play football with you. I then replied that all fathers in wheelchairs were egoistic fathers in his view. (I still was quite quick-witted in those days.) Your youth would be spoiled by having to nurse the geriatric ward. 'Sorry, I can't come, I have to take out my father to feed the ducks. My mother can't come because she just had a new hip.' I retorted that this was a reason for widespread genetic screening for predispositions of late onset diseases like cancer or diseases of the brain. After all, you weren't the only one who ran the risk of losing parents at a young age. That was an altogether different situation according to him. One had the right not to know about these risks. 'Does one?', I asked. 'Think of your poor children if you die from a debilitating disease in the near future.' He countered that by saying that his wife was very young, a lot younger than he was. One of his students, I presume. (Dirty old man, hence the respect for old fathers.) 'That's no guarantee for not dying in the near future,' I said. He also argued that our expectations of you would be too high and therefore detrimental to your mental health. Why? What a strange idea. Probably 90 per cent of all parents would be disqualified if that was a criterion. Did he have low expectations of his children? (Probably the reason he had five children: bigger chance of at least one living up to expectations. That's what I thought, I didn't say it.) He then focused his attack on physicians. Where was the good old principle of *in dubiis abstine*? I never liked that principle, I think it has a cowardly, too careful, and conservative side. It was very *bon ton* then to speak condescendingly of technology. Rather ungrateful and stupid. I have to admit I was almost reverent, also exaggerated. Optimism about the accomplishments of technological progress was considered to be dangerous, or at best naïve.

Looking back now, there was no problem regarding our stamina in the first ten years of your life. We could easily keep up with you. In fact I did everything with you a young or younger mother does. I was tired. But I'm convinced that all the mothers of young children were tired. The difference, of course, was that I would rather have bitten my tongue off than admit it out of fear of reactions like 'well, you made your own bed, now lie on it'. I remember the shock when uncle John told us he had bought an apartment in this 'silo for the fossils' (your father's words for it) and that he didn't want his grandchildren to stay because he found that too exhausting. We then realized how big the gap between uncle John and us was. I think nobody really thought of the possible effects on the friendships of the older parents, how estranged they were from their generation. Our friends started to talk more and more about the past (oh, how boring these reminiscing sessions were), whereas I was concentrated on the future (your future, but also inextricably mine).

When you were 10 you all of a sudden decided that you did not want me to go swimming with you any more; you felt ashamed of my old body. 'You have so many wrinkles, mum.' Your father was allowed to accompany you. He was better conserved. (Oh, the unfair ways of nature.) That was the day I decided to have a facelift.

The risk that you would lose us young was in fact a risk. We had asked uncle Charles and aunt Sally to look after you if something happened. They solemnly promised they would. For us this was very important, precisely because we were very much aware of the risk. Was it too big? Every parent has these moments of sheer panic: 'I hope I don't die in a traffic accident, I hope I won't get breast cancer when I'm 35.' Should one be paralysed by it? Of course, in our case the chances were greater, but I had a life expectancy of 82. You would—statistically speaking—be 27 when I died. I found it scary, but not irresponsible. I

244 *Inez de Beaufort*

can hear you say now, 'easy to talk about risks with somebody else's life'. But the inevitable essence of parenthood is that you take risks with somebody else's life, whether you are a post-menopausal mother, travel with your children through Italy in a caravan, don't look for genetic information, or do look for genetic information. No parent has the guarantee that his child will have a happy life with both his parents at his side until the mid-life crisis. Parents don't come with a best before label. Who am I kidding? My God, how relieved I was each time after the yearly check-up. And how relieved on all your birthdays: another year closer to adulthood and independence. Looking back now our conversion to an incredibly healthy lifestyle was almost funny. From the day your father fell ill, now five years ago, my fear of dying and leaving you behind has become more poignant. But how were we to know that he would get Alzheimer's disease? He could just as well not have contracted it. Then everybody would have said, 'well, weren't they lucky'. Now they said, 'that's what you get, they have been asking for problems'. Although I suppose that it comes because you miss him so much I think that you can be very harsh about it. 'I refuse to go out with this batty father.' Have you forgotten his patience, his mildness? The games, the beautiful things he made for you, the journey you made when I was in hospital for the facelift? I think I have never told you that when we were waiting in the hospital for the IVF I got so scared that I almost left. Your father actually had to restrain me from walking away. If he hadn't . . .

I know, I know, parents do not have a right to gratitude, what they do is taken for granted, their duty and your right. You have not asked for your existence. How children can blackmail their parents with that reproach. But respect, don't parents have a right to respect? Or at least a little understanding? I probably only realized that myself when I became a parent. Yes, indeed a little late. And maybe we spoiled you too much. I was so afraid to be old-fashioned, in the naïve presupposition that old and old-fashioned go together. Afraid that you would say, 'that's because you are so old'. Even if I knew that that wasn't the reason you often said it when you didn't get your own way. I think, unconsciously, I also wanted to compensate for the wrong I had done you in your eyes by withholding my youth from you. You always played that quite cleverly. As the victim of the ideological drive of your parents you were entitled to compensation. ('What did you want to prove with me?' We didn't want to prove anything, we wanted a child.) You often preferred not to see the advantages. When your friends were complaining about their always absent mothers who insisted on pursuing careers, you could offer them hospitality and room service because I was then retired. Over the tea I served you could be aggrieved about your 'tragic' fate. (I admit that the other 'unnatural' mothers and I sometimes laughed about this competition of wretchedness. Please don't think I'm trivializing your feelings.) It's not that I want to argue away your anger— I've never managed to do that with your anger anyway—it's just that to be able to put things in perspective might benefit you.

What I find very difficult is that I will not be around when the circle is completed because your daughter reproaches you that you're not there or too often there. You always stated that you would have your children at a very young age. If it is given to you to realize that intention, you will have other conflicts. I'm happy that the combination of work and motherhood nowadays is easier than it was in my day (that is: the day I should have had you according to you). But you will also have to face the arguments with adolescents. I'm not in favour of the cheap philosophy of 'my mother is my best girlfriend'. You're idealizing that. If we went shopping and there was something I didn't like (usually clothes, remember the pink cowboy boots) you would always say that my age had ruined my taste. Publicity for margarine in which the mother looks as young as her daughter I have always found ridiculous. (Surprise, surprise, I find myself defending some sort of natural course of life after all.) I'm sure that you will then sometimes think of me. I know: that's what mothers always say. Please know that I have also enjoyed it, the challenge, the intensity, the purity. (I suppose I'm not allowed to say that it kept me young!)

Now regarding this plan of yours to learn Italian and go to Italy to look for your genetic mother; I do not know anything about her. An Italian woman undergoing IVF treatment, who did not object to her oocytes being used for a post-menopausal mother? No, that makes her too akin, too sympathetic and modern. She probably did it for the money. You cannot find out her identity. At the time anonymous donation was still practised. Frankly, I'm happy you will not be able to find her. It may be envy. I'm your mother. I carried you, I gave birth to you. I took care of you, I put plasters on your sore knees, I helped you with your homework, I consoled you, and I looked at you at night in silent adoration. I'm your mother, whether you want it or not. (I admit, I'm jealous, very jealous. She must be a fat Italian mamma—definitely with a moustache— who wouldn't know what to do with you.) Do you know what you are looking for? Your genetic roots or a successor mother for when I'm not there any more? Sometimes I think you should accept your fate better. But then I realize these thoughts spring more from tiredness than from wisdom. That I want you to be independent so that my task is completed. And regarding the acceptance of fate I set a bad example, so why should I expect you to be compliant? Fate does not keep the agreements you thought you had bargained for. Sometimes it is wise to accept one's fate; sometimes it is stupid. Still, it would be reassuring to know that you are reconciled.

Maybe it would be useful if you met other children of older parents. As you know, your father and I were the founding 'fathers' of the International Association of Older Parents. (Others mockingly called it the Society of Prehistoric Parents.) In the first years the Association was really successful: united, because everybody suffered from the criticisms of the Pope, the ethicists, the neighbours. After five years there was a schism. Some psychologists and paediatricians wanted to do research to investigate how the children were doing, physically, mentally, and socially. You would have been compared to a group of normal children (whatever that may be) and a group of children brought up by their grandparents. Half of the members (including us) wanted to participate, the other half strongly resisted the idea. Anyway the project was never carried out. But what keeps you from organizing an association of children? Certainly the parents have not been able to hide this fact from their children. Just don't marry a boy from that group because then your children will not have any grandparents. (And they do need them with such young parents!)

There's no triumph over what I have done, I realized too often that it has been difficult for you. There were no regrets, ever. There is too much love, too much happiness, too much affection for regrets. Of course I have often wondered how life would have been if we had had 'you' twenty years earlier. Whether we would have been better parents. Whether the life of that child would have been totally different. Whether this fact has made you into who you are. I don't know. I just don't know. You once asked why we didn't adopt. I now think that for me that meant giving up the dream of having your father's child and giving birth. When I was ready to give up the dream we were too old to adopt. I cannot deny feeling pain about the part of your life I will not be able to share, this long part of your life. Although I have always known that, the pain gets worse now that I grow older and have to face my death. Even I, in spite of child and facelift, cannot escape the inevitable decay of nature. But we outfoxed her once, didn't we? (No triumph, but a profound gratitude.) I think no parent can express what his or her child means for him or her. The grief, the disappointments, the anger, and the grudges (yes, also for us, sometimes) count for little when compared to the love and the deepest closeness. I love you so much. Well, as you can hear, I'm getting sentimental in my old age. A reason to stop writing. My dearest daughter, may you be very happy the coming year. I promise to try not to break my brittle bones, not to lose my teeth, and not to end up in a wheelchair.

Your mother

Bibliography

ALPERN, K. D. (ed.), *The Ethics of Reproductive Technology* (New York: Oxford University Press, 1992).

AUSTIN, C. R., *Human Embryos: The Debate on Assisted Reproduction* (New York: Oxford University Press, 1989).

BAIRD, R. M., and ROSENBAUM, S. E. (eds.), *The Ethics of Abortion: Pro-life vs. Pro-choice*, rev. edn. (Buffalo, NY: Prometheus Books, 1993).

BARTELS, D. M., PRIESTER, R., VAWTER, D. E., and CAPLAN, A. L. (eds.), *Beyond Baby M: Ethical Issues in New Reproductive Techniques* (Clifton, NJ: Humana Press, 1990).

BAYERTZ, K., *GenEthics: Technological Intervention in Human Reproduction as a Philosophical Problem* (New York: Cambridge University Press, 1994).

BELLER, F. K., and WEIR, R. F. (eds.), *The Beginning of Human Life* (Boston: Kluwer Academic, 1994).

BEWLEY, S., and WARD, R. H. (eds.), *Ethics in Obstetrics and Gynaecology* (London: Royal College of Obstetricians and Gynaecologists Press, 1994).

BONNICKSEN, A. L., *In Vitro Fertilization: Building Policy from Laboratories to Legislatures* (New York: Columbia University Press, 1989).

BROMHAM, D. R., DALTON, M. E., and JACKSON, J. C. (eds.), *Philosophical Ethics in Reproductive Medicine: Proceedings of the First International Conference on Philosophical Ethics in Reproductive Medicine, University of Leeds, 18–22 April 1988* (Manchester: Manchester University Press, 1990).

CALLAHAN, J. C. (ed.), *Reproduction, Ethics, and the Law: Feminist Perspectives* (Bloomington: Indiana University Press, 1995).

CAMPBELL, C. S. (ed.), *What Price Parenthood? Ethics and Assisted Reproduction* (Brookfield, Vt.: Dartmouth Pub. Co., 1992).

CHADWICK, R. F. (ed.), *Ethics, Reproduction and Genetic Control* (New York: Croom Helm, 1987).

DICKENS, B. M., *Legal Issues in Embryo and Fetal Tissue Research and Therapy* (Ottawa: Royal Commission on New Reproductive Technologies, 1991).

DUNSTAN, G. R. (ed.), *The Human Embryo: Aristotle and the Arabic and European Traditions* (Exeter: University of Exeter Press, 1990).

—— and SELLER, M. J. (eds.), *The Status of the Human Embryo: Perspectives from Moral Tradition* (London: King Edward's Hospital Fund for London, 1988).

DWORKIN, R., *Life's Dominion: An Argument about Abortion and Euthanasia* (New York: Knopf, 1993).

DYSON, A., and HARRIS, J. (eds.), *Experiments on Embryos* (London: Routledge, 1991).

—— —— (eds.), *Ethics and Biotechnology* (London: Routledge, 1994).

EDWARDS, R. G., *Life before Birth: Reflections on the Embryo Debate* (New York: Basic Books, 1989).

EVANS, D. (ed.), *Conceiving the Embryo* (Dordrecht: Kluwer, 1996).

—— (ed.), *Creating the Child* (Dordrecht: Kluwer, 1996).

FORD, N. M., *When Did I Begin? Conception of the Human Individual in History, Philosophy and Science* (New York: Cambridge University Press, 1988).

FORRESTER, M. G., *Persons, Animals, and Fetuses: An Essay in Practical Ethics* (Boston: Kluwer Academic, 1996).

GLOVER, J., *et al.*, *Ethics of New Reproductive Technologies: The Glover Report to the European Commission* (DeKalb: Northern Illinois University Press, 1989).

GOODMAN, M. F. (ed.), *What Is a Person?* (Clifton, NJ: Humana Press, 1988).

GRAZI, R. V. (ed.), *Be Fruitful and Multiply: Fertility Therapy and the Jewish Tradition* (Jerusalem: Genesis Jerusalem Press, 1994).

GROBSTEIN, C., *Science and the Unborn: Choosing Human Futures* (New York: Basic Books, 1988).

GUNNING, J., and ENGLISH, V., *Human In Vitro Fertilization: A Case Study in the Regulation of Medical Innovation* (Brookfield, Vt.: Dartmouth Publishing Co., 1993).

HARRIS, J., *The Value of Life: An Introduction to Medical Ethics* (London: Routledge & Kegan Paul, 1985).

—— *Wonderwoman and Superman: The Ethics of Human Biotechnology* (Oxford: Oxford University Press, 1992).

HAUERWAS, S., *Suffering Presence: Theological Reflections on Medicine, the Mentally Handicapped, and the Church* (Notre Dame, Ind.: University of Notre Dame Press, 1986).

HOLMES, H. B., and PURDY, L. M. (eds.), *Feminist Perspectives in Medical Ethics* (Bloomington: Indiana University Press, 1992).

HUMBER, J. M., and ALMEDER, R. F., *Biomedical Ethics Reviews, 1995: Reproduction, Technology, and Rights* (Totowa, NJ: Humana Press, 1996).

HURSTHOUSE, R., *Beginning Lives* (Oxford: Basil Blackwell, 1987).

IGLESIAS, T., *IVF and Justice: Moral, Social and Legal Issues Related to Human (In Vitro) Fertilisation* (London: Linacre Centre for Health Care Ethics, 1990).

JONES, D. G., *Brave New People: Ethical Issues at the Commencement of Life*, rev. edn. (Grand Rapids, Mich.: Eerdmans, 1985).

KAMM, E. M., *Creation and Abortion: A Study in Moral and Legal Philosophy* (New York: Oxford University Press, 1992).

KAPLAN, L. J., and TONG, R., *Controlling our Reproductive Destiny: A Technological and Philosophical Perspective* (Cambridge, Mass.: MIT Press, 1994).

KLEIN, R. D. (ed.), *Infertility: Women Speak out about their Experiences of Reproductive Medicine* (London: Pandora Press, 1989).

KOLKER, A., and BURKE, B. M., *Prenatal Testing: A Sociological Perspective* (Westport, Conn.: Bergin & Garvey, 1994).

LEE, R., and MORGAN, D. (eds.), *Birthrights: Law and Ethics at the Beginnings of Life* (London: Routledge, 1989).

MCCORMICK, R. A., *How Brave a New World: Dilemmas in Bioethics*, rev. edn. (Washington: Georgetown University Press, 1985).

MCCULLAGH, P. J., *The Foetus as Transplant Donor: Scientific, Social and Ethical Perspectives* (New York: Wiley, 1987).

MCKIE, J. (ed.), *Ethical Issues in Prenatal Diagnosis and the Termination of Pregnancy* (Melbourne: Centre for Human Bioethics, Monash University, 1994).

MACKLIN, R., *Surrogates and Other Mothers: The Debates over Assisted Reproduction* (Philadelphia: Temple University Press, 1994).

MERRICK, J. C., and BLANK, R. H. (eds.), *The Politics of Pregnancy: Policy Dilemmas in the Maternal–Fetal Relationship* (New York: Haworth Press, 1993).

MULLEN, M. A., *The Use of Human Embryos and Fetal Tissues: A Research Architecture* (Ottawa: Royal Commission on New Reproductive Techno-ogies, 1992).

OVERALL, C., *Ethics and Human Reproduction: A Feminist Analysis* (Boston: Allen & Unwin, 1987).

—— (ed.), *The Future of Human Reproduction* (Toronto: Women's Press, 1989).

RAGONE, H., *Surrogate Motherhood: Conception in the Heart* (Boulder, Colo.: Westview Press, 1994).

RAYMOND, J. G., *Women as Wombs: Reproductive Technologies and the Battle over Women's Freedom* (San Francisco: HarperSanFrancisco, 1993).

ROBERTSON, J. A., *Children of Choice: Freedom and the New Reproductive Technologies* (Princeton: Princeton University Press, 1994).

ROSNER, F., *Modern Medicine and Jewish Ethics*, 2nd edn. (Hoboken, NJ: Yeshiva University Press, 1991).

ROTHMAN, B. K., *The Tentative Pregnancy: Prenatal Diagnosis and the Future of Motherhood* (New York: Penguin Books, 1987).

—— *Recreating Motherhood: Ideology and Technology in a Patriarchal Society* (New York: Norton, 1989).

SEN, G., and SNOW, R. C. (eds.), *Power and Decision: The Social Control of Reproduction* (Boston: Harvard School of Public Health, 1994).

SINGER, P., KUHSE, H., BUCKLE, S., DAWSON, K., and KASIMBA, P. (eds.), *Embryo Experimentation* (New York: Cambridge University Press, 1990).

—— and WELLS, D., *Making Babies: The New Science and Ethics of Concep-tion* (New York: Scribner, 1985).

SPALLONE, P., *Beyond Conception: The New Politics of Reproduction* (Granby, Mass.: Bergin & Garvey, 1989).

STACEY, M. (ed.), *Changing Human Reproduction: Social Science Perspectives* (Newbury Park, Calif.: Sage Publications, 1992).

STEINBOCK, B., *Life before Birth: The Moral and Legal Status of Embryos and Fetuses* (New York: Oxford University Press, 1992).

STEPHENSON, P., and WAGNER, M. G. (eds.), *Tough Choices: In Vitro Fertilization and the Reproductive Technologies* (Philadelphia: Temple University Press, 1993).

STOTLAND, N. L. (ed.), *Psychiatric Aspects of Reproductive Technology* (Washington: American Psychiatric Press, 1990).

SUTTON, A., *Prenatal Diagnosis: Confronting the Ethical Issues* (London: Linacre Centre, 1990).

WARNOCK, M., *A Question of Life: The Warnock Report on Human Fertilisation and Embryology* (New York: Basil Blackwell, 1985).

Index